D1544867

DISCARDED

The New and the Old Criminology

edited by
Edith Elisabeth Flynn
John P. Conrad

Published in cooperation with the
American Society of Criminology

The Praeger Special Studies program, through a selective worldwide distribution network, makes available to the academic, government, and business communities significant and timely research in U.S. and international economic, social, and political issues.

The New and the Old Criminology

Praeger Publishers   New York   London

Library of Congress Cataloging in Publication Data

Main entry under title:

The New and the old criminology.

"Published in cooperation with the American
Society of Criminology."
Includes index.
1. Crime and criminals—United States—Address-
es, essays, lectures. 2. Criminal justice,
Administration of—United States—Addresses, essays,
lectures. I. Flynn, Edith E. II. Conrad, John
Phillips, 1913–   III. American Society of
Criminology.
HV6789.N47   364   76-14130
ISBN 0-03-040891-1

PRAEGER SPECIAL STUDIES
200 Park Avenue, New York, N.Y., 10017, U.S.A.

Published in the United States of America in 1978
by Praeger Publishers,
A Division of Holt, Rinehart and Winston, CBS, Inc.

89   038   987654321

© 1978 by Praeger Publishers

All rights reserved

Printed in the United States of America

CONTENTS

LIST OF TABLES AND FIGURES

THE NEW AND THE OLD CRIMINOLOGY: SKETCHING THE FUTURE AGENDA OF CRIMINOLOGY
Edith Elisabeth Flynn

The purpose of this chapter is to sketch and discuss the future agenda of criminology. In view of the fact that criminology is neither a cohesive nor a well-established science, this quest is admittedly hazardous. Nonetheless, there is intrinsic value in looking ahead because man, in contrast to God's other creatures, is in a position to create, or at least alter, his future. There is further consolation in the fact that the projection of future states, which will be attempted here, is not so much concerned with what will happen but with the identification of possible future alternatives. Once the range of possible future alternatives has been identified, the prospects will have improved for taking concerted action that would either enhance the realization of those trends or alternatives deemed desirable or would inhibit or divert those trends that, although probable, are perceived as undesirable.

The task at hand is divided into three parts. The first part discusses the theoretical development of criminology from its inception to the major developments affecting the discipline today. The second part outlines some of the basic questions around which modern criminology will continue to revolve and presents a short analysis of some of the major directions the discipline will probably pursue in the future. The third part identifies and discusses in summary fashion some of the basic issues and priorities for the criminology of the future.

THE THEORETICAL DEVELOPMENT OF CRIMINOLOGY AND CURRENT MAJOR DEVELOPMENTS

Criminology's theoretical development can be traced to the eighteenth century, when such writers and scholars as Cesare Beccaria, Jeremy Bentham, and Samuel Romilly (Phillipson 1923)

reacted against the turmoil and social disorder of contemporary
society and objected to the injustices inflicted on the population by
the prevailing legal systems and criminal justice practices. Modern criminology began in the early nineteenth century when such
scholars as Guerry, Quetelet, and von Oettingen studied crime as a
social phenomenon and collected and analyzed criminal statistics in
an effort to discover society's natural laws and to provide program-
matic prescriptions for upholding the existing social order and mend-
ing the torn fabric of their societies. In the 1870s, criminology
came under the influence of the natural sciences, culminating in the
"positive school" of criminology, with Cesare Lombroso, Enrico
Ferri, and Raffaele Garofalo as its principal proponents. The
Italian positivists exerted a profound influence on the development
of criminology in the first few decades of the twentieth century both
in Europe and in the United States. Only gradually did criminologists
reject the principles of biological determinism and begin to focus, in
turn, on the study of psychological characteristics and other multiple
causes of crime.

     While there had been early attempts to merge criminology with
sociology (Parmelee 1908), a truly sociological criminology did not
emerge until the 1920s with the founding of the first university-based
sociology department at the University of Chicago. The seminal
ideas of the Chicago school had a powerful impact on U.S. criminology. The writings of Park (1925), Thrasher (1927), and Shaw (1929)
provided the foundation for the majority of subsequent sociological
research on the relationship between crime and the phenomena of
urbanization, ecological patterns, and cultural and physical environments.

     By the 1930s students of U.S. criminology could discern three
major and distinct theories of crime: differential association, social
structure and anomie, and cultural conflict. Sutherland's (1947: 6-7)
theory of differential association replaced previous multiple-factor
approaches and provided criminology with its first integrative theory.
Sutherland's theory continues to serve as one of the major theoretical perspectives in criminology today. Merton's (1938: 672-82)
theory of social structure and anomie identified society's social and
cultural structure as principal causes of crime and suggested that
different modes of adaptation to society could account not only for
the behavior of individuals but also for the differences in crime
rates. Sellin's (1938) theory of culture conflict and crime viewed
criminal behavior as the result of conflict between the norms of
conduct and stressed the need for the study of criminal law, since
the latter constitutes one form of conduct norms. Theoretical developments since the 1940s consisted primarily of extensions of
these three perspectives and their empirical testing.

The 1960s brought a major change in focus for criminology. Viewing crime as socially and legally defined phenomena and an integral part of the processes of conflict and change, criminologists began to focus their attention once again--as the founding fathers had done--on the legal processes. As such, the sphere of criminology was expanded to include the study of law enforcement, the administration of justice, societal reaction to crime, victimology, criminal behavior patterns, the formulation of criminal law, victimless crimes, among other subjects.

The late 1960s brought additional major change. In less than a decade there occurred a proliferation of different approaches within the discipline, variously labeled "new criminology," "critical criminology," and "radical criminology." Proponents of the latter approach view contemporary criminology as closely tied to the state's interests and today's criminologists as "ancillary agents" of the political power (Quinney 1975: 13). Those criminologists perceived to be following a "liberal" ideology stood accused of following a legalistic definition of crime, accepting the state's definitions; supporting reformist measures in rehabilitating criminals and ameliorative reforms of society; rejecting general theory and macroscopic historical analysis, favoring pragmatism and social behaviorism; and being susceptible to cynicism and a lack of passion, ignoring the possibility of far-ranging changes in society (Quinney 1975: 13).

There can be no doubt about the pervasive presence of radical and conservative ideas in criminology today. But it is difficult to interpret. A major source of the difficulty pertains to the uncertain and variable meaning of "radical" and "conservative." Those who would want to contrast bourgeois criminology with Marxist theory should recognize that such a view is no longer acceptable, for Marxism, in some societies, serves to inhibit criticism and preserves the political status quo (Kaiser 1976: 35). The indefiniteness of conservative and radical formulations in criminology is probably inescapable, since it reflects the muddled social conditions of today's society. After all, there is no great virtue in having a precise and accurate theoretical conceptualization if it is not connected with reality. If the radicalism of Marxism is being questioned, so too can the notion of conservatism in criminology. Criminology as part of the culture in which it is engendered cannot easily escape the influence of that culture, whatever its dominant orientation may be. But an important saving feature of criminology of whatever persuasion lies in its social consequences and how these come to be perceived in criminological thought. If the goal of criminology is the scientific study of delinquency and crime as social phenomena, which is communicated in the training of a small elite of social

engineers for the purpose of effecting social control, the process
would entail the development of a most destructive form of domina-
tion and lead, no doubt, to vicious social oppression. But if the goal
of criminology is the diffusion through society of an understanding of
crime, its etiology, its variegated manifestations, and the dissemination of the knowledge of how crime reduction could lead to an increase in the quality of life, then its effects can well be viewed as
beneficial and liberating.

     The most recent developments in criminology have had a
mixed blessing on the discipline. Chiefly, there has been a tendency
to polarize, politicize, and assume a highly critical stance to society
and social issues by those who subscribe to the criminologie critique
ou radicale. With the sharpened definitions of crime and the closer
scrutiny of the problems of criminal justice, the political implications of the new approaches to social control became more visible,
and politically motivated criminological criticism followed suit.
Polarization becomes pronounced whenever criminal justice practices come to be viewed as offensive or repressive or when radical
changes in the prevailing social structure are advocated by some.
Past tendencies to suppress the pursuit of objective, empirical
knowledge, to introduce change for the sake of change only, and to
replace the scientific stance and method with blind "actionism" have
damaged the discipline and undermined, to some degree, the credibility of criminology in the field and among the public at large.
Without detracting from some of the positive effects of actionism
and action research, it is important to recognize that the main task
of criminology as a science must remain the increase of knowledge
in this field. And if there is to be a value-free criminology--a question that has yet to be resolved satisfactorily--its function can lie
only in the search for more knowledge and truth. But since the objectives of criminology are so varied, it should not come as a surprise that there are multiple roles for the criminologist as well,
which in turn create conflict (Kaiser 1976: 51-52). The role differentiation becomes pronounced whenever the different professions are
examined which require, in varying degrees, some knowledge of
criminology. On the one hand, there are criminologically/legally
trained jurists, and the many professionals working in the criminal
justice system, who because of their criminologically oriented education, professional socialization, and occupational proximity to
jurisprudence and the administration of justice are clearly identified
with the prevailing polity. On the other hand, there is the sociologically trained and most often university-based criminologist who frequently assumes a critical stance distinct from organized society
and the existing polity. The latter is most often identified as siding
with socially visible minorities and tends to criticize existing power

relationships, the status quo, and the legal system in which he finds himself. While the sociologically trained criminologist claims to fulfill the role of critic of society, it should be noted that from a scientific viewpoint the other professionals can--and sometimes do-- not think any less critically than they do.

A compounding factor in the criminological role play is the controversy surrounding neo-Marxist criminology. Clearly, the contrast between the prevailing criminological thought and the neo-Marxist criminology propagated by a predominantly younger set of criminologists is much greater than is the contrast between the so-called bourgeois criminology and that of socialist criminology as it is practiced in today's socialist/communist countries (Kaiser 1976: 35-44). Even though neo-Marxism in Western society constitutes little more than sociopolitical sectarianism and has little, if any, scientific potential, its influence on some younger members of the criminological profession is nonetheless significant. In most instances, the development of utopian societies is pursued with vigor but little specificity and is accompanied by claims to the futurity and viability of such societies. Of even greater significance, however, is the existing communication barrier which seems to preclude any scientific communication or cross-fertilization between the two groups. Since ideological selectivity characterizes both radical and conservative positions, a relatively closed communication system ensues on either side. To bridge the gap, the problem and the existing polemic must be recognized. Once this happens, there may well emerge a readiness to utilize new frames of reference (some of which may include the Marxist point of view), not in the sense of accepting the Marxist theory of society, but in the sense of using various ideas, diversely interpreted, in order to raise new problems, introduce new perspectives, focalize new issues, and give fresh impetus and stimulus to criminological thought and the criminological enterprise.

The most recent development affecting criminology is more global and has developed in society at large. Bendix (1970), in his essay "Embattled Reason: Essays on Social Knowledge" describes it best. Bendix fears that science itself (which includes behavioral science and criminology), as the embodiment of reason in modern society, is now in danger of being rejected by the population. That this fear has some justification is indicated by the pronounced hostility to technology, which has developed and is still growing in some social groups found in every highly developed, urbanized, and industrialized society. Weber (1946: 129-56), in his wisdom, foresaw just such a development. In his writings Weber discusses the growing disenchantment of the world in Western societies as a direct consequence of rationalization and increased bureaucratic regulation of almost every sphere of social life (Weber 1946: 155). Weber also anticipated the movements of revolt and withdrawal that are now so familiar and that can be interpreted as attempts to re-create a lost quality of life of days gone by by reviving the type of intimate social relationships in which personal affection and spontaneity can be re-awakened.

When viewed in terms of the combined effect, the developments discussed above have contributed much to the present bedeviled state of criminology, in which there is neither a distinctive nor unified theory or method. If criminology seems to be going through a crisis, it is not because it did not produce a verified body of laws but because many of its descriptive generalizations, frames of reference, and interpretations appear no longer adequate. This inadequacy exists for one of two reasons: either the models have exhausted their capacity to generate new discoveries, or the social reality they attempt to describe has changed to such a degree that the models are no longer relevant. What is needed is the proposal of new subjects of study and pathfinding ideas. At this time the most promising attempt to provide such a new frame of reference and direction seems to be the concept of "postindustrial society" as it has been outlined in one form or another by such students of society as Touraine (1971), Bell (1967), and Brzezinski (1967). According to these writers, in the postindustrial society the progress of science could eliminate scarcity of resources in the sphere of vital human needs. Additional characteristics of postindustrial society would include the transfer of industrial work from men to machines, a development which would in turn transform the existing social stratification and class systems. The same kind of shift would also alter the existing balance between work, recreation, and leisure activities of mankind. According to Touraine (1971: 3):

> A new type of society is now being formed. These
> new societies can be labeled post-industrial to
> stress how different they are from the industrial
> societies that preceded them. . . . They may
> also be called technocratic because of the power
> that dominates them according to the nature of
> their production methods and economic organi-
> zation.

Touraine's description is similar to the one formulated by Brzezinski (1967: 18), who notes that "America is in the midst of a transition that is both unique and baffling . . . ceasing to be an industrial society, it is being shaped to an ever increasing extent by technology and electronics, and thus becoming the first technetronic society." And Bell (1967: 24-35), in a similar vein, albeit with a slightly different emphasis, stresses the central importance of theoretical knowledge in the system of production and the shift from a manufacturing economy to a service economy. Brzezinski and Bell envision the new society as a harmonious one, in which major social divisions have largely been erased and in which the general course of social development is determined by a relatively harmonious process of economic development. Brzezinski (1967: 18-21) writes:

> . . . it seems unlikely that a unifying ideology of political action, capable of mobilizing large-scale loyalty, can emerge in the manner that Marxism arose in response to the industrial era. . . . The largely humanist-oriented, occasionally ideologically minded intellectual dissenter, who saw his role largely in terms of proffering social critiques, is rapidly being displaced either by experts and specialists, who become involved in special governmental undertakings, or by the generalists-integrators, who become in effect house ideologues for those in power, providing overall intellectual integration for disparate actions.

Given that any form of social action and development is likely to produce both manifest and latent consequences, it is more likely that even the new postindustrial society will generate its own forms of conflicts. For example, given the rapid growth of centralized bureaucratic regulation intruding into almost every sphere of human endeavor, and given the dominance of a purely technological outlook, one can expect continued rejection of such developments within certain segments of the population already opposed to such intrusions. In addition, new kinds of social conflicts can be expected to arise between those who control the political decisions and a society's economic destiny and those who have been reduced to a condition succinctly described by Touraine (1971: 9) as "dependent participation."

If we accept the concept of the postindustrial society as discussed above, criminology will need to anticipate its development. Thus it is likely that the tasks of criminology will include the focus on the concept of the "quality of life," which will no doubt propel it further afield than its present focus on crime as a social phenomenon and on the machinery set up to deal with its manifestations.

SOME BASIC QUESTIONS OF MODERN CRIMINOLOGY
AND FUTURE DIRECTIONS

Criminology today concerns itself mainly with the key concepts of crime, the criminal, and the mechanisms of social control.
To these concepts we have added the quality of life. If these concepts are accepted as givens, all questions of definition, etiological
statements, and sanctions will depend on the problems and issues
surrounding these concepts. Further, the reciprocal relationships
between these concepts will clearly determine the specific questions
criminology must seek to answer. Within its current sphere of inquiry, criminology includes the description of the extent and structure of crime, the development of offender typologies, the assessment of differences between known and unknown offenders, the analysis of individualized sanctions and treatment approaches, victimology,
and the cost of crime, among many others. Analyzing the multiplicity of approaches as they now exist in criminology, some major
developments can be recognized and certain directions can be identified. Principal among these are the expansion of the sphere of
criminological inquiry (vergroessertes Wissensgebiet), a deemphasis
of the role of the individual offender based on the recognition that the
reduction of the problem of crime to the problem of the offender has
outlived its utility, and an increasingly critical stance and scientific
rigor on the part of the profession, which will lead to a more dynamic, scientific, and interactionist criminology.

The Expansion of Criminology's Sphere of Inquiry

Today the traditional definitions of crime and the traditional
legal mechanisms of responding to identified crime are no longer
accepted as givens by most criminologists; rather they have come
to be perceived as problematic. Further, criminology's current
focus includes within its sphere of analysis the study of victims,
victim-offender relationships, and every conceivable aspect of the
administration of criminal justice. For example, labeling theory
and the study of societal reaction to crime have contributed substantially to the widening of criminology's approach. (It should be
noted, however, that the significance of labeling theory's contribution to criminology probably lies more in its research approach
than in any actual enhancement of empirically verified knowledge or
theory.) In the future, criminology probably will expand into new
areas which will improve policy decisions aimed at reducing crime
and improving the quality of life. It is important to recognize that
the latter can be defined by both positive and negative factors. In
his discussion of an improved quality of life, Wilkins (1977) writes:

> Negative factors are particularly important as
> are "absences" of factors. Philosophers have
> dealt at considerable length with the concept of
> freedom and noted that "freedom-from" differs
> from "freedom-to," and similar issues. Free-
> dom from, or the absence of a fear of crime in
> a community may be a far more important indi-
> cator than any positive or present factor. . . .
> It is, of course, difficult to count things which
> do not exist, but the absence of "ills" is not the
> same as the presence of "goods"; indeed it is
> the former which is the more critical for the
> quality of life as seen from the perspective of
> criminal justice.

Deemphasis of the Role of the Individual Offender

For too long criminology focused almost exclusively on the
criminal and offender. The victim, the situation, the physical environment, and most other aspects of that complex event called
crime tended to be ignored (Wilkins 1977: 154). Perhaps this exclu-
sionary approach has accounted for the fact that criminology has not
been too successful in explaining criminal behavior or in accounting
for its absence. Whenever the problem of crime is reduced to the
problem of the offender, serious limitations ensue. Such an oversimplification constitutes a disservice to criminology and is not an
adequate specification of the crime problem. And no problem can
be resolved until it is adequately described and specified. There
can be no doubt that future criminological research will need to expand its scope and widen its horizons to include environmental factors, victim-offender relationships, and situational variables if it is
to improve significantly our knowledge and the state of the art.

Increasing Scientific Rigor and Critical Stance
on the Part of the Profession

With the development of the social sciences in the United States
and Europe in the past decade and a growing number of sociologically
trained criminologists, criminological thought has grown more scientific. This trend is likely to prevail. Further, the existing contrast
between the applied professions (for example, jurists, psychiatrists,
clinical psychologists working in criminal justice, and so on) and the
academically based sociologist-criminologist has probably strength-
ened the latter's scientific rigor and thought, if for no other reason

than the criminologist's research and professional opinions are so
frequently challenged or at odds with the policy makers. In addition,
criminological thought today, as it applies to the key concepts and to
empirical research, has become more dynamic than it used to be.
This development is visible from the renewed focus on questions that
pertain to such issues as victim-offender relationships, the dark
figure of crime and delinquency, criminal justice functions and
processes, and the questions of selection (and prejudice) in the application of the law. Similarly, such sociological concepts as social
control and socialization have enriched the criminological discussion.
There prevails today an increased readiness to accept interdisciplinary approaches to the problem of crime and to work toward the improvement of the quality of life in society. The time has come to
recognize that ultimate answers will probably never come from a
single discipline but will depend on the mutual cooperation and inter-
change of ideas of professionals from many disciplines. The expanded sphere of criminology unquestionably makes an ideal host for
such an approach.

On the minus side of the criminological endeavor, there has
been a decline in emphasis on criminal prognosis and treatment.
Also, the lack of efficiency within the criminal justice system and
rampant injustice in the administration of the law are appalling.
While criminal justice is in desperate need of improvement, criminology, on balance, is richer, more encompassing, multiple and
dynamic in its approaches, occasionally politicized, and more scientific today than it has been in the past. While the plurality of the
different professions within this field has created considerable ten-
sion, crisis, and conflict, it has also contributed the necessary fer-
ment to quicken the development of the discipline. What remains to
be done is to pursue equity, liberty, and justice for all citizens, the
humanization of the criminal justice process, and especially the general improvement of the quality of life of a postindustrial society
that is rapidly moving into the twenty-first century.

SOME BASIC ISSUES AND PRIORITIES FOR
THE CRIMINOLOGY OF THE FUTURE

Future criminological research needs to recognize that criminology is heavily influenced by value systems and lies tenuously between moral concerns and technology brought together by the concept of law. As a result, changes in technology will affect crime as
much as will changes in values. Wilkins (1977: 21) states that "value
systems emphasize the human actors in the situation, event or act
which is defined as criminal; technology tends to emphasize the

circumstances surrounding the event and the techniques available to those who commit crimes, as well as to those who attempt to prevent them." Since criminology's past preoccupation with the criminal often neglected to view crime as a social phenomenon, a new dimension is needed in the discussion of crime: Political, economic, and social causes of crime will increasingly need to be linked to the effects of public policy, if the state of knowledge in criminology is to advance and if crime is to be more effectively controlled. Unquestionably, crime and policy are interrelated. Modern and now postindustrial societies are increasingly "service" oriented as opposed to "production" oriented. This phenomenon, paired with the population explosion, is rapidly reducing opportunities for the poor and minority groups in such societies. The situation is aggravated by the fact that earth is finite and expansion by emigration into "new lands" is no longer possible. In addition, opportunities for the working and lower-middle classes may also be declining; this in turn could lead to a rising crime rate among these groups. Clearly, to focus on large-scale demographic, social, economic, and technological causes of crime which extends the scope of analysis beyond present simplistic concerns regarding such items as race, poverty, and crime is to introduce a new dimension into criminological discussion and research. An excellent example of such an expanded focus is the recent study estimating the social costs of national economic policy prepared for the Congressional Joint Economic Committee (1976). This study evaluates the long-term and aggregative impact on society of changes in income, prices, and employment and makes a significant contribution to economic and public policy. Seven indicators of social stress--total mortality, homicide, suicide, cardiovascular-renal disease, cirrhosis of the liver mortality, total state imprisonment, and state mental hospital admissions--were evaluated to determine their sensitivity to changes in real income, rates of inflation, and rates of unemployment. It was found that all seven of these stress indicators are directly affected by changes in the three national economic variables and that the unemployment rate has the most profound impact on these three variables (Joint Economic Committee 1976: iv).

Future criminological research will need to maintain a similarly expanded view. As a result, the following policy-relevant research is likely to gain increasing importance in the future and should yield considerably more payoff than present limited concerns and orientations: macroeconomic analyses of crime, the study and control of illicit marketplaces, organized crime, political corruption, deterrence models, operational definitions of criminal justice, equity, humane treatment, the study of the decision processes, and the use of discretion in the administration of criminal justice.

Additional profitable areas for pursuit would be the environmental control of crime to include experimental modifications of the physical (target hardening) and social environments in which crimes take place, technological and managerial efforts to make the commission of crime more difficult, corporate and collective crime, longitudinal studies of criminal causes as stochastic processes, and the restraint, delay, and prevention of criminal acts. Increased attention will also need to be paid to the development and function of incentives toward socially desirable behavior, not just to focus exclusively on the administration and effects of punishment. Finally, the criminology of the future will take cognizance of the historic tendency to saddle criminal justice with sociomedical and social welfare cases, which has resulted in overloading the machinery of justice and has severely handicapped any effectiveness the system may have. It is clearly beyond the competence and proper scope of criminal justice to deal effectively with the multitude of medically and mentally ill, alcoholics, and drug addicts. Further, the propensity for outlawing private behavior that is so common in our society simply because it is morally objectionable to a part of our society has resulted in overcriminalization. The practical effect of this is that too many laws proscribe too many kinds of behavior and too many problems are being placed into the field of law, which might be better resolved in other areas of specialization. The need is great, therefore, to unscramble the medical, mental health, moral, technological, and scientific questions which are currently intertwined in the criminological enterprise. Once this is accomplished, a clearer perspective will emerge as to which problems--medical, mental, moral, social welfare, economic, or legal--can best be solved by which discipline--medicine, mental health, religion, governmental assistance programs, or criminal justice and criminology.

REFERENCES

Bell, D.
    1967   The Public Interest 6 and 7 (Winter and Spring issues).

Bendix, R.
    1970   Embattled Reason: Essays on Social Knowledge. New
            York: Oxford.

Brzezinski, Z.
    1967   The American transition. New Republic 157 (December).

Joint Economic Committee, Congress of the United States
    1976   Estimating the Social Costs of National Economic Policy:
            Implications for Mental and Physical Health, and Crim-
            inal Aggression. Vol. 1, Paper No. 5 (October 26).

Kaiser, G.
    1976   Kriminologie. Heidelberg: C. F. Mueller Juristischer
            Verlag.

Merton, R. K.
    1938   Social structure and anomie. American Sociological
            Review 3.

Park, R. E.
    1925   The City. Chicago: University of Chicago Press.

Parmelee, M. F.
    1908   The Principles of Anthropology and Sociology in Their Re-
            lations to Criminal Procedure. New York: Macmillan.

Phillipson, C.
    1923   Three Criminal Law Reformers: Beccaria, Bentham,
            Romilly. London: J. M. Dent.

Quinney, R.
    1975   Criminology. Boston: Little, Brown.

Sellin, T.
    1938   Culture Conflict and Crime. New York: Social Science
            Research Council.

Shaw, C. R.
    1929   Delinquency Areas. Chicago: University of Chicago Press.

Sutherland, E. H.
    1947   Principles of Criminology, 4th ed. Philadelphia:
            Lippincott.

Thrasher, F. M.
    1927   The Gang. Chicago: University of Chicago Press.

Touraine, A.
    1971   The Post-Industrial Society. New York: Random House.

Weber, M.
1946   From Max Weber: Essays in Sociology. Translated by
H. H. Gerth and C. W. Mills. New York: Oxford University Press.

Wilkins, L. T.
1977   The development of assessments and inventories related
to criminal justice activities for purposes of long-range
planning. Paper prepared for the Law Enforcement Assistance Administration and United Nations Social Defence
Research Institute Conference on International Criminal
Justice Information Systems held in Rome, January 13-
15.

INTRODUCTION

The next three chapters follow the general theme discussed at length in Chapter 1. Each is concerned with the inadequacy of present-day criminological paradigms and the failure of criminological research to reduce crime or to achieve justice in our society. John P. Conrad, after discussing the mixed performance of the social scientist in the service of policy, comes to the reluctant conclusion that even an effective criminal justice system would not be able to contribute significantly to the containment of the crime problem. Enamored of stale paradigms, criminologists seem to be about as ineffectual in solving the crime problem as any layman would be. But Conrad rejects the concepts of the hard-liners now so prevalent in criminological writings as much as he rebuffs the "Marxian" critiques advanced by the "new criminologists." Calling for a reappraisal of criminology as it stands now, Conrad takes the position that to persist in traditional criminology is to accept the prospect of diminishing returns. In order to escape such a turn of events, he suggests that criminology merge with the new science of society, a merger first suggested for sociology by Birnbaum. Such a development would vastly enlarge the horizon of criminology. As a result, the phenomena of crime could be related to the society that produces them. Also, when viewed in this manner, crime becomes a symptom of the dislocation of the national order, no longer a symptom of a disease called criminality, which can be cured or eradicated as one would a medical illness. Conrad's suggestions agree in principle with the new approach and concepts discussed in Chapter 1. In combination, they may be viewed as the first preliminary outline of the criminology of the future.

The chapter by Don Gibbons and Kelly Hancock shares with Conrad's writings a pronounced pessimism concerning the future of criminal justice and the ability of contemporary criminologists to help reduce crime in modern America. Crippled by overload, the system could easily become ever more ineffectual. Both authors see criminal justice enmeshed in a vicious cycle of increasingly insistent challenge on the part of the disenfranchised and an ever-more inadequate system response. Gibbons and Hancock even question whether we will be able to keep society "patched" up in view of the continued emergence of new types of crime that seem to develop in response to pervasive repression and racism. The authors note a considerable continuity between conventional, liberal, and radical criminological thought. The differences that seem to exist are

largely a matter of degree only. Both radical and liberal criminologists are beginning to note an increase in political forms of crime,
but neither group sees any imminent danger to the existing social
order. Disagreeing with both points of view, Gibbons and Hancock
note an ominous withdrawal of legitimacy from the social order by
many individuals in U.S. society. Their point of view was recently
reinforced by the writings of the Task Force on Disorders and Terrorism, which note the considerable potential and probability for
civil disorder, including terrorism, in our pluralistic society (National Advisory Commission 1976). Both this report and Gibbons
and Hancock raise some crucial questions concerning many unresolved problems that will continue to plague our society for some
time to come and which cry out for resolutions.

The final chapter in Part I by Joseph Scimecca and Sara Lee
represents a significant contribution to criminological theory.
Analyzing recent developments in criminology from a sociology-of-
knowledge perspective, the authors note the major shifts in focus in
criminological theory from functionalism to interactionism to conflict theory. Their basic premise is that there is a relationship between theory, the theorist, and the world in which he lives and works.
Building on and modifying Kuhn's The Structure of Scientific Revolutions (1973), the authors posit that change in social theory can be said
to come from three sources: internal technical developments based
on the rules and decision-making processes within a discipline,
changes in the infrastructure (which concern the important assumptions of a particular theory), and from the interaction effects between
the first and second points. Scimecca and Lee argue convincingly
that the acceptance or rejection of various schools in criminology
and deviance has less to do with the truth or falsity of any particular perspective but with how social conditions shape the assumptions
of the practitioners within the field. As a result, empirical support
has little, if anything, to do with the continued acceptance (or rejection) of a particular paradigm. Indeed, one can always find both
supportive and nonsupportive research given the second-order nature
of social scientific constructs in criminology and deviance. The
authors go on to argue that conflict theory came into prominence with
a shift in societal ethos during the late 1960s and early 1970s. Social
thought during these difficult times was clearly no longer characterized by a desire to understand and explain individual and group
problems but by a desire to understand the political and economic
order of society. Taking an extremely relativistic position, and
one which shifts the focus of understanding to the level of the sociology of knowledge, the authors provide a much broader perspective
from which one can begin to make sense of the various perspectives
and the often contradictory findings derived from these perspectives.

Even though Scimecca and Lee seem to assume that the conflict paradigm will continue to be dominant in criminology for some time to come, we can only reiterate the urgent need of the discipline to transcend this particular frame of reference in the hopes of moving the field from the old to the real new criminology.

CHAPTER

2

**THE USES OF CRIMINOLOGY:
COMPLAINT FROM AN
UNGRATEFUL CURMUDGEON**
John P. Conrad

In his contribution to a recent symposium musing over the
public disenchantment with social science, Wilson (1976: 356-59)
recalls a heyday, the years of the Kennedy and Johnson administra-
tions. Those were the times when social scientists streamed into
Washington at the behest of confident and hopeful presidents to
assist in the making of a better and happier America. Wilson concludes that in spite of illusions and claims, the impact of social
science on policy making was inconsequential. America is neither
better nor happier as a result of our efforts or those of our political patrons.

The services we were called on to perform were more modest
than the expectations with which we went to Washington--I write as
one of the migrants--but more in keeping with what we had to offer.
As Wilson sees the interplay of social science with public policy,
there are three kinds of work for which we may be useful. Because
it seems to me that these three patterns constitute most of the possible contributions of the criminologist to the public good, I will
begin this complaint by considering them.

First, Wilson reminds us, the social scientist was summoned
by the political leadership to supply ideas. On the whole, he says,
not many ideas emerged. Speaking only for criminologists, I think
he gives us too little credit. Plenty of ideas erupted as a result of
our exposure to the commissions, agencies, and bureaus which re-
cruited us. Cloward and Ohlin (1960) advanced their theory of the
opportunity structure, from which a number of social experiments
were generated. At a less-imposing paradigmatic level, the assem-
bly of criminologists who composed the task forces of the Katzenbach
Commission created victimology with the conduct of the nation's first
survey of the victims of crime. Commission consultants and staff

proposed an interesting model for the reorganization of the police, with which little has been done so far, owing to the conservatism of police administrators. Decriminalization of at least some of the victimless crimes was vigorously recommended; considerable progress has since been made toward a more reasonable disposition of the drunks, prostitutes, homosexuals, and marijuana smokers who used to populate our still-noisome county jails. Much was made of community-based corrections as an alternative to incarceration at least as effective as our "training schools" and prisons in the rehabilitation of offenders. Progress in this direction has been modest, in spite of the widespread acceptance of the idea in principle.

It would be foolish to claim that we met President Johnson's demand for programs to banish crime from the U.S. scene, but ideas were supplied, more than the nation or its leaders could translate into action. A new idea is not an immediately digestible offering for the most eager policy maker. Social engineering is an imperfect discipline at best, and it has seldom excelled in the application of ideas to practice. Too much was expected too soon. Impatient presidents induced us to stir ideas into the stagnation of criminal justice. They did not get the transformation for which they hoped, but they did create a criminal justice research community. Things will never be the same again in the nation's police stations, court rooms, and cell blocks.

Second, Wilson suggests, the social scientist was called to Washington to solve puzzles. There were and are many of them on which the public has expected the president and Congress to take action. Our unsafe streets have not become safer nor have the miseries of unemployment been eliminated as a result of the studies we have conducted to solve these and other puzzles. Morosely, Wilson (1976) remarks that at this task none of the social science disciplines has done well. Scholars have not succeeded in explaining the inexplicable, largely because of the "crisis-oriented, hurry-up-and-act-yesterday atmosphere of a presidential commission trying to calm a worried nation. . . ."

We can hardly claim that criminologists have exceeded the performance of our colleagues in other disciplines. We have had the advantage of four amply funded and prestigious commissions during this last decade, but we cannot claim that the recommendations we have propounded have abated crime in our tormented cities. We have not explained the inexplicable because we have proceeded on the assumption that crime is the puzzle, or that crimes are puzzles. The quest for "root causes" hypnotizes us. We acted on the notion that these causes could be traced by methods peculiar to our discipline, and that when found, the causes would be as peculiar to the phenomenon of crime as the spirochete is to syphilis. This delusion survives, and I will return to it.

Finally, the third role of the social scientist in the service of policy is to tell the administrator "what works." Wilson observes that the presidents of the 1960s received little guidance of this sort; innovation was going on at too fast a pace. But for the contemporary criminologist, "what works" is a phrase which reverberates with the vocabulary of Martinson (1974: 22-54) and his colleagues in their summary of the effectiveness of correctional treatment. Their melancholy conclusion, "nothing works," has transfixed the criminal justice system despite the cautious disavowals of its putative exponents.

Does anything "work" in the criminal justice system? There are many disquieting indications that by the measurements now available to us, neither the reduction of crime nor the ends of justice are achieved according to the expectations of an anxious public or the hopes of the social scientist himself. Our contributions to the public disillusionment have been unpleasant and stark. The belief dies hard that a truly effective criminal justice system has a definitive part to play in containing the crime problem, but it is dying amid general apprehension for a future without the hopes that such a faith made possible. Indeed, alarmed pessimism grows as the criminal justice system, increasingly crippled by its overload, becomes more ineffectual in the discharge of its mission. The spiral of ever more insistent challenge and ever more inadequate response is vicious and the means for its interruption is not on the horizon.

So the recent performance of criminologists gets a mixed report. We are not without ideas, but we lack the engineering skill to get them into practice. In thrall to stale paradigms for the study of crime, we are as ineffectual as any layman in solving the puzzles of crime. Our evaluative critique of the criminal justice system has demonstrated its inadequacies for the execution of the tasks to which it is assigned or for the mistaken expectations of the public. In the space of a decade or so, the face of criminology has changed beyond recognition.

Some think of the predicament as a disarray which is remediable only by their particular vulgarization of Marx. We are told that the crime problem is only to be solved by a recognition of the social and economic contradictions inherent in our capitalist culture. The coming of the socialist state, it is predicted, will remove from criminal law all those provisions a capitalist society requires for its protection from the poor it oppresses. The evidence that this outcome can be expected is hard to find in all of Eastern Europe, but in any case, until such a socialist state takes hold of us, the criminologist must persevere in the study of crime in the existing culture.

Others proclaim that the disarray is only the discrediting of a
"liberal" ideology which has assumed that crime can be most effectively dealt with by changing criminals. Because criminals cannot
be changed in the ways we had expected, we should therefore be concentrating on punishing criminals more severely and thereby deter
more crime. This currently popular contention mistakes rhetoric
for reality. In even the most hopeful days of the ideology of rehabilitation, precious little of it was being attempted. Punishment and deterrence were the reigning objectives of the criminal justice system.
They were adulterated by expectations of rehabilitation, making possible a magnanimous posture in the actions of punishment but not
seriously altering its imposition, except to introduce an element of
uncertainty as to its stringency. It is likely that punishment and deterrence might be more efficaciously administered, but as matters
stand now, there are neither the police to catch more criminals, nor
the courts to try them, nor the prisons in which to lock them up.
The draconian measures advocated by van den Haag (1975) and Wilson
(1975) have the same degree of unreality as the "Marxian" critiques
advanced by the "new criminologists" (Taylor, Walton, and Young
1973). It is fanciful to expect the convulsive changes required for a
vastly enlarged criminal justice system such as the advocates of hard
line envisage. This country is not ripe for revolution in criminal
justice from either the right or the left.

In this volume we present a cross section of the interests and
accomplishments of today's working criminologists. In a way, their
work defines their profession. They have built on the intellectual
foundations of the past ten years of turbulence. It is a good time to
appraise the discipline as it stands now and to consider how well it
is fitted to contribute further to the development of criminal policy,
the task to which they were called by Presidents Kennedy and Johnson.

It will be noted that few of the chapters presented here dramatically break new ground. Rather, they represent accretions of knowledge from which the improvement of the criminal justice system can
be planned. Invalid assumptions are readied for discard, and support is mobilized for those processes which have hitherto rested only
on a priori arguments. We should be grateful and we are.

But around us we hear the rattle of discontent from both the
managers of the criminal justice system itself and from the lay public. One prominent criminologist asks how long the taxpayers will
continue to support our increasingly costly research, which seems
to be so unproductive in achieving the desired objective of a reduction in the kinds of crime which have made some of our streets
gauntlets of fear. Another attacks his colleagues because of our
concentration on the causes of crime when society needs a wider
selection of measures to prevent it. Our increasing esoteric

methodology impresses only ourselves, and our findings too often demonstrate the power of our methodology to lead us to conclusions of no great moment, if any. Indeed, the notion is not at all far-fetched that too much contemporary criminology is hardly better than so much scientism, applying as it does the formidable mathematical procedures of natural science to issues which can be as well investigated by fairly elementary statistics. It is probably good for us to stretch our muscles with Markov chains and path analyses, but not much advance in knowledge can yet be claimed from such exercises. Relief from our discontents must be sought elsewhere.

In his presidential address to the Society for the Study of Social Problems, Wheeler (1976: 525-34) called for a return of criminology to the study of the criminal and what he does. He argued that we have gone about as far as is useful to go in the development of theories of deviance and the study of the systems of social control. The great work of the Chicago school of criminology has fallen into an honored desuetude. We all admire the great studies of Thrasher, Shaw, Sutherland, and MacKay, but not many of us have been inclined to follow in their footsteps. It may well be that this criticism is as inappropriate as the charge that modern composers are letting us down because they no longer produce concertos like those of Mozart and Beethoven. Sutherland wrote the annals of Chic Conwell and his like in part because the opportunity to do so presented itself, but also because it seemed that this was the kind of information society required at the time. We needed that kind of description of the life styles of thieves if we were ever to arrive at a sufficiently reliable understanding of the individual career thief to enable us to theorize about the epidemiology of thievery and to propose strategies for its control.

It is doubtful that Sutherland would choose to pursue his study of the deeds of Conwell if he were to return to Chicago today. But I think there is a continuity between his great work and that of the names listed in the contents of this volume, just as a continuity of musical standards and tradition extends from Mozart and Beethoven to Stravinsky and Boulez. The question for the theoretical criminologist to consider now is where this continuity will take us in the future. If we have moved from the study of criminal activity to an analysis of the mechanisms of social control and now find ourselves running out of useful issues to resolve, where is our next emphasis?

Some will argue that we have much more to do in the study of social control. Economists in considerable numbers have zestfully applied their techniques of study to the problems of deterrence. Some of us find a useful outlet for our investigative talents in exploring effective incapacitation of various kinds of offenders by means of various kinds of restraint. I will concede that there is more work to be done before we have an adequate estimate of the capabilities of

social control by the criminal justice system. Nevertheless, the
limits of such studies can be clearly seen, long before their conclusions can be predicted. The study of the criminal justice system
was brought into vogue by a succession of presidential commissions
dominated by lawyers and their interests in the world in which they
work. The end of these studies is in sight. We now know better
what we should have known all along: that the administration of justice can do little more than collect and dispose of the debris of social
dislocation and pathology. Our studies have explained the behavior
of the courts, the police, and the jails and in doing so we have been
more useful than our critics understand. We now have to move on.
    In a recent essay, Birnbaum (1975: 466) says:

> Many of us are primarily interested in society
> and secondarily in sociology. The analysis of
> society presents problems, some of them very
> profound, none of them easy. Many of our con-
> temporaries are doing interesting work on so-
> ciety, much of it quite unclassifiable in the con-
> ventional academic categories. Why not join
> them on the frontiers of thought instead of per-
> sisting in the attempt to construct a solipsistic
> universe of discourse? Sociology may gradual-
> ly lose its distinctiveness as our efforts combine
> in a new science of society. That would hardly
> be a tragedy: the new science would continue
> that attempt at synthesis and contemporaneity
> which gave dignity to the sociological tradition.
> That, however, is a somewhat distant prospect.
> For the moment, the most effective way to be
> loyal to the tradition is to accept the conse-
> quences of its ending.

    Whether the kinship between sociology and criminology is
parental or avuncular is a metaphorical nicety for others to resolve.
But what ails sociology is a malaise which is ominously similar to
the symptoms manifested by criminology. To persist in traditional
criminology is to accept the prospect of diminishing usefulness. To
take our impressive continuity into the new science of society suggested by Birnbaum is to multiply those uses by relating the phenomena of crime to the society which produces them. It is in the
social system as a whole that the solution to the modern, or perhaps
postmodern, plague must be sought.
    At the turn of the century, Durkheim plunged himself into a
bitter and never-resolved controversy with his less-immortal

antagonist, Gabriel Tarde, concerning the normality of crime (Lukes 1973: 307-10). To this day, his contention is unacceptable to many social scientists as well as incomprehensible to most laymen. His dictum is invaluable in the context of the perceived crisis.

Arguing that the desirable condition of society may be defined in the same way as in defining good health, Durkheim (1938: 75) wrote that

> the object of our efforts is both given and defined at the same time. It is no longer a matter of pursuing desperately an objective that retreats as one advances, but of working with steady perseverance to maintain the normal state, of reestablishing it if it is threatened, and of rediscovering its conditions if they have changed. The duty of the statesman is no longer to push society toward an ideal that seems attractive to him, but his role is that of the physician: he prevents the outbreak of illnesses by good hygiene, and he seeks to cure them when they have appeared.

Weary of the "medical model" as a paradigm for the rehabilitation of the criminal, social scientists are naturally cautious about using a metaphor drawn from medicine and hygiene in considering social policy. Like any metaphor, Durkheim's analogy is valuable only for bringing an idea to notice. The practice of political hygiene is not launched by suggesting its possibility.

It is fair to say that neither social scientists nor political leaders have done much with Durkheim's cue. Instead, we have dealt with crime as a symptom of a disease called criminality which affects individuals and which may be cured or even eradicated, just as we have seen the last of smallpox and have come close to eliminating tuberculosis. Durkheim would not have us disregard the individual crimes which afflict us, nor would he recommend against their punishment. But he thought that criminal behavior should be seen in the context of a larger social pathology, enabling us to chart the changing morbidity of the community and its consciousness. Seen this way, crime is a symptom of the dislocation of the national order. The anger and resentment of the unskilled farm laborer who moves from the rural South to the streets of the Northern cities expresses itself naturally in mugging just as similar anger and resentment moved Sicilian peasants on the same streets 50 years ago to reproduce a conspiratorial kind of criminal entrepreneurship which had been familiar to them in the old country. In the study of society into which criminology should gradually merge its traditions and continuities of scholarship, we will wish to study the anger and resentment, not the crime. We have nearly outgrown the old criminology, but we can still be proud of contributions such as those appearing in this volume. Nevertheless, the new criminology is an urgent need. Its uses in diagnosing and curing the ills of a society afflicted with the analogs of degenerative diseases will be of far greater significance than our past accomplishments. Call this the churlish ingratitude of an ungrateful curmudgeon, if you will. But what we have here gives us reason to believe that the greatest contributions of criminology are still to come.

REFERENCES

Birnbaum, N.
    1975   An end to sociology? Social Research 42, no. 3 (Autumn).

Cloward, R. A., and L. E. Ohlin
    1960   Delinquency and Opportunity: A Theory of Delinquent Groups. Glencoe, Ill.: Free Press.

Durkheim, E.
    1938   The Rules of Sociological Method. Translated by S. Solovay and J. H. Mueller. New York: The Free Press.

Lukes, S.
    1973   Emile Durkheim: His Life and Work. London: Allen Lane.

Martinson, R.
    1974   What works? questions and answers about prison reform. The Public Interest 35 (Spring)

Taylor, I., P. Walton, and J. Young
    1973   The New Criminology. London: Routledge and Kegan Paul.

van den Haag, E.
    1975   Punishing Criminals. New York: Basic Books.

Wheeler, S.
    1976   Trends and problems in the sociological study of crime. Social Problems 23 (June).

Wilson, J. Q.
    1975   Thinking about Crime. New York: Basic Books.

    1976   Social science: the public disenchantment. The American
           Scholar 45 (Summer).

3

SOME CRIMINOLOGICAL THEORY
AND FORECASTS FOR A SOCIETY
THAT IS COMING APART

Don C. Gibbons
R. Kelly Hancock

This chapter consists of two related parts. The first examines the development of criminological thought over the past 50 years or so, but with particular emphasis upon modern liberal-cynical criminology and recent radical-conflict perspectives (Gibbons and Garabedian 1974). This section will deal with the emergence of conflict perspectives, will show the earlier versions of this kind of theorizing, and so on. It will argue that for all the radical, polemical language involved in radical criminology, this sort of analysis actually is rather highly "intellectualized" and detached in character, with the criminological exponent of these views not really involved in uttering apocalyptic visions of impending doom. Nor do they act upon their diagnoses of the social order's defects, for most of them refrain from engaging in revolutionary activities. Instead, they hang around universities, leading the life of the mind. Most radicals are involved in suggesting that perhaps we ought to try to bring about a socialist revolution so as to get rid of the root causes of crime, but one also gets the sense that these people back off from any sort of argument that our society is in such terrible shape that if we don't create a revolution we are all going to be doomed, and in the very near future. Stated differently, we seem to have a choice: either continue to repress people, keep the lid on racism and sexism, with perhaps some increase in turmoil but still at manageable levels, or work for a more humane, socialist society.

The second part of this chapter goes on to ask whether events in the real world have been occurring that will mean that criminological thought will have to be modified further in a conflict direction, taking account of massive increases in new forms of crime that are direct responses to repression, racism, and so on. Then, too, these recent events may mean that we can no longer be sanguine

about the possibilities of keeping the society patched up. There may
be more urgency to the need for dissolution of modern corporate
capitalism than criminologists acknowledge. Failure to move in
these directions may mean markedly greater levels of turmoil and
greater tendencies toward the unraveling of the social and moral
order than suggested by most radicals.

   This second part of the chapter will draw upon various recent
events in the United States that may be harbingers of things to come.
We have in mind here such events as the "Zebra killings" in San
Francisco and various facets of the Patty Hearst kidnapping and the
Symbionese Liberation Army (SLA) movement. We would hope that
this second section, which is predictive in character, would be sol-
idly grounded in whatever empirical evidence can be marshalled
regarding current developments in the United States, and in extrapo-
lations from revolutionary periods and patterns from the past. Let
us elaborate upon some of these notions.

THE DEVELOPMENT OF CRIMINOLOGICAL THOUGHT

   Some brief mention should be made of premodern thought
about criminality as represented by Lombroso (1896) and others of
that ilk. These views took the criminal law as "given" and thought
of it as the codification of moral law. "Criminals" were seen as
morally defective persons who were flawed in other ways too, with
the view often being advanced that they were members of the "criminal classes." The thrust of causal analysis was to ask how moral
weaklings are produced, and the usual hypotheses pointed in the
direction of hereditary taint, aberrant family life, or other conditions
of that sort. Societal defects were heavily underplayed.

   Then, early sociological criminology (1900-30) in the United
States tended to run parallel to such notions. Here again, the laws
were taken as "given" and merely the codification of mores, moral
laws, and so on. The etiological focus was almost entirely upon the
question, "Why do they do it?" and the answers were located in
heredity, bad families, and the like.

   More modern, liberal-cynical criminology (1930-70) also has
tended to center about queries regarding the behavior of criminals,
rather than on the criminality of behavior, as pointed out by Vold
(1958), Turk (1964, 1969), and a number of others, including Jeffery
(1956). That is, until recently criminologists rarely asked: "How
come certain kinds of behavior (and people) have come to be defined
by some social process as 'criminal'?" Instead, the behavior-of-
criminals query is the sort of thing involved in differential association
theory, where the concern is with the question: "How do people come

to learn to be burglars, rapists, and so on?" This is the question addressed in Merton's (1957) anomie formulation too: Why do people engage in deviant acts (rather than why are these acts defined as "deviant" in the first place)?

However, this whole business is a relative matter. One can find some attention to the criminalization process, that is, the making of laws and tagging of persons as "criminals" even in the writings of early figures such as Parmelee (1908). We will also show that Vold (1958) had quite a bit to say about the need to study law making, the conflict origins of law, and so on. The same can be said about some of Sutherland's (1947) writings. Hence the modern radicals are not uttering entirely new ideas about the social origins of laws. Instead, what is most noticeable about statements by such persons as Quinney (1971, 1974) is that they argue that all or nearly all laws are the outgrowth of conflict in which the "overdogs" create laws so as to repress "underdogs," so that radicals don't concede that any criminal laws are related to widely shared moral sentiments (incest laws, for example). Also, there is a conspiratorial tone in the writings of Quinney (1971, 1974) in which loose assertions are made about how "society" does various things or how the "power structure" creates repressive laws. The "looseness" resides in the reification of notions such as "society" and the failure to articulate the details of the social processes that are presumably operating in the creation of laws. But in all of this, one can argue that there is some continuity between conventional, liberal views in criminology and more recent, radical ones.

But again, the heaviest emphasis in liberal criminology has been on the behavior-of-criminals question. The hypotheses and theories developed here have been quite sophisticated and sociological. We have abandoned those notions that criminals are outsiders who are thrust upon us from time to time by social aberrations. Instead, we have formulated arguments about basic flaws in the social order that produce criminality, for example dislocations due to rapid social change, urbanization, anomie.

One would be hard-pressed to argue that recent radical diagnoses of the causes of criminality are distinctly different from those involved in conventional or liberal-cynical criminology. Rather, the differences are a matter of degree. Surely the notion advanced by radicals that corporate capitalism is at the heart of crime etiology would not be entirely foreign to criminologists such as Sutherland and various other well-known figures. However, radical criminology tends to be more emphatic than liberal versions in stressing the workings of racism, sexism, and economic exploitation in criminality. Also, radical theorists link these matters directly to basic characteristics and functional needs of corporate capitalism, leading therefore to more pessimistic conclusions about our ability to deal with racism, sexism, and so on. Racism and sexism are fundamental to the successful operation of corporate capitalism. If so, one can hardly argue that we can eradicate these root causes of criminality if they are inevitable features of corporate capitalism. By contrast, the liberal theorist sees some relationships between the economic order and racism and sexism but does not perceive or does not agree that these are inextricably linked; hence we can eliminate or reduce some of these problems (racism, sexism) while still retaining the basic form of social order that we now enjoy.

Another difference in degree between conventional and radical criminology has to do with the radical attention to the international ramifications and consequences of corporate capitalism in the United States. Radicals are more prone to discern connections between exploitation of the peoples of the Third World by U.S. and multinational corporate interests and criminality in the United States than are old-style liberals. That is, the radical theorist argues that corporate capitalism is involved in exploitation of persons in places like Chile and that these forms of activity are generically similar to, or part and parcel of, the economic exploitation of persons in the United States. In the case of the latter, the precarious economic situation of large masses of individuals drives them into crime.

One might conclude this section by directing attention to the writings of Gordon (1971), the Harvard economist. His commentary is radical but not bombastic, with the central tenets of radical criminological thought being laid out quite clearly. One can see that Gordon and others of that persuasion are surely involved in advancing a position that is more radical and pessimistic than what is contained in books such as Gibbons' Society, Crime, and Criminal Careers (1977), even though not entirely alien to the latter.

On this general matter of differences in degree between conventional and radical criminologists, one could also take note of the question of enforcement and social control. Traditional liberal thinkers such as Reiss (1968) contend that the police sometimes misbehave, but not markedly. Quinney (1971, 1974) and others, by contrast, view the police as "pigs" and lackeys of the power structure, employed to repress and harass the underdogs. Traditional criminologists acknowledge that the criminal justice system is often more accurately described as a criminal injustice system, but radicals go further in their claims, viewing prisons as devices through which corporate interests are able to warehouse surplus workers such as blacks and also to defuse their potential for creating trouble by keeping them locked up. This is the core proposition in the argument that blacks are in prison as "political prisoners," found in the writings of black writers like Cleaver (1968) and Jackson (1970) and

voiced also by radicals. Contemporary liberal criminologists tend
not to go this far in their assertions about differential enforcement
and use of the criminal justice system. So here again one can draw
contrasts between radicals and liberals, but we can also see that
these differences are just that: differences in degree rather than
totally separate perspectives.

Regarding the business of corrections, crime prevention, and
amelioration of crime, liberal criminologists of an earlier decade
did often show considerable faith in the ability of such people as applied scientists and trained correctional workers to make significant
inroads upon crime and to reduce criminality. Thus we see a batch
of earlier, liberal criminologists engaged in constructing parole
prediction devices, examining various forms of correctional therapy,
and discussing various improvements to be made in the correctional
machinery so as to bring about crime control. An excellent example
of traditional liberal criminology and its views on crime control can
be found in the 1967 President's Commission on Law Enforcement
and Administration of Justice, The Challenge of Crime in a Free
Society (1967). That document argues that we can win a "war on
crime" if we spend enough money on various kinds of improvements
in the criminal justice system and do some relatively minor
tinkering with the economic order.

However, growing numbers of contemporary liberal criminologists are at least markedly more pessimistic and cynical about the
prospects for reducing crime in contemporary America. I don't
suppose that we are alone in our perception of the massive Law Enforcement Assistance Administration (LEAA) program as constituting
a new form of WPA for middle-class, young, college-trained persons. LEAA money is going to support a variety of things, including
police weaponry, but a major chunk of the money is being spent on
"the crook business" which occupies the time of hordes of criminal
justice planners, treatment workers, and kindred types. Witness
the rapid proliferation of college degree programs in "criminal justice," training young adults for jobs in the "crook business." This
is a kind of business that needs criminals and delinquents to work on
and which would be in bad shape indeed if the offenders were actually
converted into law-abiding citizens. If we did not have conventional
criminals for these college-trained young adults to work upon, we
would have to invent criminals or find some other group of humans
upon which to focus attention. In this sense, at least, crime is
functional in modern U.S. society, where the economy is not up to
the task of providing jobs for all of its middle-class, "good" citizens.

Although we have yet to be convinced that the radical view of
LEAA as a monstrous invention, a domestic CIA designed for purposes of massive repression, is correct, we surely would not argue

that this operation is likely to achieve its manifest goals of crime reduction.

Pessimism is in order, too, when we realize that the principal thing we could do to get criminals out of crime and into law-abiding careers would be to provide them with a meaningful "stake in con- formity" through jobs that offer them some kind of intrinsic rewards in the way of giving them a sense of making meaningful contributions to the social order through the fruits of their labor. But what is the situation we face in trying to get jobs for conventional offenders? The jobs that are available are menial, dead-end ones in such areas as flunky in a car wash, bus boy, or other low-rank, tedious, and meaningless jobs. No wonder, then, that offenders often return to criminality and are not insulated against recidivism by the feeble linkages that we establish for them to the conventional social order.

Still on this same point, many contemporary liberal criminolo- gists would be prone to voice quite pessimistic views about the pros- pects for crime control and crime reduction because of the influence upon their thinking of recent "labeling" lines of argument in the field of deviance. That is, the arguments of labeling theorists suggest that lawbreakers often get enmeshed in patterns of secondary deviance and careers in lawbreaking, in considerable part because of the nega- tive social reactions directed at them after they have become en- tangled in criminality. This view of things maintains that the social stigma and other social liabilities visited upon offenders make it ex- ceedingly difficult for the criminal to disentangle himself from crim- inality.

Now the posture of many contemporary liberal criminologists is one of considerable pessimism about the prospects for winning a war on crime. But the contemporary, conventional criminologist does not engage in explicit arguments of the form holding that the social order of corporate capitalism makes the solution of the crime problem an impossibility because that same corporate capitalism is responsible for the creation of crime in the first place. By contrast, the radical theorist holds that we can achieve a society with a low crime rate or a crime-free society, along with greater maximization of human dignity and individual rights, only if we manage to get rid of corporate capitalism through some kind of social revolution. Various visions of the socialist, crime-free society of the future have been put forth, including the one by Quinney (1971, 1974).

This seems to us to be the distinctive feature of radical criminol- ogy as compared to more popular, liberal versions of criminological thought. The liberal theorist does not allow himself to follow his diag- nosis of the criminogenic features of U.S. society to the conclusion that the society, and particularly corporate capitalism, must be dras- tically restructured. The liberal criminologist "sees" many of the same defects in U.S. society as does the radical theorist, but the former refrains from calling for the overthrow of the current economic order. The radical theorist, by contrast, advocates radical reconstruction of society along socialist lines.

If we examine the writings of radical theorists, we would find considerable variation among these persons. Take Gordon's (1971) writings, on the one hand. He argues that organized crime, white-collar criminality, and garden-variety street crime are all responses of citizens in a society where economic survival, at any level in the economic order, is precarious. He also talks about differential enforcement of the law, economic exploitation in other countries, and so on. But in general, his prose is tempered and similar to academic cant uttered by liberals. By contrast, Quinney (1971, 1974) writes in a much more bombastic, polemical fashion. Further, Quinney's writings are frequently flawed by poorly thought-out arguments and are full of mystifications, reifications, and so on.

But in all of the radical criminological writing, although there are calls for reconstruction of society along socialist lines, these arguments seem to lack a certain emotional fervor. One does not get the sense from these writings that we may be sitting on a powder keg in the form of a volatile, problem-ridden society that is about to blow up. One does not get the impression that we may be living in the last days before the society comes to be rent and torn by violent revolution. In short, radicals tell us that a socialist order is needed, but no sense of great urgency requiring that drastic steps in that direction be undertaken immediately is apparent in those writings.

In both liberal and more recent radical writings in criminology, one can find numerous expressions of the general argument that criminality such as garden-variety theft and robbery, white-collar crime, and other forms of lawbreaking are the product of the economic order. Then, too, some commentary exists in both of these sources regarding expressive criminality taking the form of protests against social and economic injustice. Although radicals are the ones who most frequently point to political crime, and particularly to alleged "bum beefs" in which the alleged political criminals have not actually been engaged in conspiratorial acts, liberals too have noted the increase in political forms of crime in the United States. For example, Sykes (1974) has recently discussed some emerging forms of new crime, of which political protest acts of the "trashing" variety are representative.

Radical theorists are most prone to see instances of repressive injustice in political crimes, holding that the state has acted immorally to use the criminal justice machinery to silence persons whose only crime has been to direct attention at fundamental defects in the social order. Liberals, by contrast, tend to acknowledge that most political protest criminals have, in fact, engaged in illegal acts.

But differences between radicals and liberals aside, what strikes us as most noteworthy about these views regarding political protest as an emergent form of criminality is that neither of these groups of theorists apparently sees any imminent danger to the existing social order manifested in these activities. That is, although radicals would apparently applaud the overthrow of corporate capitalism, the sense of much of their analysis is that such an occurrence is not terribly likely in the immediate future. Reading between the lines, then, the radical message would seem to be that the social order of corporate capitalism is probably going to limp along for some time, maintaining control over the masses through continued exploitation, and so on, lamentable as that might be.

However, we think that another, more ominous forecast about the United States may be in order. We intend to turn at this point to the question: "Is the United States about to blow up?" We want to explore the possibilities that there is underway a massive withdrawal of legitimacy from the social order by individuals in U.S. society. Our attention will focus upon signs of impending doom, whatever they might be. For example, what are the implications, if any, of the SLA, particularly the joining of forces of traditional oppressed persons (such as blacks) and children of privilege such as Patty Hearst? What does that say about a crisis of morality in the United States? Are we going to see the return of long, hot summers soon? Or has the volatile potential of the black ghettos been somehow removed? If it has, it surely is not clear to us how this was accomplished, in light of the continued precarious existence of ghetto blacks that has not been modified by any governmental programs or other efforts. Along the same line, what are the implications of Watergate and related events, where we now see that we have been ruled in recent years by a thoroughly amoral government where anything goes? What about the "energy crisis," where we see that oil companies will apparently go to any lengths to increase profits and rip off millions of average citizens? What about the apparent fact that hordes of citizens disbelieve that there is or was a bona fide energy crisis, believing instead that such oil companies as Standard Oil have been victimizing us?

REFERENCES

Cleaver, E.
    1968   Soul on Ice. New York: Dell.

Gibbons, D. C.
    1977   Society, Crime, and Criminal Careers. 3rd ed. Englewood Cliffs, N.J.: Prentice-Hall.

Gibbons, D. C., and P. Garabedian
  1974   Conservative, liberal and radical criminology: some
          trends and observations. Criminologist. Crime and the
          Criminal 51 (C. Reasons, ed.).

Gordon, D.
  1971   Class and economics of crime. The Review of Radical
          Political Economics 3, no. 3 (Summer).

Jackson, G.
  1970   Soledad Brother. New York: Bantam.

Jeffery, C. R.
  1956   The structure of American criminological thinking. Journal
          of Criminal Law, Criminology and Police Science 46
          (January/February).

Lombroso, C.
  1896   L'uomo delinquente. Torino, Italy: Bocca.

Merton, R. K.
  1957   Social structure and anomie. Chapter 4 in Social Theory
          and Social Structure. Glencoe, Ill.: Free Press.

Parmelee, M. F.
  1908   The Principles of Anthropology and Sociology in Their Re-
          lations to Criminal Procedures. New York: Macmillan.

President's Commission on Law Enforcement and Administration of
Justice.
  1967   The Challenge of Crime in a Free Society. Washington,
          D.C.: U.S. Government Printing Office.

Quinney, R.
  1971   The Social Reality of Crime. Boston: Little, Brown.

  1974   Criminal Justice in America. Boston: Little, Brown.

Reiss, A.
  1968   Police brutality--answers to key questions. Transaction 5
          (July/August).

Sutherland, E. H.
  1947   Principles of Criminology. 4th ed. Philadelphia: J. B.
          Lippincott.

Sykes, G.
    1974   The rise of critical criminology. Journal of Criminal
            Law and Criminology 65, no. 2.

Turk, A. T.
    1964   Prospects for theories of criminal behavior. Journal of
            Criminal Law, Criminology and Police Science 55
            (December).

    1969   Criminality and Legal Order. Chicago: Rand McNally.

Vold, G. B.
    1958   Theoretical Criminology. New York: Oxford University
            Press.

4

PARADIGM SHIFTS IN CRIMINOLOGY AND DEVIANCE: A SOCIOLOGY-OF-KNOWLEDGE APPROACH

Joseph A. Scimecca
Sara Lee

The 1960s witnessed the transformation of orthodox criminology into the sociology of deviance as emphasis on the behavior of the individual criminal gradually shifted to a focus upon social definitions of criminality. The assumption that the law was an instrument of justice--a notion that had characterized the 1950s--became problematic as interactionism and the conflict perspective opened up new areas of investigation. While any number of recent works in the area of deviant behavior have documented this change, none so far have offered any cogent explanation for the shifts in emphasis (Rock 1973). What is necessary is to approach the area of deviance from the much broader field of sociological theory. What follows is an attempt to analyze criminology and the sociology of deviance from a sociology of knowledge perspective, in particular through the use of the ground-breaking work in the philosophy of science, Kuhn's The Structure of Scientific Revolutions (1973).

THE STRUCTURE OF SCIENTIFIC REVOLUTIONS

Put simply, Kuhn invokes the concept "paradigm" to explain the history of the natural sciences. A paradigm is a model or dominant theory upon which additional theories and research are based. "To be accepted as a paradigm, a theory must seem better than its competitors, but it need not, and in fact never does, explain all the facts with which it can be confronted" (Kuhn 1973: 17-18). Paradigms gain a dominant status because they help those practitioners who accept them to successfully solve a number of problems recognized as acute. Individuals who do not work within the paradigm are either ignored or move into some other group. Research, then, is based

on a shared paradigm with a commitment to the same rules and
standards for scientific practice. "The commitment and the apparent consensus it produces are prerequisites for normal science,
i.e., for the genesis and continuation of a particular research tradition" (Kuhn 1973: 11). Kuhn thus sees the practitioner's work as a
mopping-up operation in a puzzle-solving framework, "an attempt to
force nature into the preformed and relatively inflexible box that the
paradigm supplies. Indeed, . . . that which will not fit the box is
often not seen at all" (Kuhn 1973: 24). The puzzle-solving nature of
the enterprise is of paramount importance because the major requirement of a puzzle is not that it be interesting or important but
that it be solvable (Kuhn 1973: 37).

> To a great extent these [puzzles] are the only
> problems that the community will admit as scien-
> tific or encourage its members to undertake.
> Other problems including many that had previous-
> ly been standard, are rejected as metaphysical,
> as the concern of another discipline, or some-
> thing just too problematic to be worth the time.
> A paradigm can, for that matter, even insulate
> the community from the socially important prob-
> lems that are not reducible to the puzzle form,
> because they cannot be stated in terms of the
> conceptual and instrumental tools the paradigm
> supplies.

Kuhn also introduces the concept "community paradigm,"
which consists of textbooks, lectures, and professional journals.
The community paradigm provides the means by which the paradigm's practitioners learn their trade (Kuhn 1973: 43). Paradigms,
therefore, in the Kuhnian sense, are neither universal nor eternal.
(This is an important point in our own analysis and will be developed
later.)
    Up to this point we have only summarized Kuhn's thesis. In
order for his approach to be of any explanatory use, the question of
what causes a change in the acceptance of one paradigm over another by the scientific community must be analyzed. According to
Kuhn (1973: 52), the first step toward change is the "awareness of
anomaly." When an anomaly develops to the point where it can no
longer be ignored, a crisis develops. Or as Kuhn (1973: 84) puts it,
"all crises begin with the blurring of a paradigm and the consequent
loosening of the rules for normal research. . . . [A] crisis may
begin with the emergence of a new candidate for paradigm and end
with the ensuing battle over its acceptance." A paradigm remains

valid until an alternative one becomes available to take its place and
when the transition from one paradigm to another finally becomes
complete: "the profession will have changed its view of the field, its
methods, and its goals" (Kuhn 1973: 85). It is at this point that we
propose a modification of Kuhn for social science in general and
criminology in particular. It is our contention that given the second-
order nature of social scientific constructions and the general state
of empirical research, the role of an anomaly is relatively unimportant. Anomalies or contradictory findings are found throughout social
science, and if their discovery caused paradigm shifts, scientific
revolutions would be an everyday occurrence. Instead, the explanation for shifts in thinking occurs at another level in social science:
at the level of what Gouldner (1970) calls background assumptions
and domain assumptions. Background assumptions are very general
orientations to the world which are internalized very early and are
so much a part of us that we may not even be consciously aware of
them. Domain assumptions (Gouldner 1970: 31) are

> the things attributed to all members of a domain;
> in part they are shaped by the thinker's world
> hypotheses and, in turn, they shape his deliber-
> ately wrought theories. They are an aspect of
> the larger culture that is most intimately related
> to the postulations of theory. They are also one
> of the important links between the theorist's work
> and the larger society.

The social scientist's gestalt is thus a function of the ethos of
the broader society. "Social science is a part of the social world as
well as a conception of it" (Gouldner 1970: 13). Basically, one's
assumptions influence the social career of a theory. If one's background assumptions are in agreement with the assumptions of the
theory, the theory will likely be accepted. If these assumptions
differ, dissonance occurs and the probability of the rejection of the
theory becomes greater. The important assumptions are, thus,
what Gouldner (1973: 46) labels the "infrastructure" of the theory.
Changes in social theory come from three sources. One concerns
the internal technical development based on the rules and decision-
making processes in the discipline. The second is due to a change
in the infrastructure, and the third and most important has to do
with the interaction of the first two. In short, our thesis is that the
acceptance or rejection of various schools in criminology and deviance has very little to do with the "truth" or "falsity" of any one
perspective. Ours is a relativistic position which argues that the
various shifts in criminology and deviance have less to do with

questions of accuracy than with how social conditions shape the
assumptions of practitioners within the field. We should point out,
though, that while we see a different process causing paradigm
shifts in criminology and deviance than that which occurs in the
natural sciences, the perceptions of practitioners in all areas are
basically the same. When Kuhn (1973: 85) speaks of the natural
science practitioners of the ascendant paradigm not necessarily seeing things in a completely different light but in a new relationship
within a different framework, he could just as well be speaking of
criminologists. His assertion, that older practitioners usually do
not embrace the new paradigm but cling steadfastly to the old and
that only when they retire or die off is an older paradigm finally discarded, seems to be on the level of a truism. Indeed, this would
begin to explain why criminological research is still being done using
different paradigms.

With our modification of Kuhn's premise now stated, we turn
to recent events in the field of criminology in order to demonstrate
our thesis.

FUNCTIONALISM, SYMBOLIC INTERACTIONISM, AND CONFLICT: THREE PARADIGM SHIFTS

It is the contention of this chapter that the field of criminology
has undergone three major paradigm shifts since the late 1940s: a
shift from functional analysis to symbolic interactionism and then
to conflict analysis.

Functionalism: The 1940s and 1950s

As was the case in sociology, the predominant model underlying criminological research in the 1940s and 1950s was functionalism. Two basic functional approaches are discernible during this
period: pure functionalism or deviance as norm violation, and
anomie theory. Examples of the first are such works as Davis'
(1971) analysis of prostitution, Bloch's (1951: 215-21) explanation
of gambling in American society, Mizruchi's (1959: 114-20) description of a Bohemian community, and Dentler and Erikson's (1959:
98-107) thesis on the functions of deviant behavior in groups. The
stress is on the social structure and the individual's adaption to it.
The second and more important variant of functionalism derives
from Merton's (1957: 131-94) famous anomie "paradigm." The
major focus, here again, is on social structure, with a greater emphasis on the system's goals and means. According to Merton, an

individual who is unable to attain societal goals through normal or legal institutional means may turn to deviant or illegal means to attain these socially prescribed goals. Such theories as Cohen's (1958) "delinquent sub-culture," Miller's (1958: 5-19) "focal-concerns," and Cloward and Ohlin's (1961) "differential-opportunity," to cite the more well-known, are derivatives of Merton's notion of anomie.

For the most part, the first, or pure functionalist, approach generated little systematic research to test its major assumptions--this in spite of Merton's famous dictum that theory and research be mutually supportive. Basically, deviance was taken as given and the functions of various types of deviant behavior were described. The second functionalist perspective, that of "anomie," did, however, generate a plethora of research. For example, Glaser and Rice (1959: 679-86), Meir and Bell (1960: 645-65), Reiss and Rhodes (1961: 720-32), Mizruchi (1960: 645-54), Hanson and Graves (1963), and Landis, Dinitz, and Reckless (1963: 408-16), to mention a half dozen or so researchers, all tended to support Merton's anomie theory. Yet if our thesis is correct, empirical support has little, if anything, to do with the continued acceptance of a paradigm. More important than any supportive research was the fact that the complacent 1950s gave rise to the critical era of the 1960s. Black, student, and women's movements cried out for analysis, and the functionalist model could not explain their occurrence. The tremendous change that had occurred was just too abrupt and disruptive to fit the functional model. A theoretical shift occurred as soon as a more individualized approach became needed. Whereas the theoretical frameworks of the 1950s saw the deviant as maladjusted, the new paradigm, the interactionist perspective, perceived the deviant as one swept along by societal pressures. Becker (1963: 4), for example, one of the founders of the interactionist perspective, describes his outlook as one of "unconventional sentimentality," seeing the deviant as the underdog and society as the offender.

It is interesting to note that nonsupportive research, anomalies in Kuhn's terms, occurred well after functionalism had lost its role as the dominant, and indeed only, paradigm in criminology. Reeder and Reeder (1969: 451-61), for instance, tested the hypothesis that unwed women would be more socially isolated than those who were wed, and that this social isolation would produce anomie. Their research failed to support this hypothesis. Sandhu and Allen (1969: 107-10) studied female delinquents with regard to goal obstruction and anomie. They found that delinquent girls were less committed to institutionalized goals than were nondelinquent girls.

Winslow (1967: 468-80), in a study of anomie and delinquency, found that "youngsters of lower status are subject to lower success pressures . . . [therefore] perceived opportunities do not vary significantly with a youngster's position in the social structure." And there are others, but the essential point has been made: anomalies seem to be unnecessary agents of change; paradigmatic change occurs with or without them.

Interactionism

The interactionists drew upon such early symbolic interactionists as Cooley (1902) and Mead (1964) for their theoretical base. The ongoing interaction between the individual and those around him, from whom he derived his self-definition, became the center of attention. The interactionist approach attempted to explain how and why an individual became deviant.

Labeling theory is an outgrowth or extension of the interactionist model. An individual is deviant after he has been so defined, or "labeled," by society and his significant others. This results in a change of self-definition and the acceptance of a deviant role. Deviant behavior is thus "caused" by definitions which are seen as generating the symbolic processes by which individuals come to be labeled as inferior or morally unfit, thereby undergoing a transformation of status (N. J. Davis 1972: 451).

The interactionist paradigm and labeling theory, like the functionalist paradigm which preceded them, have had both supportive and nonsupportive research generated from their premises. Examples of the former are Goffman's (1963) study of stigma, Becker's essay (1963: 46-58) on the marijuana user, and Lemert's (1967) analysis of the check forger, to cite the more well-known studies. As for nonsupportive studies, just to mention the most recent ones, there are Ball's (1967: 293-301) study of abortion clients, Gove's (1970: 873-84) findings on the mentally ill, and Fisher's (1972: 78-83) analysis of stigma and deviant careers in a school setting.

What can be stressed here is Lofland's (1966: 155-58) assertion that interactionism and labeling theory have suffered from a "methodological inhibition." This derives from an internal conceptual impoverishment facilitated by an absorption with general imagery and a resultant unsystematic, elusive, and suggestive empirical presentation rather than definitive tests of the interactionist framework. Labeling theory, therefore, has never, despite the disclaimers to the contrary of Schur (1971), fully answered Gibbs' (1966: 14) four famous questions:

First, what elements in the scheme are intended to be definitions rather than substantive theory?

Second, is the ultimate goal to explain deviant
behavior or to explain reactions to deviation?
Third, is deviant behavior to be identified exclusively in terms of reactions to it? Fourth,
exactly what kind of reaction identifies behavior as deviant?

And more importantly, we contend, labeling theory does not
have to answer these questions because its acceptance or rejection
is based on other factors, which have little to do with its explanatory
powers. Therefore, the reasons why interactionism and functionalism (which has still managed to survive, although not in the manner
it had been accustomed to) are being challenged by a new paradigm,
that of conflict, have more to do with shifts in domain assumptions
of younger sociologists than research findings of older ones.

Conflict

The conflict paradigm purports to overcome the narrowness
of the other two approaches by treating deviance in terms of a political conflict model of social change. It examines the activities of
organizations as political organizational structures. Its major
"focus is upon the conflict process during which organizations manufacture and manipulate definitions, procedures, bureaucratic priorities and administrative instruments of control" (N. J. Davis 1972:464).
The conflict paradigm suggests that social control produces deviance.
Its major proponents--Quinney (1970 and 1974), Turk (1966: 338-52),
Lofland (1966), and their students--are just beginning to accumulate
research using this perspective; therefore, even attempting to list
anomalies is premature. Basically, we hold that the conflict paradigm came to prominence with a shift in the societal ethos of the
late 1960s and early 1970s, characterized no longer by a desire to
understand and explain individual and group problems but by a desire
to understand the political and economic order of society. In light
of the tighter economic strain on the status quo and the unprecedented
attack on politicians in the United States, this shift in attention seems
plausible. And if a recent Yankelovich poll (Knickerbocker News
1972: 11a), which showed that 60 percent of youth aged 16 to 25 believed that America is a democracy in name only and is run by
special interest groups, is an indication, the conflict paradigm may
be with us for a long time.

SUMMARY AND CONCLUSION

In this chapter we have tried to show that the paradigmatic changes that the field of criminology and deviant behavior have recently undergone have less to do with empirical research generated by competing paradigms than with shifts in the societal ethos, what Gouldner refers to as domain assumptions. Kuhn's notion of anomalies as precipitating change, therefore, has little applicability in the social sciences.

While we have not explicitly stressed the implications of our thesis, they have nevertheless been implicit in our analysis. We have postulated an extreme relativistic position,[1] one which shifts the focus of understanding to the level of the sociology of knowledge, a perspective which has been conspicuously absent from criminological theory. Our position, stated simply, is that there is a relationship between theory, the theorist, and the world within which he lives and studies. To deny this is to forever be confronted with anomalies in research, a condition due to the very nature of the data studied and the methods used in the studies. Only when we approach criminological theory and research from a broader perspective--that of the sociology of knowledge--can we begin to make sense of the various perspectives and the oftentimes contradictory conclusions derived from these perspectives which comprise the field of criminology and the sociology of deviance today.

NOTE

1. For a more detailed presentation of this position, see Joseph A. Scimecca, "C. Wright Mills and the Sociology of Knowledge," a paper presented at the meeting of the Eastern Sociological Society, Philadelphia, April 1974.

REFERENCES

Ball, D. W.
   1967   Ethnography of an abortion clinic. Social Problems 14 (Winter).

Becker, H. S.
   1963   Outsiders: Studies in the Sociology of Deviance. Glencoe, Ill.: The Free Press.

Bloch, H.
    1951   The sociology of gambling. American Journal of Sociology
            57 (November).

Cloward, R. , and L. Ohlin
    1961   Delinquency and Opportunity. Glencoe, Ill,: The Free
            Press.

Cohen, A.
    1958   Delinquent Boys: The Culture of the Gang. Glencoe, Ill.:
            The Free Press.

Cooley, D. H.
    1902   Human Nature and the Social Order. New York: Scribner.

Davis, K.
    1971   Sexual behavior. In R. K. Merton and R. Nisbet, Con-
            temporary Social Problems. New York: Harcourt,
            Brace, Jovanovich.

Davis, N. J.
    1972   Labelling theory in deviance research: a critique and re-
            consideration. Sociological Quarterly 13 (Fall).

Dentler, R. , and K. Erikson
    1959   The functions of deviance in groups. Social Problems 7
            (Spring).

Fisher, S.
    1972   Stigma and deviant careers in school. Social Problems
            20 (Summer).

Gibbs, J. P.
    1966   Conceptions of deviant behavior: the old and the new.
            Pacific Sociological Review 9 (Spring).

Glaser, D. , and K. Rice.
    1959   Crime, age and employment. American Sociological
            Review 24.

Goffman, E.
    1963   Stigma: Notes on the Management of Spoiled Identity.
            Englewood Cliffs, N.J.: Prentice-Hall.

Gouldner, A. W.
    1970   The Coming Crisis of Western Sociology. New York: Avon.

Gove, W. R.
    1970   Societal reaction as an explanation of mental illness: an
            evaluation. American Sociological Review 35 (October).

Hanson, R., and T. Graves
    1963   Objective access, anomie and deviance in a tri-ethnic com-
            munity. Paper presented at the meeting of the American
            Sociological Association. Los Angeles (August).

The Knickerbocker News
    1972   Albany, New York. May 22.

Kuhn, T.
    1973   The Structure of Scientific Revolutions. Chicago: Uni-
            versity of Chicago Press.

Landis, J., S. Dinitz, and W. Reckless
    1963   Implementing two theories of delinquency: value orienta-
            tion and awareness of limited opportunity. Sociology and
            Social Research 47.

Lemert, E. M.
    1967   Human Deviance, Social Problems, and Social Control.
            Englewood Cliffs, N.J.: Prentice-Hall.

Lofland, J.
    1966   Deviance and Identity. Englewood Cliffs, N.J.: Prentice-
            Hall.

Mead, G. H.
    1964   George Herbert Mead on Social Psychology: Selected
            Papers. Edited and with an introduction by Anselm
            Strauss. Chicago: University of Chicago Press.

Meir, D., and W. Bell
    1960   Anomie and differential access to the achievement of life
            goals. American Sociological Review 25.

Merton, R.
    1957   Social Theory and Social Structure. New York: The
            Free Press.

Miller, W.
    1958   Lower class culture as a generating milieu of gang de-
            linquency. Journal of Social Issues 14.

Mizruchi, E.
    1959   Bohemianism and the urban community. Journal of
            Human Relations 8 (January).

    1960   Social structure and anomie in a small city. American
            Sociological Review.

National Advisory Committee on Criminal Justice
    Standards and Goals
    1973   Corrections. Washington: U.S. Government Printing
            Office.

Quinney, R.
    1970   The Social Reality of Crime. Boston: Little, Brown.

    1974   Critique of Legal Order. Boston: Little, Brown.

Reeder, L., and S. Reeder
    1969   Social isolation and illegitimacy. Journal of Marriage
            and the Family 31.

Reiss, A., and A. Rhodes
    1961   The distribution of juvenile delinquency in the social
            class structure. Sociological Quarterly 26.

Rock, P.
    1973   Deviant Behavior. London: Hutchingson University
            Library.

Sandhu, H., and D. Allen
    1969   Female delinquency: goal obstruction and anomie.
            Canadian Review of Sociology and Anthropology 6 (May).

Schur, E. M.
    1971   Labelling Deviant Behavior: Its Sociological Implications.
            New York: Harper and Row.

Turk, A.
    1966   Conflict and criminality. American Sociological Review
            31 (June).

Winslow, R.
    1967   Anomie and its alternatives: a self-report study of de-
            linquency. Sociological Quarterly 8 (Autumn).

PART

II

METHODOLOGY

Students of criminology and criminal justice are beginning to note the accelerating inadequacy of the existing social institutions designed to deal with delinquency and crime. There is accumulating evidence that the criminal justice system in the United States is unable to serve the interests of all segments in our society and that it is in the slow but obvious process of breaking down. It is also evident that the dominant theories on delinquency and crime causation are grounded on a weak base of factual knowledge and are insufficiently supported by research. And on those rare occasions when reputable and meaningful research does occur, it is well known that such efforts manage to exert relatively little influence over criminal justice policy formation.

It is unfortunate that this dismal state of affairs occurs at a time when social attitudes toward crime seem balanced precariously on a watershed between an exhausted liberal reformism and the current revival of neoclassic concepts of punishment and "just deserts." While traditionally the offender, not the crime, has been the focus of crime-control policy, the pendulum is now swinging to the other side and the crime is becoming more important than the person who has committed it. In light of these developments, there is an urgent need not only to improve the caliber of criminological research and theory development but also to engage in the systematic testing of competing theories in order to arrive at an empirically grounded knowledge base.

If criminological research is to exert a greater (and much-needed) influence in the field of criminal justice, a number of developments will need to occur. First, the field will need to transcend the "phantom" character of the demand for services, which it shares with the rest of the social sciences. Criminologists tend to write mainly for one another and thereby generate an apparent demand for their services. This observation, although unpalatable, appears to be a fair assessment, since most criminological research--with a number of distinguished exceptions--is characterized by a considerable inapplicability to empirical settings and practices. A quick look at most journal offerings will convince the inquisitor of many an author's diligent pursuit of the "significance of insignificance."

A second problem with criminological research is that there is entirely too little experimentation going on. Criminology as a science involves the proposing of theories, hypotheses, and models and the acceptance or rejection of these on the basis of some external criteria or bench marks. While experimentation cannot prove a particular theory--it can only test, probe, or disprove theories--it does constitute a highly efficient way for rejecting, modifying, or accepting a particular theory or hypothesis. Yet the political climate characteristically has been and continues to be adverse to experimentation in criminal justice. The image of the mad scientist wielding a scalpel performing psychosurgery or sterilization is alive and well in the public mind and has generated substantial fear. With the growth of the prisoners' rights movement came a number of studies exploring psychiatric justice and other behavior modification programs. And public fears were anything but attenuated by the revelation of a limited number of abuses of operant conditions and other behavior modification techniques that had been inflicted on some juvenile and adult prisoners. Criminal justice practitioners, most of whom utilized various innocuous schemes of "positive" behavior control (whereby appropriate, nondeviant behavioral responses are encouraged by rewarding their occurrence), clearly underestimated the publicity dynamite in behavior modification. Nor did they foresee what the news media or other vested interest groups could do with a topic laden with such emotion. Before any significant and definitive research and evaluation could be conducted into the wide range of behavior modification techniques in existence, the programs and concepts came into instant disrepute, whether or not they deserved it. Program development, experimentation, and modification stopped in their tracks, lest the new techniques be misused. The rhetoric accompanying the demise of behavior modification programs has not helped to enhance the image of experimental criminology. The future of experimentation in terms of programs and research will depend on clearing up these and other misconceptions. For example, decision makers and program administrators show little understanding for the need for control groups and randomization in research. But there are other reasons for the notable lack of enthusiasm for experimentation in criminal justice. Program administrators whose cherished programs have just been demolished by evaluative research or who had to suffer through a rejection of their favorite hypothesis may well develop a syndrome of "avoidance-conditioning." Repeated negative findings can easily lead to the avoidance or outright rejection of any subsequent attempts at research and experimentation. And if the very nature of social science is one in which there are available many more wrong responses than right ones, we had better prepare for many disappointing results. Nonetheless, practitioners and researchers will have to recognize that experimentation, while not a panacea for all research problems, constitutes the basic language of proof and may well be one of the most important avenues to cumulative progress.

A third major problem hampering criminological research is the notable lack of sophistication on the part of policy makers (most of whom have legal, not scientific, training), program administrators, and even funding agency staff, in matters of methodology, statistical manipulation, and in the development of adequate and appropriate data bases to which statistical procedures can be applied. The last-mentioned problem is probably the most frequent "crime" of commission in criminal justice today. Who, for example, has not been tempted when embarking on a new research venture to apply the "shotgun" technique (without the benefit of a guiding hypothesis) in an effort to capture every conceivable variable in the hopes of finding unexpected significance in some relationship? Granted, social science operates under recognized and distinct disadvantages when compared to natural science. While the goals of any scientific endeavor--social or natural--can be reduced to explanation and prediction in order to facilitate intervention in some course of events, the social scientist is frequently confronted by the fact that elements composing an explained situation experience sufficient change to interfere with his ability to predict and hence his capacity to intervene.

A fourth and final problem facing criminological research is the fact that criminology shares with the rest of the social sciences an inherently weak theoretical underpinning. Theory consists largely of general orientations toward available information, suggesting types of variables which somehow need to be taken into account, rather than clear and testable statements of relationships between specified and measurable variables. Merton's dictum on social science theory is applicable to criminology as well: We have many concepts but few confirmed theories. There are many points of view, but few theorems. And while there are many approaches, there are few arrivals. More often than not, the degree of validity attached to research findings is unclear. Yet greater clarity may not be sought because the results may possibly prove offensive. In this manner, fallacies manage to stay alive and opinions may be more a function of ideology than scientific fact.

There is no question that the current trend toward quantified research is improving the dismal state of the art, especially if such research is well integrated with an underlying theoretical structure. The following chapter by William Doerner and Anthony Meade exemplifies such an effort. After generating their own data base guided by theory and previous findings, and applying rather sophisticated data analysis and manipulation techniques, the authors take cognizance of the wider theoretical significance of their findings. By doing so, this type of research achieves something greater than the usual sterile excursions in computational gymnastics so frequently found in journals today. On the basis of a study of structural-level conditions as they influence aggregate-level rates and patterns of criminal behavior, the

authors manage to shed light on a significant number of highly contro-
versial issues. For example, in Atlanta, the city they analyzed,
crowding of housing and especially household density have the highest
correlation with the violent crime rate, while economic status has the
highest correlation with the property crime rate. This finding of a
highly pernicious effect of high-density housing contradicts highly pub-
licized studies by Freedman (1975) and Altman (1975) and is therefore
of great significance. The authors found that 76 percent of the variation in the violent crime rate can be explained by the variables of
crowding, quality of housing, housing tenure status, and employment
status. When examining the influence of race composition on crime
rates, the authors found this variable to be a redundant predictor.
This result contrasts with several studies in which the race variable
was found to be a prominent correlate of violent crime. Apparently,
race composition decreases in importance when the focus of analysis
is shifted from between-area to within-area crime rate variation.

It should be noted that this study is significant not because it es-
tablishes a direct cause-and-effect relationship between the variables
discussed above and crime but because it corroborates the growing
realization that crime is related to the larger social issues. This is
of course precisely the point which today's hard liners in criminal
justice either deny or tacitly ignore. In this sense the study com-
plements and expands the recent work by Harvey Brenner for the
Joint Economic Committee of the Congress of the United States (1976).
This report links rises in unemployment to a wide range of pathological social conditions such as an increase in the disease death, homicide, and suicide rate, as well as to increases in mental hospitali-
zations and imprisonment. Studies of the caliber discussed above
are important because they offer evidence on the basis of which
ideology and prejudice can be overcome. It is economic deprivation
and urban blight and not ethnic or racial concentration which seem
to account for many social ills, including variations in our crime
rates. And policy development had better take heed of these findings
lest society will soon have to bear the full toll of its mounting neglect.

REFERENCES

Altman, I.
  1975   The Environment and Social Behavior. Monterey, Calif.:
         Brooks/Cole Inc.

Brenner, H.
   1976   Estimating the Social Costs of National Economic Policy:
           Implications for Mental and Physical Health, and Crim-
           inal Aggression. A study prepared for the use of the
           Joint Economic Committee, Congress of the United States.
           Washington, D. C.: U.S. Government Printing Office.

Freedman, J. L.
   1975   Crowding and Behavior. New York: Viking.

CHAPTER

5

ON REPLICATION AND THE
IMPLICATIONS OF FINDINGS
OF NONLINEARITY IN CRIME RESEARCH

William G. Doerner
Anthony C. Meade

The application of polynomial regression to describe nonlinear relationships between independent and dependent variables was the topic of concern in a recent criminological study by Beasley and Antunes (1974: 439-61). Aggregate-level personal and property crime rates served as dependent variables in that study. While their ecological study of Houston, Texas, was based upon analyses of 20 geographic areas, the authors encouraged reexamination of their investigation in different cities and at a smaller areal unit level of analysis (Beasley and Antunes 1974: 460).

What followed from this work was a rather feeble replication effort by Mladenka and Hill (1976: 491-506). These authors did nothing more than repeat the study using 1973, as opposed to 1970, crime data. Inconsequential changes included unit reclassification where police districts had been restructured and the exclusion from analysis of extreme independent variable cases. In that their analysis also originally involved only 20 data points, the latter operation had the rather obvious result of modifying the form of the regression curve toward linearity.

In sum, the Mladenka-Hill work failed to address important replication issues. First, they repeated the Beasley-Antunes work at the same unit level (police district). Regarding this point, Slatin (1969: 889) has shown that differences in aggregation levels result in changes in correlation magnitudes. His research demonstrated that the larger the aggregation level, the stronger the between-unit correlation. Thus, investigating the generalizability to smaller aggregate levels of analysis of the crime rate-independent variable relationships observed by Beasley and Antunes would seem to be the proper and more instructive exercise. Second, Mladenka and Hill repeated the study in the same geographic setting. This seems a rather pointless undertaking when the crime data are separated by only a three-year period, and even more so in that the replicators' independent variable operational measures are the identical ones used in the original study. Beasley and Antunes urged testing of their findings in other settings and not the reexamination of the relationships of the same 1970 census data to crime rates in the same city three years later.

Other issues concern both of the Houston studies. For example, though Boggs (1965: 899-908) has correctly emphasized the importance of both offender residence and offense location data, the former seem more consistent with etiological investigations which incorporate demographic characteristics of resident populations as hypothesized explanatory variables. When the dependent variable is constructed in terms of the offender's residence it represents a barometer of the incidence of criminality among a resident population which is limited only by the overall geographic boundaries of the study. This of course does not mean to deny the certain deficiencies of official-record crime data. While individuals (city residents in this case) do commit offenses outside the jurisdiction of the record-keeping agency, they represent a more randomly distributed phenomenon than the case of "outsiders" (interunit or intercity) contributing to offense location rates. As Mladenka and Hill (1976: 505) acknowledge, operationalizing the dependent variable on the basis of offense location is not the most satisfactory procedure when conceptualizing the etiology of crime in terms of the ecological life situation of a resident population. Crime location measures result in areal unit rates which simultaneously involve elements of the structural-level situation which are conducive to producing criminal behavior on the part of the resident population, and characteristics of the area which make it attractive for, or vulnerable to, crime on the part of residents and nonresidents alike. The focus of the Houston studies was clearly the behavior of aggregates as it relates to the structural characteristics of those aggregates. Though the replicators indicated an awareness of the shortcomings of location data for this purpose, they apologetically proceeded to use it as the dependent variable indicator.

Most important is the fact that the researchers in both studies ignored the wider theoretical significance of their findings. It is such implications which make this type of research something more than sterile excursions in computational gymnastics. The Beasley-Antunes results suggest that important theoretical modifications concerning the nature of variable relationships are called for. It was basically for this reason that the present verification study was undertaken. Furthermore, in that both Houston studies highlight the empirical demonstration of nonlinear bivariate relationships in the ecological analysis of crime rates, it seems reasonable for this study to test other assumptions of their methodology pertaining to variable relationships. One such consideration is the extent to which the multiple regression analyses presented in those studies should have assumed an additive model of variable effects. This question, as well as the issues introduced above, will be addressed in the following sections of this chapter.

PROCEDURE

Crime data were collected from the official files of the City of Atlanta Police Department. Thus, the City of Atlanta represents the geographic boundaries of the study. Collection operations involved the transferring of case numbers and offenses from the daily arrest log to information cards for all adults arrested during 1970. This step was followed by retrieval of each arrested person's file, thereby allowing procurement of this individual's address at the time of arrest. Each address was then located within its appropriate census tract through use of an ADMATCH directory compiled by the Atlanta Metropolitan Housing and Planning Commission. The effort identified approximately 8,500 city residents charged with roughly 9,900 offenses. For the purposes of this study, arrests were classified as either violent or property offenses. Victimless crimes were excluded from the analysis. Violent offenses included murder, forcible rape, assault, battery, robbery, and kidnapping. Included under property offenses were burglary, larceny, theft, auto theft, forgery, embezzlement, fraud, and arson. Violent and property resident arrest rates were computed for each census tract within the city by summing the number of offenses in that category, dividing by the census tract population age 17 and above, and then multiplying by a constant of 1,000. This age criterion was used because in 1970 the jurisdiction of the criminal court in Georgia began at age 17. The dependent variables in this study are census-tract violent crime rate and census tract property crime rate.

Loftin and Hill (1974: 718) dramatically demonstrated the importance of assuring a rigorous variable set when investigating the reliability of results, as well as the validity of the conclusions, of earlier research. Therefore, selection of the proposed correlates of census tract resident crime rates in this study was based upon a close review of the literature regarding the ecological analysis of intracity variation in the distribution of crime (Beasley and Antunes 1974; Bensing and Schroeder 1960; Green 1970: 476–90; Harries 1974; Moses 1947: 411–20; Quinney 1964: 149–55; Schmid 1960: 351–57; Wilks 1967). Eleven independent variables were selected. Table 5.1 lists these variables, their respective operational indicators, and the direction of their hypothesized statistical relationship with census tract crime rates.

TABLE 5.1

Proposed Independent Variables, Operational Measures, and
the Direction of Their Hypothesized Relationship
to Violent and Property Crime Rates

Variable	Index	Relationship Direction
Economic status	Mean annual income of families and unrelated individuals	Negative
Education status	Mean number of school years completed by those age 25 and above	Negative
Employment status	Percent civilian labor force classified as unemployed	Positive
Housing-tenure status	Percent occupied housing units occupied by owners	Negative
Quality of housing	Percent occupied housing units lacking some or all plumbing facilities	Positive
Crowding of housing	Percent occupied housing units having a person-per-room ratio in excess of 1.00	Positive
Land-area density	Number of persons per square mile	Positive
Residential mobility	Percent individuals relocating their residence in the past five years	Positive
Race composition	Percent population age 17 and above classified as black	Positive
Sex composition	Percent population age 17 and above classified as male	Positive
Age composition	Percent population age 17 through 24	Positive

Source: Compiled by the authors.

Each variable in Table 5.1 represents an aggregate-level measure for a census tract unit and is proposed as a structural correlate of tract crime rates. The mean, rather than the median, was chosen as the operational summary measure of income and education on the basis of the recommendation and justifications presented by Bogue (1969:440). The decision to percentage from the age 17 and above base for the race and sex variables was made because this was the legally defined criminal population -at-risk for Georgia in 1970. This seems to be the correct base, especially where the dependent variables refer to residence of offender rates rather than place of offence rates.

RESULTS AND INTERPRETATION

Table 5.2 presents zero-order correlations between the 11 independent variables and each of the dependent variable forms. The values in columns 2 and 4 refer to Pearson product-moment correlations between independent variables and violent and property crime rates, respectively, where independent variable values have been transformed to their natural logarithms. Both independent and dependent variable values are in their original states in columns 1 and 3. The logarithmic transformation is commonly used as a check for linearity in sociological research.

Levels of statistical significance are not appropriate for decision making in this study since correlations are based upon variable scores for all census tract units making up the city of Atlanta. Those 108 tracts are the population rather than a random sample of elements. Coefficients equal to or greater than .20 will, however, be regarded as substantively significant. Support for this decision can be found in the literature (Frideres and Taylor 1972: 462-72; Quinney 1966: 47). Though this criterion value is of course arbitrary, it should be remembered that selection of a specific statistical significance level is also a conventionally based arbitrary decision. In any case, the primary objective of this study is not that of inferential theory testing. This study does, however, attempt to demonstrate methodological operations which should contribute to greater precision in correlation-based theory testing.

The values shown in columns 1 and 3 indicate that 8 of the 11 independent variables exceed the .20 criterion in their relationship to both forms of the dependent variable. Only sex composition, age composition, and residential mobility showed negligible relationships with violent and property crime rates. With respect to the other eight variables, all were related to crime rate in the predicted direction at magnitudes of .40 or greater. Crowding of housing had the highest correlation (.64) with violent crime rate, while economic status had the highest correlation (-.63) with property crime rate.

TABLE 5.2

Correlations between Independent Variables and
Crime Rates for Census Tracts, 1970

Independent Variable	Dependent Variable			
	Violent Crime		Property Crime	
	r		r	
	(original)	(log of X)	(original)	(log of X)
Economic status	-.52	-.63	-.55	-.66
Education status	-.57	-.61	-.56	-.58
Employment status	.54	.56	.54	.59
Housing-tenure status	-.59	-.62	-.63	-.68
Quality of housing	.52	.50	.46	.44
Crowding of housing	.64	.56	.61	.57
Land-area density	.38	.41	.41	.44
Residential mobility	.08	.09	.11	.12
Race composition	.47	.50	.48	.52
Sex composition	-.05	-.09	-.13	-.18
Age composition	.05	.09	.09	.14

Source: Compiled by the authors.

The correlation values presented in columns 1 and 3 would underestimate the true degree of association between independent and dependent variables if the actual relationships were nonlinear (Blalock 1972: 103; Schuessler 1971: 387). However, the decision as to when an independent-dependent variable relationship departs from linearity is also an arbitrary one in this study. An observed change of .10 or more correlation units was selected as the criterion. Again, this decision is based on an authoritative precedent (Davis 1971: 103-04). The only relationships in Table 5.2 which meet or exceed this criterion were those between economic status and the crime rate variables. The relationship between economic status and violent crime rate increased from -.52 to -.63 where mean income values were transformed to their natural logarithms. The increase for the economic status-property crime rate relationship was from -.55 to -.66.

The logarithmic model often arises in instances where an independent variable (X) "takes on a wide range of values but where once a certain value has been reached, further increases produce less and less effect on the dependent variable" (Blalock 1972: 409). In these cases the nonlinear relationship can be handled by transformation of X scores such that the dependent variable (Y) becomes a linear function of log X. Taking the logarithm of the original values will lessen the bending effect of extreme values. Other ecological studies of crime and delinquency have utilized the logarithmic transformation in testing for linearity (Schuessler 1962: 314-23; Fleischer 1966). In this study the logarithmic test uncovered only one variable (mean income) which was nonlinearly related to dependent variable measures.

Polynomials of the nth degree represent other nonlinear functions characterized by simple equations beyond that of a straight line. A second-degree polynomial is a U-shaped type of curve, while the third-degree polynomial has two bends in it and could be described as an S-shaped curve. Beasley and Antunes (1974: 45) uncovered several notable departures from linearity in demographic variable-crime rate relationships when utilizing second-order polynomial regression.

The general technique for investigating polynomial trends is to insert an original variable and successive powers of that variable into a regression equation. For example, if X_1 represented mean income, X mean income squared would refer to a second independent variable (X_2). The multiple correlation between the dependent variable (Y) and both X_1 and X_2, when compared with the linear-based bivariate correlation between Y and X_1, indicates the extent to which a second-degree equation better fits the form of the mean income-crime rate relationship (Kim and Kohout 1975: 372). Blalock (1972: 461) points out that the nature of most distributions seldom suggests appropriate fits beyond a third-degree equation.[1] Table 5.3 presents correlation values obtained through the cubic power of the original independent variables.

The logarithmic transformation operation noted curvilinear trends only for the economic status-dependent variable relationships. Polynomial regression did not appreciably improve the predictive ability of this variable beyond that demonstrated by the logarithmic transformation. Table 5.3 does show an increase of .10 correlation units for the relationship between age composition and property crime rate for a second-degree curve. Despite this increase, however, the correlation value still remains less than .20. Both quality of housing and sex composition demonstrate large increases in their relationship to the dependent variables where third-degree equations are used. This part of the analysis involved an initial check of the magnitude of the difference in the statistical relationships yielded by first- and third-degree equations. If the difference was equal to or exceeded .10 correlation units, it was concluded that the data were best fit by a nonlinear function. A third-degree curve was regarded as the appropriate relationship form where there was at least a .10 unit difference between the correlation values yielded by the first- and third-degree equations, as well as at least a .05 unit difference between the second- and third-degree correlation values. A parabola was regarded as the appropriate form of the relationship where the difference between the second- and third-degree values failed to meet this criterion, but there was at least a .10 difference between the first- and second-degree correlation values. Logarithmic transformations did not uncover curvilinear trends in the relationship of either of these independent variables to violent and property crime rate. Even a second-degree equation would have uncovered only the curvilinear relationship between percent male and property crime rate. Even more notable is the fact that the six composition-dependent variable relationships were found to exceed the .20 criterion level of substantive significance only after utilization of polynomial regression.

TABLE 5.3

Correlations Based upon First-, Second-, and
Third-Degree Polynomial Assumptions

Independent Variable	Dependent Variable					
	Violent Crime			Property Crime		
	rij	Ri x jk	Ri x jkl*	rij	Ri x jk	Ri x jkl
Economic status	-.52	.65	.65	-.55	.68	.68
Education status	-.57	.62	.63	-.56	.58	.59
Employment status	.54	.55	.58	.57	.58	.62
Housing-tenure status	-.59	.63	.63	-.63	.69	.69
Quality of housing	.52	.52	.64	.46	.47	.57
Crowding of housing	.64	.64	.64	.61	.61	.62
Land-area density	.38	.45	.46	.41	.45	.47
Residential mobility	.08	.08	.08	.11	.12	.18
Race composition	.47	.48	.51	.48	.50	.53
Sex composition	-.05	.14	.23	-.13	.23	.32
Age composition	.05	.11	.11	.09	.09	.19

*k refers to j^2 and l refers to j^3.
Source: Compiled by the authors.

Tables 5.4 and 5.5 present multiple correlation results for violent crime rate and property crime rate where all the substantively significant independent variables (in their original forms) were entered into the regression equation through a forward stepwise inclusion procedure.

TABLE 5.4

Violent Crime Rate Multiple Regression Summary Table with Significant Independent Variables in Their Original Form

Independent Variable	R^2	R^2 Change
Crowding of housing	.404	.404
Quality of housing	.587	.183
Housing-tenure status	.682	.095
Employment status	.700	.018
Race composition	.709	.009
Education status	.714	.005
Land-area density	.715	.001
Economic status	.716	.001

Source: Compiled by the authors.

TABLE 5.5

Property Crime Rate Multiple Regression Summary Table with Significant Independent Variables in Their Original Form

Independent Variable	R^2	R^2 Change
Housing-tenure status	.396	.396
Crowding of housing	.554	.158
Quality of housing	.649	.095
Employment status	.678	.029
Race composition	.692	.014
Education composition	.697	.005
Land-area density	.698	.001
Economic status	.698	.000

Source: Compiled by the authors.

These tables show that after crowding of housing, quality of housing, housing-tenure status, and employment status are entered into the equation, none of the remaining independent variables appreciably improve the variation-explained term for violent crime rate. An increment of at least 1 percent in R^2, beyond the contribution of a previously included variable, was regarded as an appreciable increase. Percent unemployed, itself, only adds about 2 percent to the explained variation. These four variables account for 70 percent of the variation in census tract violent crime rate. The same four variables, with the addition of race composition, account for 69 percent of the variation in property crime rate. Economic status, education status, and land-area density again make negligible contributions, while percent unemployed and percent black increase the variation-explained term only by about 3 percent and 1.4 percent, respectively.

Tables 5.6 and 5.7 represent multiple correlation results which take into account those polynomial terms suggested as appropriate by the results presented in Tables 5.2 and 5.3. Essentially, violent and property crime rates are predicted from a number of substantively significant independent variables where linear models are assumed for some of the variables and nonlinear models for others. [2] Crowding of housing, quality of housing, employment status, and housing-tenure status explained 76 percent of the variation in violent crime rate. Again, the remaining independent variables failed to appreciably increase the variation-explained term after these four variables were entered into the equation. For property crime rate, only land-area density and the sex composition variable made negligible contributions to the explained variation. Percent unemployed, percent black, and mean education all showed increment increases of less than 3 percent. Economic status, quality of housing, crowding of housing, housing-tenure status, employment status, race composition, and education status do, however, explain 75 percent of the variation in census tract property crime rate.

These results confirm several of Beasley and Antunes' conclusions.

First, as they suggested, a few selected variables can statistically account for almost all of the variation in intracity crime rates (about three-fourths of the variation for both violent and property crime rates in the City of Atlanta). As would be expected on the basis of the Slatin work (1969), however, the R^2 values based on census tract unit data (Atlanta) were not as great as those observed when the more inclusive police district represented the unit of analysis (Houston).

Second, tests for nonlinear independent-dependent variable relationships did uncover several notable departures from linearity. Furthermore, the criterion used in making the decision as to whether curvilinear models better fit the data in this study was more demanding than that used by Beasley and Antunes. The results do indicate that the influence of income differentials upon crime rate variation

TABLE 5.6

Violent Crime Rate Multiple Regression Summary Table
with Significant Independent Variables in Either
Their Original or Transformed State

Independent Variable	R^2	R^2 Change
Crowding of Housing	.404	
Quality of housing*	.679	.275
Employment status	.733	.054
Housing-tenure status	.757	.024
Race composition	.766	.009
Sex composition*	.773	.007
Education status	.779	.006
Economic status (log)	.781	.002
Land-area density	.782	.001

*Third-degree polynomial transformation.
Source: Compiled by the authors.

TABLE 5.7

Property Crime Rate Multiple Regression Summary Table
with Significant Independent Variables in Either
Their Original or Transformed State

Independent Variable	R^2	R^2 Change
Economic status (log)	.434	
Quality of housing*	.619	.185
Crowding of housing	.656	.037
Housing-tenure status	.697	.041
Employment status	.722	.025
Race composition	.737	.015
Education status	.748	.011
Land-area density	.748	.000
Sex composition*	.748	.000

*Third-degree polynomial transformation.
Source: Compiled by the authors.

decreases as the upper income levels are approached. The relationships between percent male and percent of housing units of substandard quality with crime rate, however, were found to reverse themselves over the total distribution of the variables. For example, at the lower end of the independent variable distribution, increases in percent of housing units of substandard quality are associated with increases in crime rate. The nature of this relationship then bends to the negative only to resume a positive form at the higher levels of the independent variable distribution. The opposite pattern (negative, positive, negative) describes the percent male–crime rate relationship. With respect to interpretation, the results for the income and housing variables represent contradictions for any criminological theory which might posit a simple relationship between socioeconomic well-being as indicative of constructs such as anomie, stake in conformity, or value diversity and the distribution of crime.

Third, a central-tendency income measure was found to have the highest correlation with property crime rate. It is interesting to note that such summary measures of economic well-being as mean or median income have shown negligible positive correlations with crime when the topic of study was interurban crime rate differentials (Dansiger and Wheeler 1975: 113–31; Meade 1973). In these studies measures of within-unit income inequality were found to be better predictors (in the expected direction) of interarea crime rate variation.

The interurban studies alluded to above used the standard metropolitan statistical area (SMSA) as the unit of analysis. These studies classified units on the basis of within-area income distribution inequality. The basis for this operation is the assumption that SMSA residents interpret their economic situation not by reference to residents of different metropolitan areas, but rather in comparison to residents of the metropolitan area in which they reside. In sum, between-unit, central tendency income comparisons seem less appropriate when differences in geographical location reflect considerable variation with respect to the financial cost of a living standard. The standard of living cost is more likely to be comparable, however, when the units of analysis are census tracts within a single urban area. Further support for the appropriateness of central tendency income measures as indicators of relative economic well-being in intraurban studies is the presumption that tract units demonstrate greater homogeneity than do SMSA units.

Fourth, while population per square mile emerged as the strongest predictor of violent crime rate in the Beasley and Antunes study, it was found to be a redundant predictor in the present study. However, the percent of housing units having a person-per-room ratio greater than 1.0 (household density, if you will) did have the highest correlation with violent crime rate in this study. This finding regarding the comparative predictive value of land-area density and housing overcrowding is precisely that hypothesized by Harries (1974: 83).

Fifth, as was the case for Houston, race composition was found to be a redundant predictor of area crime rates. This result contrasts with the results of the above-mentioned interarea studies in which the race variable was found to be a prominent correlate of violent crime. Thus, race composition as a variable decreases in importance when moving from the analysis of between-area to within-area crime rate variation. When the focus of study is intraurban crime rate differentials, indicators of material resources and quality of life are found to be more influential than race composition. While collinearity among the independent variables in this study requires a cautious approach toward discussing their relative effects upon the dependent variables, the results do suggest that material quality-of-life indicators deserve to be further explored in regard to their relation to the phenomenon of intraurban crime rate differentials.

The observed contribution of statistical corrections for nonlinear trends to optimal-explained-variation results suggests the relevance of at least one other procedure. A stepwise regression solution assumes that all variable effects are additive, that is, that an independent-dependent variable relationship is the same over all values of the remaining independent variables. Interactive relationships reflect departures from this assumption. For example, the effect of racial composition upon the crime rate might not be the same for census tracts at different economic status levels. Where such relationships exist, but are ignored, there will result a poorer fit of the regression equation than would have been the case if the interaction between the independent variables had been taken into account. The multiplicative term is a commonly used approach to the interaction problem. This approach allows retention of the additive format through creation of "new" predictor variables which represent products of the values of the original set of independent variables.[3] A first-order interaction is a cross-product term involving two of the original predictor variables while a second-order interaction refers to a triple-product term.

Table 5.8 is a multiple regression summary for violent crime rate where all first-order interaction terms were introduced after the substantively significant predictors, as identified in Table 5.6, were entered into the equation. Four interaction effects showed explained variation increments of at least 1.0 percent. Those interaction effects occurred between quality of housing and housing-tenure status, quality of housing and employment status, crowding of housing

TABLE 5.8

Violent Crime Rate Multiple Regression Summary Table
Including Interaction Terms That Yielded
Appreciable Increment Increases

Independent Variable	R^2	R^2 Change
Crowding of housing = X_1	.404	
Quality of housing* = X_2	.679	.275
Employment status = X_3	.733	.054
Housing–tenure status = X_4	.757	.024
$X_2 X_4 = X_5$	.811	.054
$X_2 X_3 = X_6$	.849	.038
$X_1 X_3 = X_7$	.864	.015
$X_1 X_4 = X_8$	.875	.011

*Third–degree polynomial.
Source: Compiled by the authors.

TABLE 5.9

Property Crime Rate Multiple Regression Summary Table
Including Interaction Terms That Yielded
Appreciable Increment Increases

Independent Variable	R^2	R^2 Change
Economic status log = X_1	.434	
Quality of housing* = X_2	.619	.185
Crowding of housing = X_3	.656	.037
Housing–tenure status = X_4	.697	.041
Employment status = X_5	.722	.025
Race composition = X_6	.737	.015
Education status = X_7	.748	.011
$X_2 X_4 = X_8$	.805	.057
$X_2 X_5 = X_9$	.823	.018

*Third–degree polynomial.
Source: Compiled by the authors.

and employment status, and crowding of housing and housing-tenure status. With these four cross-product terms considered, the R^2 value for violent crime as the dependent variable did increase from .76, where additivity was assumed, to .88. For property crime rate (Table 5.9), only two of all possible first-order interactions showed explained variation increments of at least 1.0 percent. Inclusion of the interaction effect between quality of housing and housing-tenure status and that between quality of housing and employment status did, however, increase R^2 from .75 to .82.

DISCUSSION

The findings of this study, as well as those of Beasley and Antunes, indicate that propositions derived from theories of crime etiology need not, and possibly should not, be stated in terms of linear relationships. Even where such bivariate propositions are appropriate, it might be necessary to state them in qualified terms, that is, with reference to values of other variables. While this could be interpreted as restriction of the range of casual statements, it can also be seen as propagation of more complex and precise theoretical propositions.

The present work tested for the existence of departures from linearity in bivariate relationships, and for the presence of interaction among a set of independent variables. Upon identifying such properties, an effort was made to achieve a prediction model of maximum power by exhausting the residual variance. This was accomplished by transforming variables where it was found to be appropriate and then cumulating a variable set (original and transformed) through multiple correlation. In all frankness, the study must plead guilty to a brute-force strategy of data manipulation. It is hoped, however, that the work redeems itself on the following grounds: first, by completing a disciplined and instructive verification study which extended the generalizability of earlier findings; second, by expanding such findings as those observed in the earlier study through the introduction of further analytical techniques; third, by its strong advocacy of the need to incorporate the study results within future efforts at theory construction and testing in crime etiology at the ecological level.

It is regrettably conceded here that structural-level, criminological theory is a critically underdeveloped area. This situation can undoubtedly be attributed to a predominance of descriptive, as opposed to interpretive, research goals, and to the unrelenting criticism, both technical and substantive, that ecological studies have encountered (Robinson 1950: 351-57; Gordon 1968: 592-616).

Despite the pitfalls of ecological, aggregation, regression, and reification fallacies, much can be said for promoting theory construction efforts and attendant empirical investigation at the aggregate level (Robinson 1950; Slatin 1969; and Gordon 1968). None of these problems is insurmountable. The classic ecological fallacy can be avoided through appropriate caution at the interpretive stage. The aggregation issue can be addressed by simultaneous analyses of different unit levels. Collinearity trends among aggregate-level variables can be technically rectified at the index construction stage by means such as factor analysis, which has been used to provide composite (nonrelated) explanatory variables (Meade 1973).

With respect to reification, sociologists have probably erred more on the side of timidity than bravado when interpreting ecological data. This is not the case for other disciplines, economics for example, which have studied crime at the aggregate level (Dansiger and Wheeler 1975; Fleisher 1966; Sjoquist 1973: 439-46). A reverse in this trend in sociology is represented by Blau (1974: 613), who has gone as far as maintaining that the study of structural parameters is "the distinctive task of sociology." A corollary to the Blau pronouncement for the area under discussion in this work might read: The study of structural level conditions as they influence aggregate-level rates and patterns of criminal behavior is the distinctive task of criminology. This chapter takes just such a position. It further recommends the utilization of structural parameter data as contextual factors, that is, as indicators of the macrolevel life situation of a person, when studying crime etiology at the individual level of analysis (Lazarsfeld and Menzel 1961). A vigorous approach toward identifying the structural correlates of crime should yield empirical models from which an inductively based, aggregate-level theory of the distribution of crime can emerge.

CONCLUSION

In this study structural-level, material quality of life indicators were shown to be appreciably related to aggregate, between-unit criminal behavior patterns for city residents. Violent crime was found to be more closely associated with an urban-blight situation involving crowding, high levels of substandard housing, unemployment, and low levels of home ownership. The noted interaction tendencies among these variables, however, warn the researcher that the effects of the variables within this set vary at different levels of the other variables. Property crime rates also are not immune to an urban-blight situation, though a central-tendency measure of economic status is the primary correlate of this type of crime. The logarithmic form of its relation to property crime indicates, however, that the linear pattern of decrease in rates with increasing levels of income bottoms out at a certain income level.

The findings regarding the race composition-crime rate relationships are seen as having important interpretive implications. Race composition was shown to be a relatively low correlate, and an essentially redundant predictor, of census tract crime rates (both violent and property) within the city of Atlanta. It should be underscored that such results were observed regardless of the fact that the crime data source for this study was an officially recorded arrest.

It cannot be emphasized enough that it is the discouraging aspects of urban blight and economic deprivation, and not ethnic or racial concentration, which account for intracity crime rate variation. This admonition is made in consideration of the fact that the nation's major cities will increasingly have to upgrade and accelerate their planning efforts in order to avoid both fiscal and social problem crises of unprecedented magnitude. Finally, while the distribution of most of the predictor variables used in this study could be assumed to have remained relatively constant since 1970, it would be interesting to investigate the consequences, with respect to crime-rate variation, of the striking increases in unemployment which have plagued the latter part of this decade.

NOTES

1. For a more sophisticated discussion and inclusive presentation of techniques for addressing nonlinearity, see Kmenta, Elements of Econometrics, 1971: 451-72.

2. Where polynomial regression suggested curvilinear relationships, the original independent variable values were transformed to reflect the power that best fit the form of the regression curve such that:

$$X_{n + 1i} = (X_{1i}b_1 + X_{2i}b_2 + X_{3i}b_3 + X_{ni}b_n).$$

For example, X_{4i} = a newly created independent variable value for the ith tract reflecting the percent male's curvilinear relationship to property crime rate; Y_1 = property crime rate; X_1 = percent male; X_{1i} = percent male for the ith tract; b_1 = the unstandardized partial regression coefficient of Y_1 on X_1; $X_2 = X_1^2$; X_{2i} = percent male squared for the ith tract; b_2 = the unstandardized partial regression coefficient of Y_1 on X_2; $X_3 = X_1^3$; X_{3i} = percent male cubed for the ith tract; b_3 = the unstandardized partial regression coefficient of Y_1 on X_3. See Blalock 1972: 461.

3. For example, the new variable value (X_3) might refer to the cross product (X_1X_2) where:

X_1 = the census tract percent unemployment value, and
X_2 = the census tract percent black value. See Blalock 1974: 462, and Kim and Kohout 1975: 373.

REFERENCES

Beasley, R. W., and G. Antunes
   1974   The etiology of urban crime: an ecological analysis.
          Criminology 2, no. 4.

Bensing, R. C., and O. Schroeder
   1960   Homicide in an Urban Community. Springfield, Ill.:
          Charles C. Thomas.

Blalock, H. M., Jr.
   1972   Social Statistics. New York: McGraw-Hill.

Blau, P. M.
   1974   Presidential address: parameters of social structure.
          American Sociological Review 39, no. 5.

Boggs, S. L.
   1965   Urban crime patterns. American Sociological Review 30.

Bogue, D. J.
   1969   Principles of Demography. New York: John Wiley.

Dansiger, S., and D. Wheeler
   1975   The economics of crime: punishment or income redistri-
          bution. Review of Social Economy 33.

Davis, J. A.
   1971   Elementary Survey Analysis. Englewood Cliffs, N.J.:
          Prentice-Hall.

Fleisher, B. M.
   1966   The Economics of Delinquency. Chicago: Quadrangle.

Frideres, J. S., and K. W. Taylor
   1972   Issues versus controversies: substantive and statistical
          significance. American Sociological Review 39, no. 4.

Gordon, R. A.
  1968   Issues in multiple regression. American Sociological
          Review.

Green, E.
  1970   Race, social status and criminal arrest. American
          Sociological Review 35, no. 3.

Harries, K. D.
  1974   The Geography of Crime and Justice. New York:
          McGraw-Hill.

Kim, M. H., and M. Kohout
  1975   Special topics in general linear models. In Statistical
          Package for the Social Sciences, ed. N. Nie, H. Hull,
          J. Jenkins, K. Steinbrenner, and D. Bent. New York:
          McGraw-Hill.

Lazarsfeld, P. F., and H. Menzel
  1961   On the relation between individual and collective prop-
          erties. In Complex Organizations: A Sociological
          Reader, ed. Amitai Etzioni. New York: Holt, Rinehart
          & Winston.

Loftin, C., and R. H. Hill
  1974   Regional Subculture and homicide: an examination of the
          Gastil-Hackney thesis. American Sociological Review
          39, no. 5.

Meade, A. C.
  1973   Metropolitan areas and violent crime: 1971. Unpublished
          research report to the Center for Studies on Crime and
          Delinquency, National Institute of Mental Health.

Mladenka, K. R., and K. Q. Hill
  1976   A reexamination of the etiology of urban crime. Crim-
          inology 13, no. 4.

Moses, E. R.
  1947   Differentials in crime rates between Negroes and Whites
          based on comparisons of four socioeconomically equated
          areas. American Sociological Review 12.

Quinney, R.
  1964 Crime, delinquency and social areas. Journal of Research
        in Crime and Delinquency 1.

  1966 Structural characteristics, population areas, and crime
        rates in the United States. Journal of Criminal Law,
        Criminology, and Police Science, no. 57.

Robinson, W. S.
  1950 Ecological correlations and the behavior of individuals.
        American Sociological Review 15.

Schmid, C. F.
  1960 Urban crime areas: part 1. American Sociological Re-
        view 25.

Schuessler, K.
  1962 Components of variations in city crime rates. Social
        Problems 9.

  1971 Analyzing Social Data: A Statistical Orientation. Boston:
        Houghton Mifflin.

Sjoquist, D. L.
  1973 Property crime and economic behavior: some empirical
        results. American Economic Review 58.

Slatin, G. T.
  1969 Ecological analyses of delinquency: aggregation effects.
        American Sociological Review 34, no. 6.

Wilks, J. A.
  1967 Ecological correlates of crime and delinquency. In Task
        Force Report: Crime and Its Impact--An Assessment.
        President's Commission on Law Enforcement and Admin-
        istration of Justice. Washington, D.C.: U.S. Government
        Printing Office (Appendix A).

PART

DETERRENCE

INTRODUCTION TO PART III

The concept of deterrence, first promulgated by the classical school of criminology, is firmly embedded in the theory of utilitarianism. It holds that the objective of punishment should be to deter offenders. For the purpose at hand, it is useful to differentiate in terms of function between general, special, and marginal deterrence. General deterrence has as its object the population at large. Through the employment of public threat, notice is served that a given punishment will follow a wrongful act. In modern societies, the agencies of criminal justice (the police, the courts, and corrections) are vested with the responsibility to maintain social order, uphold prevailing moral standards, norms, and regulations by means of an organized readiness to impose penalties on those who choose to violate them. Special deterrence has as its object the individual offender. It refers to the threat of further punishment of those who have already been through the conviction and punishment process for a previous offense. Within the framework of criminal law, criminal justice agencies have considerable discretion in the severity and type of punitive sanctions they can impose on law violators. It is through the judicious application of such discretion which encompasses arrest, charge, conviction, and type of sentence decisions that criminal justice agencies seek to control the frequency and seriousness of criminal events. As a result, criminal justice decision makers perennially seek to answer such questions as whether more severe penalties would more effectively deter criminal behavior as opposed to less severe sanctions. Or whether increased efficiency at the point of crime detection (or arrest) would produce better results in terms of deterrence than would the improvement of operations at the judicial or correctional level. The concept of marginal deterrence concerns itself with these issues. It refers to increasing the effectiveness of deterrence through variations in the application of criminal justice system strategies and in the employment of the conditions of legal threats.

Today, there is renewed interest in deterrence. Advocates of the "just deserts" model in criminal justice, such as Ernest van den Haag, James Q. Wilson, and David Fogel, to name a few, look upon the rising crime rate as the result of society's failure to deter through punishment. A plethora of judicial reforms, sentencing revisions, and swift punishment are being proposed (and enacted in a growing number of states) as the cures to the crime problem. Conceptualizations such as these are based on the inherent assumption that most crimes are deterrable and that celerity and certainty of punishment is what deters. At this time, however, it seems premature and sophistic to say that the criminal justice system's failure to deter has led to the increases in crime. Such a view ignores the fact that obedience to the law, and obversely criminal behavior, is brought about by many factors, among which criminal justice plays but a minor role. Crime is clearly related to many social problems: prejudice; discrimination against certain social or ethnic groups; immigration and concentration of the poor, the uneducated, and the unskilled in city enclaves; the outmigration of industry and business to rural areas and the suburbs, with a concomitant loss of jobs; the racial revolution; the notable decline and disintegration of the family and the institution of the church; the destructive effects of Vietnam and political corruption; the widespread and increasingly documented failure of the schools; the substantial increase in mobility brought about by the automobile; and the corrosive effects of television, with its glorification of violence and the possession of material things. Individually and interactively these factors contribute to the crime problem. While the quality of justice, police clearance rates, and the judicious disposition of offenders are most assuredly important in deterrence, it must be recognized that deterrence exerted by the criminal justice system alone will never be able to replace the influence of the other, more traditional, and mostly informal, social control. In other words, the marginal rate of technical substitution between criminal justice and social deterrence is probably not as elastic as current hardliners make it out to be. As a result, increases in punitiveness (that is, deterrence), without accompanying social change, will not be able to reduce our crime rates sufficiently to warrant the social costs that would build up as a result of such a development. The intrinsic social value that is currently being attached to retribution and the mandatory sentence mania that is sweeping the nation already reflect more shades of George Orwell's 1984 than any reasonable man could possibly be comfortable with. In view of the impending repercussions of these developments on the administration of criminal justice--for example, the accelerating prison and jail populations in this country--the careful examination of deterrence as a concept, as a process, and in terms of actual results could not be more urgent. Such research and theory development must come about if societal efforts designed to prevent and reduce crime are to be based on empirically verified knowledge instead of on belief systems shaped by ideology or outright prejudice.

 The following chapter by Charles Tittle and Alan Rowe is one of a growing number of studies seeking to provide insight into deterrence theory on the basis of empirical analysis. Using arrest clearance rates as one measure of certainty of sanction, the researchers found that the probability of apprehension seems to be negatively related to the crime (as predicted), but only when the degree of certainty had reached a minimal level or "tipping point." It appears that once the certainty of arrest reaches approximately 30 percent in a jurisdiction, increases in police efficiency do seem to be related to decreases in the volume of crime. The opposite relationship to deterrence seems to occur if arrest certainty falls below the tipping point. While the findings of this study offer some support for deterrence theory, they also indicate that statements about deterrent effects based on correlational studies using official data bases must be advanced carefully. Nonetheless, given appropriately comprehensive, valid, and reliable data, it is possible and useful to measure the consequences for crime control of alternative strategies in the selective application of criminal justice resources and in the employment of criminal justice sanctions.

But before much more progress can be made in this subject area, there will need to be a general improvement in the reporting and recording of crime statistics. Ideally, a uniform reporting system of disposition decisions on the part of criminal justice agencies should be created, which would include information on the rationale for these decisions. A laudable effort occurred in this direction when the Law Enforcement Assistance Administration of the U.S. Department of Justice funded the development of project SEARCH with the purpose of designing a prototype of a criminal justice information system. The development of an offender-based transaction statistics system (OBTS) demonstrated the feasibility of a computerized statistics system based on an accounting of individual offenders as they proceed through the criminal justice system. But since the implementation of OBTS and similar information systems in the United States depends on the voluntary participation of interested jurisdictions, it will take decades to develop comprehensive national information and statistics systems. And while new and promising concepts and technology are on the horizon for criminal justice, the majority of decision makers and administrators will continue to make their decisions on the basis of flawed data and severely limited information systems, and research will be similarly handicapped.

In sum, deterrence studies are still in their infancy. What knowledge we do have seems to indicate that deterrence operates in a very specialized way which may be contingent upon any number of conditions, such as the level of certainty involved in the threat of sanctions, or the certainty and celerity of apprehension. Perhaps deterrence is limited to particular kinds of threats. Possibly each of the various patterns of sanctions available to criminal justice has a different consequence for the problem of general and specific

deterrence. For example, we know that deterrence works differently on different people. Most assuredly, crime control can be
achieved in a variety of ways. Among these could be increases in
the certainty of arrests, as the Tittle and Rowe study seems to suggest, which could be paired for enhanced effectiveness with a high
certainty of conviction without necessarily severe sentencing dispositions. Yet another mode might entail assuring a high arrest rate
without a high certainty of conviction but coupled with severe sentencing sanctions, and so on, with all the many possible permutations allowable under existing discretionary practices. Only carefully documented research and experimentation will be able to determine the characteristics of optimal sanction patterns among the
many possibilities that exist. Yet in view of the current trend in
criminal justice toward retrenchment and punishment, inordinate
care will need to be taken that the current crop of legal sanctions do
not involve the criminal justice system in a most vicious cycle. In
the worst of possible scenarios, abuse of discretion and unduly harsh
sentences could well reduce a people's (or group's) disposition to
obey the law and thereby increase the crime rate. This in turn
could lead to increasingly excessive and repressive practices. In
such a development the principles of individual liberty would be sacrificed at the altar of law and order, while freedom and justice would
be lost.

CHAPTER

6

ARREST AND CRIME:
MORE ON THE DETERRENCE PROBLEM
Charles R. Tittle
Alan R. Rowe

The possible effect of sanctions in deterring deviance has at-
tracted considerable attention in recent years, and a number of
studies have reported findings consistent with deterrence ideas
(Tittle and Logan 1973). However, much of the evidence has been
produced by correlational studies (Antunes and Hunt 1973; Bailey
et al. 1971; Chiricos and Waldo 1970; Ehrlich 1972; Gibbs 1968;
Gray and Martin 1969; Jensen 1969; Kobrin et al. 1972; Logan 1971
and 1972; Salem and Bowers 1970; Tittle 1969; Tittle and Rowe 1974;
Waldo and Chiricos 1972) and for that reason is not compelling
(Zimring and Hawkins 1973: 253-70). Survey designs suffer from
an inability to control for all the extraneous variables which might
produce spurious relationships between sanctions and deviance, and
they usually do not provide the means to establish the direction of
causality. Even if the effect of extraneous variables could be ruled
out, a strong negative relationship between a measure of the certainty or severity of apprehension/punishment and some measure of
rule violation would be subject to varied interpretations. Such an
association could be taken as evidence of deterrence or it could indicate that the amount of rule breaking determines the level of certainty or severity of punishment (Tittle 1969: 420-21; Tittle and
Rowe 1974; Bowers and Salem 1972).
    This chapter reports a replication and extension of a correla-
tional study which found evidence interpreted as supportive of deterrence theory (Tittle and Rowe 1974). Using arrest clearance
rate as a measure of certainty of sanction, Tittle and Rowe found

The authors would like to thank David W. Britt for his helpful
analytical comments on earlier drafts of this chapter.

that the probability of apprehension was negatively related to crime rate but only when the degree of certainty had reached a minimal level (tipping point). This chapter makes use of more recent data, and it goes a step further and attempts to establish the direction of causality using information for two points in time. The basic idea underlying the use of penal analysis in establishing causal direction is that a presumed effect should be more closely associated with a prior rather than a subsequent cause. Therefore, a presumed cause at time one should correlate higher with a presumed effect at time two than does the presumed effect at time one with the presumed cause at time two (Campbell and Stanley 1963: 68–70; Pelz and Andrews 1964). Thus by analyzing cross-lagged relationships between arrest and crime data for the same ecological units at two points in time it is possible to evaluate the credibility of a directional inference (Heise 1970).

METHOD

Data for the study were extracted from the 1971 and 1972 annual reports of the Department of Law Enforcement of the State of Florida (UCR, State of Florida 1971 and 1972). The reports include arrest clearance and crime rates for each municipality and each county in the state, although not for each offense separately. In this chapter the interrelationships among the probabilities of arrest and crime rates for the two years are examined using data for municipalities with populations of 2,500 or more. Municipalities of this size were used because census data to enable control for other variables were not available for smaller places. Aggregate data for counties were excluded because they include such great variability among the subunits within each county that it is difficult to justify the assumption that the overall probability of arrest is a meaningful measure of certainty of apprehension for a given crime at various locations within the county.

Probability of Apprehension

Two different indexes of the probability of apprehension, both rooted in the clearance rate, are employed. In one analysis, the probability of arrest is used as the independent variable. This is simply the proportion of crimes known to the police that are cleared by arrest. In a second analysis the number of crimes cleared by arrest is standardized by dividing by the number of police in each city. This procedure produces an indicator of police efficiency, which is the clearance rate per policeman.

Arrest clearance means that the police have satisfied themselves that they have taken into custody the person who committed
the crime (UCR 1970: 30). Because they are the produce of police
discretion, arrest data are subject to some distortion. For example, in order to improve their performance record, police departments may too easily satisfy themselves that the perpetrator of a
given crime has been apprehended, or they may induce suspects to
confess to crimes they did not actually commit in exchange for favorable treatment in prosecution of the instant crime (Skolnick 1966).
Although these possibilities clearly exist, there are good reasons
to doubt that they greatly contaminate the data (Logan 1971: 119-21),
especially since the clearance rates are so low. It is possible that
some departments are more demanding than others in satisfying
themselves of a clearance, but such variations would appear to be
unsystematic and therefore unlikely to account for the findings to be
reported.

Despite these possible distortions, arrest data appear to be
superior to data that have been used in other studies of the deterrence question (Logan 1971: 117-19). First, arrest clearance reflects, although imperfectly, the probability of getting caught for a
criminal act. Some evidence indicates that it is this possibility
which is most likely to influence criminal behavior rather than the
fear of actually being sanctioned (Kobrin et al. 1972: 257-68). In a
survey of the adult populations of three states, it was found that
people make almost no distinction between the unpleasantness involved in arrest, conviction, or incarceration (Tittle 1974). Furthermore, some evidence suggests that arrest may stigmatize, even
though conviction does not ensue (Schwartz and Skolnick 1962). Thus
the threat of arrest would seem to capture much of what is implied
in theoretical discussions of deterrence. Second, the clearance rate
unambiguously indexes the probability of punishment for specific
criminal acts. Other indexes permit no clear interpretation of the
difference between punished criminal acts and punished individuals
who may have been responsible for many or few crimes (see Gibbs
1968; Tittle 1969; Chiricos and Waldo 1970). Third, unlike other
data that have been used, arrest clearance data are compiled by similar agencies using common rules of procedure, thus making the information and categories directly comparable. Finally, since arrest is
the first step in the process by which all legal sanctions are imposed,
its probability predetermines the maximum probability of any legal
sanction.

Volume of Crime

The index of crime which is employed is simply the number of
Federal Bureau of Investigation (FBI) "index" crimes known to the

police per 1,000 (modified from the reported "per 100,000 population"). While the unreliability of crime statistics is widely acknowledged (Cressey 1957; Beattie 1960), they still represent the most comprehensive and systematic crime data available. Until better data are produced, the only alternative is to continue to work with these records and alter the conclusions when more adequate ones are produced. Moreover, this chapter analyzes internal variation within a body of data. Thus the question of the validity of the total body of data is of secondary importance.

Analysis

First, using 1972 data, correlations between arrest clearance and crime rate for the municipal units and for subgroupings by certainty of arrest were examined. Then cross-lagged path coefficients using both 1971 and 1972 arrest and crime data were calculated (Heise 1970).

Two forms of analysis were undertaken. In one the objective was to test the idea that an increase in the simple probability of apprehension causes a decrease in crime. In this case the clearance rate and the crime rate were used in the calculations. In the second analysis, the objective was to test the idea that an increase in police efficiency would lead to a decrease in crime. In this, the number of cases cleared by arrest was standardized by the number of sworn police personnel.

RESULTS

As indicated in Table 6.1, the pattern of simple correlations between clearance and crime rates is consistent with that which was reported using 1971 data (Tittle and Rowe 1974). For all cities included in the study, the correlation is -.19 in 1972 and 1971. When the cities are divided into those with low certainty of arrest (under 30 percent) and those with high certainty of arrest in order to see if there is a threshold at which deterrence becomes operative, a tipping effect is again clearly suggested. In 1971 the correlation for low-certainty cases was .19, while it was -.48 for the high-certainty cases. In 1972 the corresponding figures are .13 and -.34. Thus the 1972 data are similar to the 1971 data in suggesting that a moderate deterrent effect may be occurring but that it is contingent upon a minimal level of certainty of apprehension having been reached.

TABLE 6.1

Correlations and Cross-Lagged Path Coefficients

	All Cities	Low Certainty	High Certainty
Correlations			
$A_1C_1(N)$	-.19(178)	.19(150)	-.48(28)
$A_2C_2(N)$	-.19(178)	.13(138)	-.34(40)
Cross-lagged path coefficients			
Using probability of arrest			
$P_{A_1C_2}(N)$	-.01(178)	.04(150)	.02(28)
$P_{C_1A_2}(N)$	-.18(178)	-.23(150)	.08(28)
Using police efficiency			
$P_{A_1C_2}(N)$	.05(178)	.13(150)	-.11(28)
$P_{C_1A_2}(N)$	.08(178)	-.04(150)	.25(28)

A_1 = Apprehension, 1971.
A_2 = Apprehension, 1972.
C_1 = Crime, 1971.
C_2 = Crime, 1972.
Source: Compiled by the authors.

Examination of cross-lagged path coefficients using simple clearance and crime rates, however, calls into question the deterrent interpretation. If the probability of arrest (A_1) "causes" the crime rate (C_2), then the cross-lagged path coefficient $P_{A_1C_2}$ should be negative and larger than the cross-lagged path coefficient $P_{C_1A_2}$ (Figure 6.1). Considering all the cities together, the data indicate just the opposite pattern (-.01 versus -.18). However, examination of the data for the cities subgrouped by level of arrest certainty for both years fails either to support or counter the tipping-effect argument. For the low-certainty cities it appears that if any predominant direction of causality exists, it is from crime rate to arrest clearance (.04 versus -.23). The direction for the high-certainty cities (those with above 30 percent clearance rates) in 1971 on the other hand is not clear (.02 versus .08). Hence these data are ambiguous when considered as a whole, and for low-certainty cases the evidence suggests that crime influences the arrest probability more than arrest influences crime. The direction of causality suggested by the deterrent argument, however, cannot be ruled out where sufficient levels of certainty have been achieved.

FIGURE 6.1

Path Model Showing Cross-Lagged Path Coefficients
Using Crime Clearance and Crime Rates

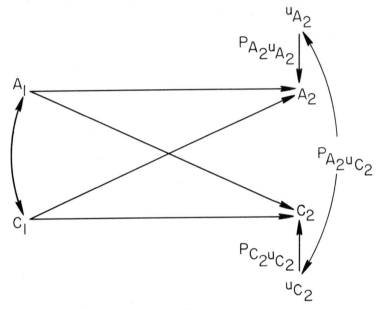

Source: Compiled by the authors.

Cross-lagged path coefficients using measures of police efficiency rather than simple arrest probabilities indicate a clearer
pattern. Considering all the cities and the low-certainty cities, we
find little consistent evidence of predominant influence (.05 versus
.08 and .13 versus -.04, respectively), but figures for the high-
certainty cities clearly suggest that arrest efficiency leads to reduced crime (-.11 versus .25). Thus the data imply that once the
certainty of arrest reaches approximately 30 percent, increases in
police efficiency (that is, increases in number of clearances per
policeman) lead to decreases in the volume of crime. However, below the 30 percent level no such causal effect appears to occur, and
in fact the opposite direction of causality may be operative.

DISCUSSION

These results offer some support for the hypothesis that a deterrent effect occurs once the certainty of arrest reaches a critical
level, at least when the independent variable is a measure of police

efficiency. This conclusion must be tempered with caution, however. For one thing, the use of a two-wave model for causal analysis assumes a number of conditions which have not been met in the present analysis (Heise 1970: 10-12). Although Heise has shown that failure to meet some of these assumptions has little effect on the accuracy of results, at least two assumptions remain troublesome in the present case.

The model used here assumes that the "time required to measure one sample unit on all variables is less than the causal lag period" (Heise 1970: 11). We are dealing with annual measurements and a one-year lag period, thus violating this assumption. However, since crime figures for the year are usually multiple functions of crime figures for any given month,[1] it seemed justifiable to act as if we had measurements for a given month with a one-year causal lag.

Second, the effect of measurement imprecision on the accuracy of results is dependent upon the size of the sample. The smaller the sample, the greater is the effect of measurement error. In this study, our sample sizes, especially in the subgroup of high certainty, are small. Therefore, the possibility of distortion is very real.

Nevertheless, the findings do support the conclusion that the deterrent hypothesis is at least tenable under some conditions. This is particularly true since the coefficients reported here are probably very conservative. The amount of crime, the size of the population, and the number of police are all interrelated. Therefore, standardizing the number of crimes cleared by number of police removes much of the legitimate variation in the independent and dependent variables, thus attenuating the coefficients (see Gordon 1968).

It does remain a puzzle, though, why the data are relatively clear when a measure of police efficiency is used in the analysis but are ambiguous when simple arrest probability is considered. Several possibilities come to mind.

First, the relationship between simple arrest probability and crime rate may be more susceptible to reciprocal effects than is police efficiency. It is easy to imagine that the causal effects of arrest probability could be masked by the feedback produced when increased crime leads to more police and finally to increased arrests. Still it is difficult to convince oneself that this is more likely to occur in the case of simple arrest probability than for a standardized measure of police efficiency.

Second, it may be that we are dealing with a complex and recurrent causal chain which is restricted because we are looking only at a one-year span. Thus one could imagine that a decline in police efficiency such as might occur with an increase in population might lead to an increase in crime, which eventually would produce an increase in the number of police. More police could inflate the arrest rate and thereby cause a decrease in the volume of crime.

If this were an accurate description of reality it would be reasonable to find evidence that police efficiency influenced crime at the same time that crime was causing changes in the arrest rate.

However, a less complex yet more plausible possibility is simply that the causal lag period for simple probability of arrest is greater than for police efficiency. If this were the case, an effect for arrest probability would not become apparent during this one-year lag analysis. Tittle and Rowe (1973) found that while certainty of apprehension reduced deviance, the more credible sanctioning agent had a greater initial effect. Since police efficiency is more likely to be immediately visible to potential lawbreakers than is the abstract general probability of arrest, it would seem logical that police efficiency would have a more immediate effect. Inclusion of data for a longer time span might, therefore, turn up a causal linkage between simple probability of arrest and crime rate. But even if this did not occur, the argument would still seem to be tenable since the deterrent hypothesis is most logical the closer the threat is to the potential deviant.

CONCLUSION

The findings offer some further support for the deterrent hypothesis, but they clearly indicate that statements about deterrent effects, especially those based on correlational studies using official police data, must be advanced cautiously and in very specific terms. Indeed the data suggest that below the tipping point of certainty, the opposite relationship to deterrence occurs and that arrest certainty is a function of crime. Thus deterrence seems to operate in a very specialized way which is contingent upon a number of conditions such as the level of certainty involved in the threat and perhaps even limited to particular kinds of "threats" (in this case the threat implied by greater police efficiency). The job that remains is to specify empirically the conditions under which sanctions or sanction threats influence behavior.

NOTE

1. There is some seasonal variation in crime data, but it is minimal in the state of Florida and is confined primarily to violent crime, which is a small proportion of the total (UCR 1972: 17-18).

REFERENCES

Antunes, G., and A. L. Hunt
  1973   The impact of certainty and severity of punishment on
         levels of crime in American states: an extended analysis.
         Journal of Criminal Law and Criminology 64 (December):
         486-93.

Bailey, W. C., J. D. Martin, and L. N. Gray
  1971   Crime and deterrence: a correlation analysis. Unpub-
         lished paper. Mimeograph.

Beattie, R. H.
  1960   Criminal statistics in the United States. Journal of Crim-
         inal Law, Criminology and Police Science 51 (May-June):
         49-65.

Bowers, W. J., and R. G. Salem
  1972   Severity of formal sanctions as a repressive response to
         deviant behavior. Law and Society Review 6 (February):
         427-41.

Campbell, D. T., and J. C. Stanley
  1963   Experimental and Quasi-Experimental Designs for Re-
         search. Chicago: Rand McNally.

Chiricos, T. G., and G. P. Waldo
  1970   Punishment and crime: an examination of some empirical
         evidence. Social Problems 18 (Fall): 200-17.

Cressey, D. R.
  1957   The state of criminal statistics. National Probation and
         Parole Association Journal 3 (July): 230-41.

Ehrlich, I.
  1972   The deterrent effect of criminal law enforcement. Journal
         of Legal Studies 1 (June): 259-76.

Gibbs, J. P.
  1968   Crime, punishment and deterrence. Southwestern Social
         Science Quarterly 48 (March): 515-30.

Gordon, R. A.
  1968   Issues in multiple regression. American Journal of
         Sociology 73 (March): 592-616.

Gray, L. N., and J. D. Martin
1969   Punishment and deterrence: another analysis of Gibbs'
        data. Social Science Quarterly 50: 389-95.

Heise, D. R.
1970   Causal inference from penal data. In Sociological Methodol-
        ogy, ed. Edgar F. Borgatta. San Francisco: Jossey-Bass.

Jensen, G. F.
1969   "Crime doesn't pay": correlates of a shared misunder-
        standing. Social Problems 17 (Fall): 189-201.

Kobrin, S., S. G. Lubeck, E. W. Hansen, and R. Yeaman
1972   The Deterrent Effectiveness of Criminal Justice Sanction
        Strategies: Final Report. Los Angeles: Public Systems
        Research Institute.

Logan, C. H.
1971   Legal sanctions and deterrence from crime. Ph.D. dis-
        sertation, Indiana University.

1972   General deterrent effects of imprisonment. Social Forces
        51 (September): 64-73.

Pelz, D. C., and F. M. Andrews
1964   Detecting causal priorities in panel data. American
        Sociological Review 29 (December): 836-48.

Salem, R. G., and W. J. Bowers
1970   Severity of formal sanctions as a deterrent to deviant be-
        havior. Law and Society Review 5 (August): 21-40.

Schwartz, R. D., and J. H. Skolnick
1962   Two studies of legal stigma. Social Problems 10 (Fall):
        133-42.

Skolnick, J. H.
1966   Justice without Trial. New York: John Wiley.

Tittle, C. R.
1969   Crime rates and legal sanctions. Social Problems 16
        (Spring): 409-23.

1974   Perceptions of sanctions and conformity. NSF funded
        project in progress.

Tittle, C. R., and C. H. Logan
1973 Sanctions and deviance: evidence and remaining questions. Law and Society Review 7 (Spring): 372-92.

Tittle, C. R., and A. R. Rowe
1973 Moral appeal, sanction threat, and deviance: an experimental test. Social Problems 20 (Spring): 488-98.

1974 Certainty of arrest and crime rates: a further test of the deterrence hypothesis. Social Forces 52 (June): 455-62.

Uniform Crime Reports
1970 U.S. Department of Justice. Washington, D.C.: U.S. Government Printing Office.

Uniform Crime Reports, State of Florida
1971 Crime in Florida. Tallahassee: Florida Department of Law Enforcement.

1972 Crime in Florida. Tallahassee: Florida Department of Law Enforcement.

Waldo, G. P., and T. G. Chiricos
1972 Perceived penal sanction and self-reported criminality: a neglected approach to deterrence research. Social Problems 19 (Spring): 522-40.

Zimring, F. E., and G. J. Hawkins
1973 Deterrence: The Legal Threat in Crime Control. Chicago: University of Chicago Press.

PART

IV

CRIMINALIZATION AND DECRIMINALIZATION

Few reasonable people would advocate the decriminalization of violent and predatory crimes--such as homicide, injuries to the person, threats to persons--or major incursions to property--such as housebreaking and burglary. But whether criminal law should proscribe such acts as homosexuality between consenting adults, abortion (when illegal), prostitution, the use of marijuana or even hard drugs, gambling or public drunkenness has come under serious question for some time. Activities such as these are often considered to harm no one except possibly those who engage in them. Nevertheless, whether this behavior is really victimless remains an open question. There are those who argue that historically criminal law has been used not only to protect citizens from harm but also to coerce people to private virtue. And when criminal law proscribes a host of so-called victimless crimes (better characterized as crimes without an effective complainant), it is considered to overreach itself. This overreach brings under the purview of the criminal justice system many individuals who rarely can be helped by it. It is simply beyond the competence and proper scope of criminal justice to deal effectively with the alcoholic, the drug addict, the gambler, or the prostitute. Correctional "treatment," if offered, often exacerbates the problem of these persons and thereby contributes to the revolving-door syndrome characterizing our jails and other penal institutions. In addition, the attempt to control such behaviors is costly in both economic and social terms and is deemed by many to be a major obstacle to the development of a rational and effective criminal justice system.

A position contrary to that described above argues that such behavior is indeed socially harmful because it weakens social values and norms, undermines society's cohesiveness and moral fiber, and tends to produce a significant amount of harm to others, such as the victimization of persons by narcotics users who must support their habit by stealth or worse.

The social, scientific, ethical, and moral dilemmas which permeate the area of victimless crimes are deep. They involve a wide range of scientific disciplines, moral philosophy, religion, the law, criminal justice agencies, and the human service professions. It seems unlikely, therefore, that there will soon be any breakthrough in terms of etiological explanations, predictions and control, or a unified policy. In view of this deadlock, there has been a recent shift in focus by many criminologists from such value-laden considerations of personal and/or interpersonal harm to the actual transactions that occur between consenting persons, such as buyers and sellers and consumers of illicit goods and services. Once the focus of analysis has shifted from questions of morality and ethics to the consequences of proscribing legislation, one can begin to assess empirically the "costs of criminalization." Among the generally recognized costs are staggering enforcement costs, socially harmful economic consequences, costs arising from the corruption of agents of the law and other governmental officials, as well as rising contempt for the law and the costs due to crime proliferation.

The cost of fighting victimless crimes is staggering and siphons off badly needed resources from fighting serious crimes, such as homicide, rape, robbery, and aggravated assault, to name a few. In this sense, victimless crime statutes place a serious burden on our already overtaxed criminal justice system. Further, many such laws are notoriously difficult to enforce. To obtain evidence on consensual transactions occurring in private most of the time, law enforcement agents frequently have to stoop to unsavory techniques which come dangerously close to entrapment. Worse, such efforts at policing private morality are singularly ineffective. In most cases, law enforcement achieves a temporary containment or displacement of the undesirable activities, conducts a few skirmishes, and exerts some regulatory control over illicit behavior and vice. But it never manages to eradicate the offensive behavior.

Among some of the socially harmful economic consequences is the fact that once a commodity is outlawed, a crime tariff is placed on it: The tougher the law enforcement, the higher the risk to the entrepreneur, the higher the cost of the goods to the consumer, be they hard drugs, illegal abortions, or illicit sex. A related economic consequence to criminalizing moral foibles is the fact that the enormous profits involved have provided the cornerstone on which organized crime grows and flourishes.

Police and government official corruption is yet another consequence of "criminalization" of victimless crimes. The huge sums of money involved in drug traffic frequently prove too much of a temptation for many who are charged to enforce the law. There is mounting evidence that police officers and narcotic agents are part and parcel of the drug problem in major urban areas. And ubiquitous drugs in jails and penitentiaries are due in part to corrupt correctional staff. But corrupting influences of laws against victimless crimes are not limited to drug traffic alone. Bookies and numbers runners, prostitutes and pimps look upon bribing police and other officials as a normal cost of doing business. Public knowledge of bribery and corruption evokes cynicism and contempt for the law and gradually erodes the standards and principles on which good government is built.

Legislating against victimless crimes has tended to produce more crime, not less. Drug addiction, for example, generates a host of secondary crime to procure the money needed to support drug habits. While there is much speculation among scholars and practitioners as to the extent of this type of crime, it is generally estimated at 20 to 30 percent of the total crime rate in major urban areas, and is therefore highly significant. The simple act of legislating against such prevalent types of behavior as marijuana use, gambling, homosexuality, and so on, creates new categories of "criminals," new illicit enterprises, illegal dealers and procurers, and literally drives users and consumers into black market operations and criminal haunts, thus leaving them vulnerable to a vast array of victimization ranging from usury, to blackmail, to extortion, to dangerous merchandise (such as impure and contaminated drugs), to physical injury and even death. The impact of such legislation on the behavior and self-image of such persons is well documented and shows a steady progression of increasing alienation and deeper involvement in the subculture of crime.

In light of these considerations, an increasing number of scholars and experts on crime are recommending one of two options: decriminalization of existing statutes proscribing victimless crime, or at least instituting some form of regulatory, licensing, or other control mechanisms not involving the police or the courts. There are even some suggestions to include under such regulatory mechanisms such other "illicit practices" as corporate crime, embezzlement, price fixing, tax offenses, and trafficking in drugs (as opposed to using drugs). Among the principal reasons offered for removing these types of activities from the purview of criminal law are the following: first, police are not deemed to be the best possible enforcement agents when it comes to these illegal behaviors, and second, it is reasoned that if these illicit practices were combined with victimless crimes, roughly half the business of the courts and about two-thirds that of the police would be removed from these agencies, thereby freeing them to pursue violent and predatory crime.

It is because arguments such as those discussed above are so persuasive that Graeme Newman's chapter on criminalization and decriminalization is not only well-timed but worthy of thoughtful consideration. In an effort to assess public perceptions of deviant behaviors, a large cross-national survey was conducted. Countries were selected to represent a wide range of economic and social development and reflected different political structures. The range of deviant behavior included acts traditionally seen as criminal (for example, predatory crime); more common deviant acts (for example, victimless crimes), novel deviant behavior (for example, environmental pollution), and behavior not usually proscribed by law (for example, nonviolent public protest, or not helping an endangered person). It should be noted here that cross-national and cross-cultural research is difficult to conduct. Such matters as clarification of terminology and criminal law concept variations must be carefully handled. Comparative international research also mandates a wider knowledge of the legal and social culture of the countries to be studied than probably currently exists. In spite of these difficulties, there is a need for more studies such as Newman's, in view of the fact that criminological theory and criminal justice practices would have much to gain from such work. So while there must be some caveats with regard to the ability to generalize about the findings of this study, they are certainly interesting and illuminating. For example, Newman found an almost unanimous agreement among respondents across all countries surveyed (which included citizens from Belgrade, Yugoslavia; New York, United States; Orani, Italy; Djakarta, Indonesia; and Teheran, Iran) that traditional crimes should be proscribed by law. In the area of victimless crime, the researchers obtained vastly different results. While persons in industrialized and developed countries showed a predictable weakening of social taboos and favored decriminalization of such behaviors, the respondents in the developing countries showed a strong preference for criminalization. When it came to the relatively new type of "deviant" behavior of pollution, Newman was able to document the high impact of industrialization on developing countries and the extent to which this phenomenon produces (or transmits) deviance. Apparently, pollution has been unanimously criminalized in all countries, as though crimes such as this one were traditional crimes. One additional intriguing finding should be mentioned here. The usually accepted universal taboo of incest was overwhelmingly criminalized by respondents from all countries with the exception of persons from New York, where almost 21 percent of the respondents thought that this act should not be proscribed by the law. This finding shows rather clearly one of the deleterious effects of industrialization, urbanization, and heterogeneity: that is, the degree to which these influences can be assumed to weaken previously almost sacrosanct traditional norms of morality. In sum, Newman's study (in spite of some methodological difficulties) provides valuable support for a number of sociological theories: there is a weakening of traditional norms in modern industrialized countries; there is a gradual universalization of culture; there is considerable disagreement about sanctioning and proscribing deviant (for example, victimless) crimes as opposed to criminal behavior; and finally, only four deviant acts received a less than 50 percent criminalizing response in the countries that were surveyed: public protest in Italy and Yugoslavia; abortion in Yugoslavia and the United States; and homosexuality and "not helping others" in the United States. As a result, those currently advocating decriminalization of a wide range of human behaviors might do well to pause and consider the almost universally strong support of the public for the legal sanctioning of deviant behavior.

The second chapter in this section by Carl Eklund also addresses itself to the problem of overcriminalization. It takes cognizance of the fact that court systems in the United States are dangerously overburdened with case loads. In most urban courts, criminal as well as civil case delays have reached epidemic proportions. In this process, victims and plaintiffs are alienated and literally "cooled out," the memory and willingness of witnesses fades, and offenders go unpunished and are thereby encouraged by the system to continue to violate the law. Again, no one will argue that persons who commit serious crimes such as homicide, armed robbery, arson, or rape should not be handled by the criminal justice system. The problem is that police and prosecutors cannot adequately handle serious crime cases because their resources are dissipated in the pursuit of victimless crimes, illicit practices, and in attempts at resolving a wide range of conflicts arising between neighbors, family members, landlords and tenants, or other persons having similar relationships of a continuing nature. Further, as was seen from the previous discussion on the high cost of criminalization, normal litigation through the criminal justice process is frequently not only inappropriate but may actually be a factor in perpetuating and increasing crime.

In light of these considerations, the need is great for new and innovative mechanisms located outside the criminal justice system to deal efficiently and equitably with a host of problem cases, such as community disputes, victimless crimes (in cases where complaints are lodged), a wide range of illicit and delinquent behavior, intrafamily offenses, and possibly with first offenders and victims of minor, nonviolent crimes. It is worth noting here that criminologists, society at large, and the legal profession are currently on the threshold of "discovering" yet another category of highly prevalent deviance, namely wife and child abuse. As research begins to unravel the magnitude and gravity of the problem, and as more women will be encouraged to speak out on their plight, there will no doubt be clarion calls for more criminalization and more punishment of this offensive behavior. But any rational consideration of the problem and the issues will be forced to conclude that the criminal justice system will not be able to take on this additional burden. First, there are not enough resources to deal with predatory crime, much less with this type of deviance. Second, existing knowledge points to the fact that criminal justice is singularly unsuited to deal with family disputes or intrafamily violence. Third, if current proscriptions and stiff penalties cannot solve the wide range of illicit behavior and victimless crimes, why should it be able to be more effective in family disputes? As a result, the need for alternative resolution and dispute settling techniques will be even greater within the near future than is presently recognized.

Responding to this clearly identified need, there exist today a limited number of community advocacy groups, private and public organizations, as well as some governmental agencies, all of which seek to assist victims and offenders in a peaceful resolution of conflicts and petty crimes. For example, some jurisdictions have now implemented citizens' complaint units for conducting initial interviews and screening complaints of citizens who have encountered problems involving possible legal sanctions but who have little knowledge of the noncriminal, remedial, mediatory means available to solve their problems. For example, Washington, D.C., operates a citizens' complaint center under the auspices of the prosecutor's office. Attorneys working in that office may refer complainants involved in intrafamily offenses or similar difficulties to various noncriminal agencies for resolution. Generally, screening and interviewing are performed by paralegal staff, and attorneys' services are limited to conducting hearings and advising on legal action, should that be deemed desirable. Similar approaches are offered through night prosecutor programs, which serve to reduce the workload of law enforcement and the judiciary by handling many citizen complaints through administrative--not criminal--processes. Such program activities offer a number of additonal benefits: they ease interpersonal tensions without resorting to a formal criminal justice remedy; they divert a large number of complainants from the judicial system, which frees prosecutory time and energy to cases that are in the interest of protecting the public from serious, predatory crime; and they are cost-effective from the citizen point of view since the programs generally charge only nominal fees or no fees at all for their services. Carl Eklund describes in detail the program developed by the National Center for Dispute Settlement, appropriately titled Arbitration as an Alternative to the Criminal Judicial Process. Under the provisions of this program, persons are invited to submit voluntarily their dispute to arbitration before a skilled impartial arbiter. The hearing process involves the use of a technique which combines mediation and arbitration skills sensitized to meet the needs of all parties involved in order to arrive at satisfactory solutions for everyone. When a case is heard, the arbiter has as a primary objective the reaching of a consent agreement between the parties. If an agreement cannot be reached, the arbiter is vested with the authority to render a final and binding award. Consent agreements as well as awards are enforceable in court and frequently provide such remedies as restitution, governmental assistance such as victim compensation, and/or injunctive relief. The process is clearly diversionary and "decriminalizing" in nature. In view of the current state of disarray in criminal justice, programs of this nature would seem to hold much promise, especially since they have the voluntary cooperation of the people involved.

7

CRIMINALIZATION AND DECRIMINALIZATION OF DEVIANT BEHAVIOR: A CROSS-NATIONAL OPINION SURVEY

Graeme R. Newman

The data for this study are drawn from a large cross-national survey on public perceptions of deviant behavior conducted by the United Nations Social Defense Research Institute in 1973. Countries were selected to represent a range of economic and social development, as well as differing political structures and stability. A range of deviant acts was chosen in such a way as to represent acts traditionally seen as criminal (for example, robbery) through the more common deviant acts (for example, sexual deviance) to the recent "deviant" acts of environmental pollution. This chapter reports results obtained from two standardized questions which were asked concerning each act (see Table 7.1). Personal interviews were conducted by indigenous interviewers in four countries. In the United States the interview schedules were converted to self-administering questionnaires. The original schedule was designed

The data for this chapter were collected in 1973 as part of the United Nations Social Defense Research Institute's (UNSDRI) study on changing perceptions of deviance, of which the principal investigator was Marvin E. Wolfgang. Acknowledgment is also due to the Ford Foundation and the Committee on Institutional Funds, State University of New York at Albany, for funding of various phases of the project. I also wish to thank the many persons who helped in the field work in each country, especially Eduardo Vetere and Giuseppe di Gennaro of UNSDRI, Italy; Parvis Saney and Assad Nezami, University of Teheran; Assaud Hassan and Mrs. Sadli, University of Indonesia; Mrs. Helena Spadya-Djinic, Yugoslavia; and Donald Articolo, State University of New York at Albany.

in English, in close consultation with sociological and legal experts
from each country, then translated into the various languages.

TABLE 7.1

Description of Acts

Pollution (individual):	"A person puts rubbish in a stream."
Robbery:	"A person forcefully takes $50 from another person who, as a result, is injured and has to be hospitalized."
Incest:	"A person has sexual relationships with his adult daughter."
Not Helping:	"A person sees someone in a dangerous situation and does nothing."
Abortion:	"A woman who is two months pregnant seeks and obtains an abortion."
Pollution (factory):	"A factory director continues to permit his factory to release poisonous gases into the air."
Homosexuality:	"A person has homosexual relations in private with the consent of the partner."
Protest:	"A person participates in a protest meeting against government policy in a public place. No violence occurs."
Appropriation:	"A person puts government funds to his own use."
Taking Drugs:	"A person takes heroin." ("opium," "drugs")

Source: Compiled by the author.

SAMPLING

The area sampling method was used for all country samples
with the exception of the New York sample, which was constructed
by requesting a class of undergraduate college students to adminis-
ter the interview schedule to their parents after also completing the
questionnaires themselves. The sample obtained closely resembled
census data for New York State, with the exception that there was a
slightly lower proportion of New York City respondents. However,
since in a comparative study it is the difference between samples

rather than their representativeness that is important (Lerner 1958; Przeworski and Teune 1967), this should not be seen as a severe problem. No attempt was made to make each sample statistically representative of a whole country, because of each country's enormous internal diversity. Response rates were over 85 percent for Yugoslavia, Indonesia, and Iran, over 95 percent for Sardinia, and 70 percent for the New York sample. Age and sex ratios agreed with census data on each city. The lowest age category was 18 years. In addition, a small sample was taken from a rural village within 50 miles of each major city sampled for Indonesia, Iran, and Yugoslavia. The Sardinian sample taken from Orani should be considered as basically a village or rural sample.

RESULTS

Robbery and Appropriation: The "Traditional Crimes"

Table 7.2 provides us with the most straightforward measure of criminalization: Should the act be prohibited by the law? It can be seen that there was almost unanimous agreement across all five countries that the "traditional" crimes of misappropriation and robbery should be prohibited by the law. Furthermore, almost all respondents were aware that the acts were in fact prohibited by the law (see Table 7.3).

Incest: The "Universal Taboo"

The usually accepted "universal taboo" of incest was criminalized unanimously by respondents from all countries except the United States, where almost a quarter of respondents thought the act should not be prohibited by the law. Although a similar proportion reported incorrectly that the act was not against the law (see Table 7.2), cross-tabular analysis suggested that these were not the same respondents. Incorrect knowledge of the law, therefore, did not significantly influence attitudes of decriminalization. One need hardly point to the fact that the weakening of this "taboo" has first appeared in the most industrialized and developed country.

Traditionally Deviant Acts: Homosexuality, Abortion, Taking Drugs

The decriminalizing opinion of the New York respondents in comparison to all other countries is indeed striking. Only 18.3

TABLE 7.2

"Do You Think This Act Should Be Prohibited by the Law?"
(percent distribution)

	Belgrade, Yugoslavia (N=500)		New York, United States (N=169)		Orani, Italy (N=200)		Djakarta, Indonesia (N=500)		Teheran, Iran (N=475)	
	Yes	No	Yes	No	Yes	No	Yes	No	Yes	No
Robbery	98.4	0.4	100.0	0.0	100.0	0.0	99.2	0.0	97.9	2.1
Appropriation	98.0	0.0	92.3	7.1	100.0	0.0	99.8	0.2	97.1	2.9
Incest	95.0	0.8	71.0	20.7	97.5	2.0	98.0	0.6	98.1	1.9
Homosexuality	71.6	13.6	18.3	66.9	86.5	12.5	85.9	7.2	90.3	9.7
Abortion	24.8	63.2	21.9	74.5	76.5	21.5	95.3	3.0	83.9	16.1
Taking drugs	89.2	4.2	84.6	11.8	92.0	8.0	93.3	2.4	89.8	10.2
Individual pollution	92.2	3.2	96.4	3.0	99.5	0.5	82.4	14.3	94.3	5.7
Factory pollution	92.8	1.6.	96.4	3.0	96.0	3.5	94.9	1.0	97.7	2.3
Public protest	46.2	38.4	5.9	91.1	34.5	64.5	72.3	20.9	77.0	23.0
Not helping	76.6	12.2	27.8	52.7	79.5	20.0	67.7	24.4	56.4	43.6

Source: Compiled by the author.

TABLE 7.3

"Is This Act Prohibited by the Law?"
(percent distribution)

	Belgrade, Yugoslavia (N=500)		New York, United States (N=169)		Orani, Italy (N=200)		Djakarta, Indonesia (N=500)		Teheran, Iran (N=475)	
	Yes	No	Yes	No	Yes	No	Yes	No	Yes	No
Robbery	92.8	4.0	97.6	0.6	98.5	1.0	98.0	.4	91.6	3.1
Appropriation	94.4	2.0	85.2	9.5	94.0	1.0	97.8	1.2	86.1	8.8
Incest	82.6	5.0	76.9	5.3	87.5	2.5	89.5	2.6	95.6	0.6
Homosexuality	54.6	17.2	52.5	22.1	77.0*	7.5	66.0	13.6	81.9	3.8
Abortion	24.4*	62.0	8.3*	88.3	90.5	2.0	88.7	4.2	84.9*	5.5
Taking drugs	72.8*	15.2	97.6	1.2	73.0	10.0	80.3	7.2	87.0	8.6
Individual pollution	57.4*	23.4	70.4	10.7	65.5	11.0	59.1	23.4	69.1	17.0
Factory pollution	56.2*	25.0	69.2	9.5	72.5	8.0	75.0	7.9	73.7*	12.7
Public protest	57.6*	21.8	0.6*	87.6	57.0	24.5	68.8	13.2	82.1*	5.0
Not helping	30.8	37.8	7.1*	76.3	44.5	20.0	45.4	30.3	31.6*	48.6

*Indicates that "yes" would be an "incorrect" legal response. However, the law is ambiguous on a number of acts. For example, in Iran it is not against the law for a woman to obtain an abortion through a doctor. However, it is against the law for the doctor to perform one unless to save the mother's life. These assessments of the criminality of the acts were made in consultation with legal experts of each country.

Source: Compiled by the author.

percent thought the act should be legally prohibited (see Table 7.2). Only in Yugoslavia was there a weakening in the criminalizing attitude to this act. Again, we may note that this weakening occurs in the two most economically developed countries.[1] Table 7.3 also suggests that there is a considerable amount of confusion in all countries as to whether homosexuality is prohibited by the law. More than half of each sample either did not know or answered incorrectly.

The preference for decriminalization by the two more developed countries of Yugoslavia and the United States was also demonstrated for the act of abortion, with the Yugoslavians showing much greater tolerance of this act than any other. Knowledge of the law, however, was nowhere near as confused, with only the Iranians displaying considerable lack of knowledge on the criminality of this act. This may be explained by the ambiguity of the Iranian law on abortion or, perhaps more likely, the very high rate of criminalization and affirmation of illegality of the acts displayed generally by the Iranians. The act of taking drugs is the clear exception to these traditionally deviant acts. It was almost unanimously criminalized by all countries in the same way as traditional crimes of robbery and misappropriation. Furthermore, knowledge of the law was less confused in all countries except in Yugoslavia, where 72.8 percent incorrectly thought the act was against the law.

Environmental Pollution: Individual and Factory Pollution

Reactions to these acts give an excellent chance to gauge the extent to which "deviance" produced as a direct result of industrialization (and therefore indigenous to the developed countries) has been transported to other developing countries. It can be seen from Table 7.2 that both polluting acts have been unanimously criminalized in all countries as though they were traditional crimes. Knowledge of the law on pollution was somewhat confused, although not as badly as for the traditionally deviant acts. Again, the Iranians displayed an incorrectly high affirmation of the illegality of these acts.

"Nondeviant" Acts

The New York respondents are clearly the "deviant" respondents of this survey, with only a negligible proportion criminalizing public protest, and less than half the proportions of all other countries criminalizing "not helping." However, if we view responses to these acts in comparisons to responses to other acts within each

country sample, we can see that these are generally the least criminalized acts in all countries. The large discrepancy between the
developing countries (Indonesia and Iran) and Italy, the United States,
and Yugoslavia in favoring criminalization of public protest is indeed
striking, especially when these former countries are usually rated
as more totalitarian as well as less economically developed than the
former countries.

The act of not helping is also interesting, where the proportions of the developing countries criminalizing this act were less than
Yugoslavia and Italy, yet the United States was the great exception,
with only 27.8 percent criminalizing the act. This response is even
more striking when one considers that, compared to the confused
response of all other country samples, the New Yorkers were quite
clear about the legality of this act. (And this even when the criminal
law itself in New York is somewhat ambiguous about it.)

SUMMARY AND CONCLUSIONS

If one were to order the acts according to the proportions of
each country sample criminalizing them, one would find a general
consensus across all countries. When one looks at specific acts,
however, the consensus tends to fade and holds only for traditional
crimes of robbery and misappropriation, environmental pollution,
and taking drugs.

Traditionally deviant acts were significantly more decriminal-
ized by the respondents from the industrialized countries of Yugoslavia and the United States.

"Nondeviant" acts were more highly criminalized by the developing, more totalitarian countries.

Knowledge of the law seemed to be generally above confusion
in all countries only for traditional crimes. There was especially
considerable confusion concerning the illegality of traditionally
deviant acts.

Indonesia and Iran displayed extremely high criminalizing attitudes. This result, however, should be interpreted with caution
since experience with surveys in these countries has suggested that
an element of response bias may operate in the direction of acquies-
cence (the "courtesy bias," Jones 1963).

A number of classic sociological theories are supported by
these findings: modern industrialized countries display a weakening
of traditional norms of morality; there is evidence of gradual universalization of culture (the universal criminalization of environmental pollution); deviant behavior in comparison to criminal behavior is typically that about which there is extensive disagreement
about sanctioning.

Another important observation is the very extensive confusion about whether some acts are prohibited by the law or not--there was only clear certainty for the traditional crimes. The usual assumption that the criminal law makes in most countries concerning the actor's knowledge of the law appears in light of this information somewhat unfounded, especially for traditionally deviant acts.

Finally, it may be worth noting that of those acts which are actually not criminalized by the criminal law of any country, it was only the act of public protest in New York which received a negligible criminalizing response. Only six other acts of all countries received a less than 50 percent criminalizing response: public protest in Italy and Yugoslavia (46.2 percent), abortion in Yugoslavia and the United States, and homosexuality and not helping in the United States. The currently popular move toward decriminalization of criminal law would do well to note the almost universally strong support of the public for the legal sanctioning of deviant behavior.

NOTE

1. Although Italy is within the seven most developed countries of the world, Orani is a village in Sardinia, much less developed, and more of a "subculture" (Ferracuti et al. 1970).

REFERENCES

Ferracuti, F., R. Lazzari, and M. Wolfgang
1970   Violence in Sardinia. Rome: Mario Bulzone.

Jones, E. L.
1963   The courtesy bias in South-East Asian surveys. International Social Science Journal 15: 70-76.

Lerner, D.
1958   The Passing of Traditional Society. London: Collier-Macmillan.

Przeworski, A., and H. Teune
1967   Establishing equivalence in cross-national research. Public Opinion Quarterly 30.

8

THE PROBLEM OF OVERCRIMINALIZING HUMAN CONFLICT: A CIVIL ALTERNATIVE

Carl A. Eklund

Conflict in our society is inevitable and continuing, with only its nature and intensity changing. It will always be political, social, and economic. Today, however, it is also racial, ethnic, and generational. It is between those with status and those seeking status, and between those holding power and those with little or no power. Its intensity ranges from the ultimate violence, whether sudden or calculated, through the middle levels, to the totally nonviolent, and it is even genteel at the other end of the spectrum. The intensity level of conflict is determined by many factors, not the least of which is the degree and depth of alienation and frustration on the one hand and the often blind and obstinate resistance to necessary change on the other.

It is these dynamics of conflict that are the contributing factors to today's urban crisis. Perhaps the most readily recognized, and intensely studied, element of the urban crisis is the pervasive threat to the public safety of the general populace more commonly known as street crime.

Street crimes, such as assault, petty larceny, mischievous behavior, and harassment, as well as more violent crimes, are often attributed to such root causes as racism, poverty, substandard housing, inadequate education, unemployment, family unrest, alcoholism, and drug addiction. Many sociologists relate these factors to the cause-pattern leading up to high crime rates in the central city.

But, as all are well aware, crime is not limited to the inner city or its fringe areas. It is also rampant throughout suburbia, where residents clearly enjoy a much-improved socioeconomic living level. Again, particularly among youth and young adults, many of the contributing factors may be similar to those attributed to the central city such as idle time, unemployment, lack of parental guidance, and alcohol and drug abuse. Far removed from the central city and its suburbs, one still encounters the same factors, cause-patterns, and rising crime rates. Even the most remote Eskimo villages of Alaska cannot escape this pervasive threat (Hippler and Conn 1973).

Regardless of social group membership, place of residence, or socioeconomic class level, both the youth and adult populations commit street crimes and have street crimes committed against them. To be sure, habitual criminals and persons who commit serious crimes of a violent nature such as arson, rape, armed robbery, homicide, and crimes within the arena of organized crime mandate special handling by police, courts, institutions for residential confinement, and social and vocational rehabilitation agencies.

However, normal litigation through the criminal judicial process is often not only inappropriate but may actually be a factor in perpetuating crime either on the same or on an intensified level. Although the judicial process will determine guilt or innocence, the cause-pattern generally will go unresolved, thus allowing for recurrence and even acts of retaliation. Because of legal complexities, heavy court case loads, and other factors, our extant judicial process often takes so long that victims hesitate to assist in prosecution, thus giving a quasi-social sanction to both the crime and the offender which, in turn, begins to perpetuate further victimization of themselves and others. In addition, the usual judicial process can be so costly to the offender in terms of attorney fees and loss of wages that new variables, such as unemployment due to a conviction record, may become added factors for further antisocial behavior.

New and innovative mechanisms are desperately needed to deal efficiently and effectively with offenders and victims of non-violent crimes and to resolve community disputes. Serious consideration must be given to the social problems which are the contributing causes of crime, and such considerations must be included in a more modern methodology for crime prevention, particularly those of a community nature.

Such methodologies must be utilized in the private-individual sector as well as in the broad public-community sector which includes advocate groups, social institutions, and governmental agencies. When this is done, law enforcement agencies and the courts will be able to exert their full attention and resources to violent and organized crime.

The foregoing comments are not intended to be a comprehensive statement of the sociological cause-pattern of today's crime problem; they are presented only to illustrate those problems. The term "street crime" encompasses a wide variety of crimes. It

includes the well-known victimless crime found in drug abuse, for
example, as well as intentional crimes such as purse snatching,
committed by a stranger on a random victim. The methodology of
dealing with offenders to be proffered and discussed herein places
its emphasis not on the victimless or random victim crimes but on
those involving offenders and victims who have a continuing relationship. Such crimes evolve from the same cause-patterns and manifest the same antisocial conduct differing only in the nature of the
relationship of the parties. Although a part of street crime, such
activity, at least for the purposes herein and perhaps more accurately, shall be referred to as "community crime"; the "community" consisting of any of the usual social groupings of people based
on their common interests such as family, work, recreation, housing, and schools.

     This proffered method of dealing with these community crimes
will not eradicate the cause-pattern factors in our society as a
whole. However, it can lessen the impact of those factors on individuals by making available to them new skills to deal with the influences of the antisocial cause-patterns.

     The President's Commission on Law Enforcement and Admin-
istration of Justice has observed that the "arbitrary assignment to
the criminal law and its processes of a variety of human conduct
and conditions has come to be regarded as a problem of overcriminalization" (President's Commission 1967). This problem is especially acute among those minor criminal prosecutions initiated by
private complaints brought by citizens to the police or the prosecutor.

     Complaining parties often use prosecution as a means of re-
taliation in community squabbles for which both parties may actually share some degree of blame. Where the complainant and
defendant have an ongoing relationship, such as relatives or neighbors, their conflict may erupt again and again, even after a judicial disposition of their dispute or, more accurately, a disposition
of the criminal manifestation of their dispute. Moreover, these
cases contribute to an already overloaded court calendar and burden
the staffs of law enforcement, prosecutorial, and investigatory
agencies, distracting them from more serious criminal matters.

     Such community conflicts find their roots deep in society and
human nature. Too often one sees only the symptoms--the surface
evidence--of a more pervasive problem. Much like the visible tip
of an iceberg, the private criminal complaint frequently deals with
relatively minor charges growing out of deeper human conflict,
frustration, and alienation. The criminal law with its focus on the
defendant alone is ill-equipped to deal with this basic fact. A judge
or prosecutor, faced with an overcrowded court calendar, beyond-
a-reasonable-doubt criteria for conviction, conflicting stories, and

"minor" offenses, will often dismiss such a case and lecture the
defendant, perhaps threatening possible punishment for future offenses. This is not conflict resolution; it is not problem solving in
the community; nor is it intended to be. The tip of the iceberg has
been viewed briefly, but the underlying problem remains unseen and
potentially as obstructive as ever. Neighborhood tensions have not
been reduced. Relationships have not been improved. At best a
shaky truce may have been ordered.

The National Center for Dispute Settlement (the Center), a
division of the American Arbitration Association, believed that there
was a better way to handle these private criminal complaints, and
district attorneys and municipal judges agreed. As a result of this
consensus, a new approach evolved where, in appropriate cases as
determined by the district attorney's office and the courts, and when
agreed to by the citizens involved, an alternative course of action
is followed: the voluntary submission of the dispute to arbitration.
This new course of action administered by the Center is known as
Arbitration As An Alternative to the Criminal Judicial Process
(4-A Program).

This program provides an opportunity to deal meaningfully
and sensitively with human beings in conflict, to probe for the underlying causes of such conflict and to address them, to engage in
meaningful dialog, and to reach an accommodation. It also provides finality through the arbitrator's award. The process itself
makes any award rendered far more acceptable to all parties than
is a judicial determination of guilt or innocence. The conflict which
arises in the community is settled in the community under conditions of maximum involvement and participation of the parties to
the dispute.

The program begins to function when a person in the community feels wronged by another person's acts. The wronged party
(complainant) seeks criminal prosecution against the other party
(defendant) by filing a complaint at the office of the district attorney,
city prosecutor, criminal clerk, or police department, depending
on that particular jurisdiction's procedure. This complaint from a
private citizen often results in the issuance of a warrant for the
arrest of the defendant for a relatively minor criminal offense such
as harassment, destruction of property, simple assault, disorderly
conduct, or the like. Such offenses as these often arise out of arguments between friends or neighbors which result in one party's
slapping the other, a minor scuffle, a broken window, or other
activity not uncommon to urban living but which nevertheless is
criminal in nature, if only technically so.

If all such cases were prosecuted, the courts would be back-
logged everywhere as many now are. Even if the courts could
process all such cases, they could not resolve the real problems,

that is, the cause-pattern of the technically criminal behavior; the courts are restricted to finding the defendants before them either innocent or guilty of the alleged offense and must operate within the very narrow parameters of the strict evidentiary and procedural rules of criminal procedure.

To participate in the 4-A Program, a complainant might begin by going to the prosecutor's office to request the issuance of a warrant for the defendant's arrest. The prosecutor, upon listening to the complaint, finds that two or more parties have become involved in a dispute which has manifested itself in the type of criminal conduct previously described, and finds further that the parties have one of the defined community relationships making the dispute appropriate for referral to the 4-A Program. When this occurs, the prosecutor explains the program to the complainant, advising that it is a voluntary process and that if the complainant desires to submit his case to the 4-A Program rather than to the criminal court, the defendant will then also be asked if he would desire to submit.

When both parties have executed the voluntary submission form, the Center, serving as the tribunal administrator, schedules the case for a hearing at its offices before an impartial arbitrator. The court has not as of this time taken official jurisdiction of the case. There is no criminal information filed, no arrest made, and no warrant issued. This is not to say, however, that cases cannot be referred to the 4-A Program after warrants are served, arrests made, or information filed. Judges quite often have referred cases after arraignment. Judicial referrals are usually made in the more complex cases such as the one which involved 11 parties with 17 complaints and cross-complaints filed. In such instances the parties are still referred on a voluntary basis while the court continues the trial date in contemplation of future dismissal.

Prior to signing the submission form, the parties are advised by the prosecutor for example, to confer with legal counsel on their right to legal representation at the hearing, on the hearing procedure on the authority of the arbitrator, that the formal rules of evidence will not apply, that they will be able to submit evidence themselves or through witnesses, and that they will be able to cross-examine. The parties are also advised that the arbitrator has the authority to render an award on the merits for or against any party; that the award can include civil damages and injunctive relief; and that the award is final and binding and can be enforced in court. [1]

As the hearing commences, the arbitrator again advises the parties and their counsel, if any, of the procedures, parties' rights and the arbitrator's authority.

In general, an arbitrator has the singular duty of hearing the evidence presented by the parties to a dispute and then rendering an award in favor of or against the party requesting relief. This is not the case in the 4-A Program. Here the arbitrator is charged with the initial task of attempting to mediate the case to work out a consent agreement between the parties. If mediation is unsuccessful, then he may use his arbitrator's authority to render a decision. Whether a hearing is concluded by an award or with a consent agreement, there is never an assessment of the conduct of the parties in terms of guilt or innocence. Furthermore, there can be no criminal court type of sanctions, such as fines, nor any punitive damages.

The arbitration aspect of a hearing is, in essence, an adversary proceeding, but the arbitrator first works with the adversaries as a mediator to attempt to achieve a consensus solution, rather than simply listening to them and rendering his solution to their problem.[2] This process, known as "med-arb," is a quite workable blending of mediation and arbitration which are two processes generally thought of, and generally utilized, as mutually exclusive dispute settlement techniques (Cole 1973).

Mediation, a process without any powers conferred upon the intervenor, is not an adversary proceeding. The parties enter such a process voluntarily with the goal of reaching a mutual accommodation of their individual interests. The parties fully participate in all phases of the decision-making process and must all agree to the final result. This is unlike arbitration where the parties are adversaries and must all be bound by the final result whether they agree with it or not. Mediation is usually a much longer process than arbitration since the many variables of a solution are thoroughly explored. While an arbitrator has the ultimate input into a result, the mediator's input may be substantial but is seldom conclusive (Simkin 1973).

The process of med-arb has certain advantages over either of the separate processes. While incorporating the advantages of mediation already discussed, med-arb provides an inducement for parties to settle their differences. Generally, parties would rather determine their own solution than have a solution determined for them. Even if acceptable to one party, it may not be acceptable to the other, which puts the viability of the solution in jeopardy and potentially puts the parties back on the path of future conflict. In such an instance, the present problem has not been resolved; it has merely been supplanted by a new problem.

This is not to say, however, that rendering a decision by arbitration is not good. There are many cases where it is essential to have such authority. There are many people who do not understand the negotiation process which takes place in mediation. A person, in an effort to demonstrate how reasonable he is, may make more concessions than are necessary or more than he can afford.

In such a case, an arbitrator can protect that person as well as the process. This process strives to bring equity to a situation, not to provide a forum which allows the parties to engage in a win-or-lose adversary proceeding.

There are, of course, other people who will make no concessions even when such would be beneficial to their future relationships. They may take such a stance to show how tough they are or perhaps to continue the harassment of the other party. Here an arbitrator's award may be necessary to bring equity to the situation or to structure future activity by injunctive remedies so as to hopefully prevent future conflict. Another situation where the authority to render a decision is beneficial is when one or both parties may have confided to the mediator in private caucuses a willingness to make certain concessions but refuse to do so in a plenary session for fear of losing respect, status, or bargaining position. The mediator, working with the parties in private caucuses, can work out a solution known to be acceptable to the parties and then simply render it as his award in his role of arbitrator.

This last example of an advantage to med-arb can also be a disadvantage, though not as likely in 4-A hearings as in the more professional conflicts such as union-management contract negotiations. When the parties know that the intervenor can ultimately render his own solution in the event of an impasse, the parties are not as likely to confide in the mediator the limits of their concessions, thus making mediation more difficult and impasse more likely. Conversely, if the parties freely confide their concessions and bottom-line strategies in private caucuses with the mediator and impasse is reached, the mediator, who now has to function as an arbitrator, may have had his ability to act objectively on the technical evidence compromised.

The mediation role in 4-A cases is very sensitive. The incident which brought the parties before the mediator may be the first or it may be only one of a series of serious disruptions between the parties. Many studies have shown that there is a high correlation between homicide and prior disputes between parties with ongoing relationships (Missouri Police Department 1973). This dispute is at a crisis stage at least serious enough in the mind of one party to seek the assistance of law enforcement officials to aid in the defense of his person, family, or property. Morton Bard has stated that those "who have worked with the crisis concept have emphasized the importance of the earliness of the intervention in taking advantage of the accessibility which disruption of defense affords" (National Institute of Mental Health 1973).

The mediator utilizes this disruption in normal activity to intervene into the emotion-charged conflict. The mediator must be able to recognize the emotions, sensitivities, and deep personal interests involved. As he works to guide the parties toward a resolution of their dispute, the mediator must recognize and honor their various bargaining positions. While seeking modifications of these bargaining positions, the mediator must be vary careful not to destroy them. He subtly exploits any reconciliation potential which appears during his ongoing analysis of the problem, and he attempts to guide the parties in a timely fashion toward an agreement, perhaps by persuasion or by guiding the parties in the positions they take but not advising them on these positions or pressuring them into a settlement. These "do" and "don't" methods seem almost contradictory, but they are not; they simply illustrate the sensitivity required and the subtleties involved. Timing is also very important. A mediator must know when to intervene and when to let the parties proceeed at their own pace (Robins 1973). The mediator must act with humility and objectivity and with a dedication to nothing more than putting to rest the differences of the disputing parties.

An example of a 4-A case may better show the process involved. A young man goes to visit his girlfriend (neither are juveniles) at her parents' home one evening. The girl's father has tolerated the boyfriend during his relationship with the daughter but does not approve of him. The boyfriend has a habit of dropping by the house whenever he desires, often staying for meals. The mother has remained neutral in the occasional arguments between her husband and daughter over the boyfriend's habits. One evening the father loses his patience with the loud record player and demands that it be turned off. An argument ensues between the daughter and father with the boyfriend joining in to defend her. The father demands that the boyfriend leave. A heated verbal exchange ensues, resulting in a brief struggle during which the boyfriend is physically thrown out the door and down the porch steps. A window has been broken, a table and lamp damaged, and the screen door torn and broken off its hinges. The boyfriend's shirt was torn and he received several bruises, abrasions, and minor lacerations. The boyfriend leaves the yard shouting profanities and threatening retaliation. The father orders him never to return or see his daughter again. The daughter is hysterical and tries to leave with her boyfriend but is restrained by her father. The mother is in tears and is screaming at her husband.

In this incident we have seen several crimes committed, including simple assault, disorderly conduct, unlawful entry, and destruction of private property. We have also seen several civil offenses or torts committed. Either the father or the boyfriend could make a prima facie case for a criminal warrant and information. The commencement of criminal proceedings may well be

vindictively motivated. Also, one cannot discount the possible real
fear of the father that the boyfriend may follow through on his threats
of retaliation. Great numbers of cases, commenced because of a
variety of motives and arising out of an even greater variety of personal relationships, are brought daily to our court systems.

In the example just cited, a court's finding either the father or
the boyfriend guilty or innocent will not be a solution to the real
problem, the cause-pattern. It will not relieve the father of his
fear that he may at some unsuspecting moment become the victim
of the boyfriend's retaliation. It will not mend the relationship now
impaired--perhaps only temporarily, perhaps permanently--between
the father and his daughter and even his wife. In such a case, a
sensitive mediation process must ensue.

This case coming to a court would involve the father versus
the boyfriend or vice versa. In either event, the mother and
daughter would be designated and treated as witnesses. However,
once the case reached a 4-A hearing, the arbitrator would quickly
ascertain the desirability of mediating the dispute and would recognize that the mother and daughter are more than witnesses; they are
in fact parties whose input and concurrence in the solution are more
than desirable, they are essential if the solution is to be viable.

In some cases where the parties are not so closely related as
they are in the above example, the best solution may be that the
parties simply avoid each other or meet only under specially defined conditions. Such a solution may work for casual acquaintances;
it may even work for persons in the same neighborhood. Parents
often become involved in disputes with other parents because of
something their children did. Avoidance by these neighbors may be
possible, but what about their children? Are the children parties
who should be part of the solution? Should children who play together, go to school together, and who forget their problems more
quickly and easily than adults be prohibited to engage in their normal
activities? These are problems commonly faced in 4-A hearings
which are vital to human relationships but are far beyond the jurisdiction of our extant judicial system.

The 4-A Program is not referred to by its designers as a
pretrial diversion program. This is because the term "diversion,"
as commonly used by the courts, refers to the halting or suspending
before conviction of formal criminal proceedings against a person
on the condition or assumption that the person will do something in
return (National Advisory Commission 1973). "Diversion" generally
implies the use of threat or the possibility of conviction of a criminal
offense to encourage an accused to agree to do something. Some
diversionary programs even go so far as to require the entry of a
guilty plea before the diversionary program can be entered and then,

if the offender successfully completes the program, the plea will be vacated and a <u>nolle prosequi</u> entered to reflect the final disposition of the case.[3]

It is, of course, unrealistic to believe that there is not some type of coercion involved in the referral of some of the cases to the 4-A Program. Although such coercion is not overt and by design is specifically prohibited, the very presence of a person in a court or before a judge or with a police officer often will create a psychological submissiveness to the suggestion that he voluntarily submit to the 4-A Program. By advising the parties to utilize legal counsel and by again advising them of the procedures and of their rights prior to the hearing at which time they may still withdraw their submission agreement, it is hoped that the process can be kept as voluntary as its designers intended it to be.

An encouraging aspect of the 4-A Program is that several parties have brought their cases directly to the program without being referred by law enforcement or court personnel. Most of these cases were similar to those usually referred. A few were unique in that no violent action had yet taken place but the circumstances were such that the parties realized that a serious offense was quite probable and they desired that something be done before the act took place.

Three years ago the Arbitration As An Alternative concept was initiated as a pilot program in Philadelphia with the help of the Ford Foundation and later by the Law Enforcement Assistance Administration. It has now become an institutionalized process in that city's court system and is being run by city personnel. The 4-A Program concept is now functioning in several major urban areas and has even been extended to a remote Alaskan Eskimo village (Conn and Hippler 1974).

The potential and need for this alternative to our criminal justice system is overwhelming. We must stop criminalizing all human conflict for the sake of expediency or for the lack of an alternative course of action.

NOTES

1. The merits of an arbitration award will not be reviewed by a court and cannot be appealed or reversed unless it is shown that the award was procured by corruption, fraud, or other undue means, or because of the arbitrator's misconduct or exercise of power beyond his authority. Enforcement of arbitration awards was founded in contract common law but is now generally provided for by statutes in every state except Vermont and Oklahoma.

2. The terms "mediator" and "arbitrator" are used specifically herein to describe the functions of the person designated to conduct the hearing, although this person is legally an "arbitrator" throughout the entire process.

3. See, for example, the Narcotics Diversion Program, Superior Court of the District of Columbia, Washington, D.C.

REFERENCES

Cole, D. L.
    1973   A Greater Reliance Upon Reasoning and Persuasion. The Public Interest and the Role of the Neutral in Dispute Settlement. Proceedings of the Inaugural Convention of the Society of Professionals in Dispute Resolution.

Conn, S., and A. E. Hippler
    1974   Final report--Emmonak conciliation board: a model for a new legal process for small villages in Alaska. Unpublished report, University of Alaska.

Hippler, A. E., and S. Conn
    1973   Northern Eskimo law ways and their relationships to contemporary problems of "bush justice." ISEGR Occasional Papers published by the University of Alaska.

Missouri Police Department
    1973   Conflict Management Report, Northeast Task Force. Kansas City (May).

National Advisory Commission on Criminal Justice Standards and Goals
    1973   Courts. Washington, D.C.: U.S. Government Printing Office.

National Institute of Mental Health
    1973   Immediacy and Authority in Crisis Management. Proceedings NIMH Crisis Intervention Seminar, Washington, D.C.

President's Commission on Law Enforcement and Administration of Justice
    1967   The Challenge of Crime in a Free Society. Washington, D.C.: U.S. Government Printing Office.

Robins, E.
  1973   The Mediator's Role. Proceedings of the Inaugural
          Convention of the Society of Professionals in Dispute
          Resolution.

Simkin, W.
  1973   The Mediator's Role. Proceedings of the Inaugural
          Convention of the Society of Professionals in Dispute
          Resolution.

V

CRIME-SPECIFIC
RESEARCH

INTRODUCTION TO PART V

Much of the work in theoretical criminology has been concerned with the explanation of crime in general. Yet crime includes a wide and diverse range of behaviors. About the only characteristic which all the behaviors have in common is that they constitute violations of the law. Aside from this commonality, however, crimes differ from one another in a wide variety of ways: There are differences in terms of the characteristics and motives of the offenders; the characteristics and actions as well as reactions of the victims; the modus operandi employed by offenders; the injuries and damage that result; and the actions and reactions of the criminal justice system and the public. Even though homicide, fraud, kidnapping, and rape are all crimes, it is readily apparent that these activities are homogeneous with respect to causation only in a highly abstract manner.

In view of this recognition, the majority of criminologists have come to view it as unlikely that a general theory of crime will ever be precise and exact enough to explain, predict, and control the many varied types of criminal behavior that exist. This is not to say that large-scale, comprehensive criminological theory such as Sutherland's (1947) differential association or Glaser's (1956) differential identification are without value. To the contrary, such theories provide a general orientation toward understanding crime by furnishing a broad framework or matrix for empirical study. But continued progress in criminology will largely depend on the development and refinement of what Merton (1957) calls theories of the middle range. In essence, these are theories intermediate to the minor working hypotheses that evolve during routine criminological research and to such all-inclusive master conceptual schemes as differential association. There can be little question that progress in the development of middle-range theory in criminology will be contingent upon the breakdown of criminal behavior into more homogeneous units and upon a more intensive study of the types of criminal behavior than has occurred to date. While earlier criminological classification systems and typologies reflected most common legalistic, individualistic, or social schemes, today's approaches are increasingly more complex. Among some of the major procedures studying criminal behavior in terms of homogeneous (or sociological) units are typological approaches which define homogeneous units within specific crime categories; combinations of legal categories of crime which categorize certain types of crimes (belonging to different legal categories) into sociological units; and typologies based on social behavior systems. Typologies of crime based on social behavior systems probably hold the greatest promise for advancing the discipline because they take behavior systems as the unit of analysis, which enables researchers to break away from the well-known limitations of the legal framework which have long handicapped criminological research. When using this approach, particular behavior systems can be studied whether they occur in a "criminal" context or not.

Sutherland and Cressey (1970: 280) describe criminal behavior systems in terms of the following characteristics: essentially a group way of life, behavior systems are integrated units, which include the individual act, behavior codes, traditions, and direct and indirect social relationships by participants and significant others; common behavior, operating in the same way in a large number of persons, which should facilitate the identification of causal processes not unique to particular individuals; and a feeling of identification among those who participate in the behavior system under analysis.

While the number of studies taking the behavior systems approach is limited, some important conceptual work and research to support it has occurred. Conceptually, Clinard and Quinney's (1967) typology is probably one of the most comprehensive approaches to date. Grounding their typology in such sociological criteria as the criminal career of the offender, group support of the criminal behavior, correspondence between criminal behavior and legitimate behavior patterns and societal reaction, they propose eight behavior types: violent personal crime, occasional property crime, occupational crime, political crime, crimes against the public order, conventional crime, organized crime, and professional crime. Among some of the more exemplary research utilizing the criminal behavior systems approach are the following: Wolfgang's (1958) study on victim-precipitated criminal homicide revealed that one of four cases of officially recorded homicides resulted from an intense interaction first initiated by the victim. Another classic study is Lemert's (1953) analysis of naive check forgery which examined forgeries committed by persons who did not come from a criminal milieu, who had no previous criminal record, and who resorted to check forgery due to social isolation, specific situational factors, and the process of closure. Another excellent example is Cressey's (1953) work on criminal violation of financial trust. Viewing this type of behaviors as one kind of occupational crime, Cressey identifies three sequential steps in the violator's career: trusted persons become violators when they find themselves in financial difficulty which they deem nonsharable, when they become aware that they could resolve their problem by violating their position of trust, and when they are able to rationalize their fraudulent behavior.

The chapter by Margaret Zahn and Glenn Snodgrass on drug use and the structure of homicide follows the genre of crime-specific studies discussed above. While the research is not as comprehensive in focus as the previous examples, it does make a significant contribution to the study of violent personal crime by adding to or amending the existing body of knowledge. By analyzing medical examiner records in the cities of Philadelphia and Dallas, the study seeks to describe how drug use and the risks associated with it affect the structure of homicide, whether drug use is a sufficiently important variable to affect homicide events under different regional and city conditions, and whether the regional concept of violence advanced by previous theoretical conceptualizations is really of importance in explaining actual homicide occurrence. Focusing on the characteristics of the homicide victim in terms of age, sex, race, and marital status, and on the characteristics of the circumstances of homicide in terms of place of death, the assailant, and the reasons for death, the authors conclude that the transactional risks associated with maintaining a drug habit often prove lethal for the addict, that illegal drug use significantly affects the circumstances of death of those involved, and that the risks, the organization of illicit drug markets, and the drug users' relations to social control agents are affected to some degree by the city context in which they occur.

The chapter by Graeme Newman, Jean Jester, and Donald Articolo on the structural analysis of fraud makes considerable strides toward the development of a structural framework for the understanding of the variety of fraudulent activities that abound in society. The authors note that past attempts at explaining fraud have been generally confined to specific types of predominantly legally defined fraud, such as embezzlement, check forgery, price fixing, and so on. Since such approaches tend to suffer from the previously discussed legal limitations, it is of no surprise that the present state of the art in fraud research is highly fragmented. Even though the authors do not expect that their newly proposed framework would be able to explain all fraud etiologically, they do provide an excellent dissection of the basic elements of fraud which is seen essentially as a perversion of the normal exchange process in society. Among the basic components of fraudulent exchange are the object of exchange, the structural or largely unchangeable elements of economic activity, the situational factors which may assist in the perpetration of fraud, the personal skills of the offender and the personal attributes of the victim, the information which the offender possesses or manages to develop, and the predominant external controls of exchange extant in society. After an extensive discussion of the structured context of fraud, a number of crucial research issues are identified, which in turn raise a number of fascinating questions.

For example, if economic exchange is a central feature (if not a
foundation stone) of the social order, we must ask to what extent
does the structure of economic and marketing relations in society
contribute to fraudulent activity, as opposed to the behavior of individuals in society? Further, if the personality and personal skills
of offenders are important variables in the perpetration of fraud,
why is it that studies of white-collar crime do not attempt comparisons of white-collar criminals with white-collar noncriminals? In
other words, why do only some persons commit fraud when the
socioeconomic structure of society provides an apparently significant opportunity for fraud to all citizens? Research on questions
such as these would surely prove worthwhile and enhance our knowledge on this subject. But the problem of greatest significance posed
by the authors pertains no doubt to the need for research on the relationships between law enforcement and fraud. Some criminological
research and public interest (and to some degree public policy) have
only recently shifted their attention from street crime to white-collar
crime and corruption. After decades of neglect, the number of convictions and sentences to imprisonment for these crimes is slowly
beginning to rise. This development is occurring at a time when
correctional institutions are overflowing and serious questions are
being raised as to the efficacy of incarceration. If we now consider
that economic activity is largely self-regulatory and that law enforcement in this area is singularly ill-equipped to deal effectively
with such "illicit practices" as fraud, embezzlement, tax offenses,
price fixing, and corporate crime, we seriously need to ask whether
it would not be better to move toward regulatory licensing and other
control mechanisms not involving either law enforcement or the
courts. The authors point out correctly that the role of law enforcement in this difficult area can only be reactive and not preventive.
The near-total surveillance--to say nothing of the maze of red tape
that would unfold into nightmarish bureaucratic jungles--that would
be necessary to prevent white-collar crime would no doubt destroy
business, industry, and free enterprise. In view of these considerations, future research concentrating on the development of new self-
regulatory strategies for the marketplace is urgently needed. But
at the same time, there is a critical need for an objective discussion
and public debate on the larger philosophical issues behind street
crime and white-collar crime. The overall framework of such a
discussion should be less concerned with punishment (and incarceration as a means of deterrence) than with prevention and self-
regulation.

REFERENCES

Clinard, M. B., and R. Quinney
  1967   Criminal Behavior Systems: A Typology. New York:
          Holt, Rinehart and Winston.

Cressey, D. R.
  1953   Other People's Money. New York: Free Press.

Glaser, D.
  1956   Criminality theories and behavioral images. American
          Journal of Sociology 61 (March): 433-44.

Lemert, Edwin M.
  1953   An isolation and closure theory of naive check forgery.
          Journal of Criminal Law, Criminology, and Police Science
          44: 296-307.

Merton, R. K.
  1957   Social Theory and Social Structure. New York: Free
          Press.

Sutherland, E. H.
  1947   Principles of Criminology. Philadelphia: J. B. Lippincott.

Sutherland, E. H., and D. R. Cressey
  1970   Criminology. Philadelphia: J. B. Lippincott.

Wolfgang, Marvin E., and Franco Ferracuti
  1967   The subculture of violence. London: Tavistock.

CHAPTER

9

DRUG USE AND THE
STRUCTURE OF HOMICIDE
IN TWO U.S. CITIES

Margaret A. Zahn
Glenn Snodgrass

The subculture of violence and the regional concept of violence are subjects that have been advanced to explain homicide rates in various populations. These two concepts have focused primarily on rates of variation between populations, for example, blacks and whites, southerners and northerners, in an attempt to explain such differences in rates. These theories do not, however, focus on the structure of homicide and how the structure might differ between regions; for example, how is homicide different in terms of the assailant or the place of death from one region to another. Further, existing theories do not attempt to deal with how the situation of homicide might change under the impact of illicit drug use. That illicit drug use might be important in structuring the process of homicide is suggested by related theories on aggression (Van den Berghe 1974) and by earlier empirical studies (Zahn and Bencivengo 1973). It has been suggested by Van den Berghe, for example, that aggression is a result of resource competition. When resources are scarce and when access to them is not controlled by hierarchy or territoriality, then aggression results. When applying this generally untested theory to drug use and homicide, it can be argued that use of illicit drugs involves a situation of relatively high resource competition, that is, high demand in a market of scarce commodities. Further, the need

The investigators would like to thank Dr. M. E. Aronson, Medical Examiner of Philadelphia, and Drs. Charles Petty and William Sturner, Medical Examiners of Dallas, and their staffs for their gracious and helpful cooperation in the completion of this study. The research in Dallas was partially supported by a Temple University faculty summer research award.

or desire to obtain drugs or the money to buy them may put a drug
user in a variety of situations which ultimately prove lethal. One
such behavior, that is, frequent involvement in theft, may result in
deadly confrontations with law officers or other citizens who are the
victims of thefts. A second situation, that is, involvement in arguments relating directly to securing and maintaining a supply of drugs,
may arise in the buying and selling transaction where there may be
some dissatisfied customers (someone got burned), or where some
people may try to reduce competition by eliminating sellers from
the market, and so forth. These two sets of behaviors we refer to
as transactional risks.[1] Drug use, in other words, would seem to
affect the structure of the homicide event. Furthermore, given that
drug use (heroin use in particular) is illicit in all parts of the United
States and that drug use and the attendant life style are very compelling in a society where constant hustle is necessary to sustain
drug supply,[2] there should be uniformity between regions in the manner of violent death of drug users. In other words, drug-using populations should show uniformity in the circumstances of homicide
death across regions, and those circumstances should reflect participation in a drug-oriented life pattern rather than in other involve-
ments, for example, family events.

The aims of this chapter are threefold: to describe how drug
use and the risks associated with it affect the structure of the homi-
event in terms of who is killed, who is the killer, and how, when,
and where the person dies; to describe the differences in homicide
events in two cities, thereby exploring whether the regional concept
of violence is of importance in explaining actual homicide occurrence;
and to determine whether drug use is a sufficiently important variable
to affect homicide events under different regional and/or city conditions.

To test these notions, two major cities, Philadelphia and
Dallas, were selected in which to conduct the preliminary studies.
Both cities selected have excellent Medical Examiner's records systems with full-scale toxicological facilities.[3] These were vital considerations in selecting the cities for our study. The current chapter
focuses exclusively on the homicide victim and the circumstances
surrounding his/her demise.

METHODOLOGY

Data for the study were drawn from the Medical Examiner's
Offices of Philadelphia and Dallas. The records in each city provided the following data: a face sheet containing demographic information on the victim, an autopsy report which included the physician's

determination of cause of death, toxicologic findings, and findings regarding presence of track marks indicating narcotics use; and investigation reports completed either by the police and/or the medical examiner's field investigators present at the scene of the homicide. These reports provided detailed descriptions of events surrounding the homicide and witnesses' statements when available.

There were some differences in record keeping in the two cities which affected the information gathered. Philadelphia records included the arrest records of the victims; Dallas records did not (although information regarding the victim's arrest record was eventually secured). The Medical Examiner of Philadelphia or his designated representative conducted interviews with next of kin of the victim and elicited information regarding knowledge or admittance of drug use by the deceased. Dallas conducted no such interviews.

In all, while there were systematic differences in the records, the information was sufficiently comparable to complete necessary comparisons on the victim and the circumstances of the homicide death.

DEFINITION OF MAJOR VARIABLES

A point of careful consideration for the purposes of this study was the definition of a drug user. There were some difficulties, however, in that each city had different methods of identifying the drug-using victim. The Medical Examiner's Office in Philadelphia in the late 1960s began to keep listings (informally) of drug-related homicides. The criteria for inclusion on the list were: positive toxicology, track marks, admission by the victim's family that the homicide victim was a drug user, drugs or drug paraphernalia found on or near the body at the time of death, two or more arrests for illegal possession of narcotics during the five-year period prior to death (as determined by FBI or city police arrest records). These five criteria were the basis for inclusion in the drug-using populations in Philadelphia.

Dallas did not maintain such a list. Toxicologies for presence of drugs, however, were performed whenever there were circumstances of death of suspicious nature which indicated possible drug involvement. A listing of all drug-positive toxicologies for the years 1971-73 was made available to the investigators.[4] Therefore, the initial Dallas drug sample was based entirely on positive toxicology. The researchers felt that if a selected large nondrug sample failed to produce additional drug-related homicides on the basis of the other criteria used in Philadelphia, then the existing list based on toxicology alone was sufficient for an analysis. Such was the case.

A sample of 157 nondrug cases revealed no additional drug-related homicides.

For purposes of this study, homicides included both justifiable and unjustifiable killings. The Medical Examiner's Offices in each city did not exclude justifiable homicides from their records. These include, for example, cases in which the victim was killed by a police officer, storekeeper, or homeowner while attempting to commit a felony. Because of the inclusion of these cases, the total number of homicides for each year exceeds figures submitted to the FBI by the Philadelphia and Dallas Police Departments. These cases were included, however, since we were also interested in determining if drug-using victims were more likely than nondrug-using victims to be killed during the commission of a felony.

SAMPLE

Since drawing a simple random sample of homicide victims might not have produced a sufficiently large number of drug-using victims, a disproportionate stratified sample was used. The population studies consisted of all homicide victims in Philadelphia (1969-73) and Dallas (1971-73) who were illicit drug users based on the aforementioned criteria. The population also consisted of a random sample of homicide victims who were not drug users.[5] This sample was selected by listing all homicides for each year in each city by case number. After homicides involving drug users had been identified and eliminated, a random sample was chosen from each year for the remaining homicides. In Philadelphia the number of cases selected for the sample was based on the percentage of drug-user homicides in a given year. For example, drug-user homicides made up 5 percent of the total number of homicides in the year 1969. To determine the size of the random sample, 5 percent of the remaining homicides were selected for study. This technique was used for each of the five years in Philadelphia. The final sample, then, included the universe of drug-user homicides from 1969 to 1973 (N = 372) and a random sample of nonuser homicides (N = 308).

In Dallas an oversampling of the nondrug population was made and, consequently, the number of nondrug cases for each year in Dallas was much greater than the number of drug cases. The final Dallas sample included the universe of drug-user homicides from 1971-73 (N = 45) and a random sample of nondrug homicides (N = 157).[6]

FINDINGS

Characteristics of the Homicide Victim

Sex and Homicide

Homicide victims in both cities and in both drug and nondrug populations were more likely to be males than females. In Philadelphia, 568 of 680 homicide victims were male (83.3 percent); in Dallas, 167 of the 202 victims were male (82.7 percent). Even greater likelihood of male involvement existed among the drug victim populations: in Philadelphia (N = 331) 88.9 percent and in Dallas (N = 40) 89 percent of the drug-using victims were male.

Age and Homicide

As was expected, the differences between the drug and nondrug populations of homicide victims in each city with respect to age were highly significant. In Philadelphia the difference in mean age between drug- and nondrug-using victims was 7.5 years (for the drug group the mean age was 26.5 years and for the nondrug group the mean age was 34 years). The difference in ages in Dallas between the drug and nondrug victim groups was not quite so large, yet was statistically significant. For the drug group the mean age was 29 years and for the nondrug group the mean age was 35 years (significant at the .005 level). Between cities, it is noteworthy that the homicide victims in Dallas were on the average four years older than their Philadelphia counterparts (Philadelphia mean age was 29.8 years; Dallas mean age was 33.7 years). The difference in victims' ages between cities was significant at beyond the .0005 level (t = 3.57).

Because of the significant differences based on age, this factor was controlled throughout the subsequent analyses. When the age factor affects other findings, it will be duly noted.

Race and Homicide

This study revealed findings similar to previous research regarding race and homicide, for example, Wolfgang (1958), Pokorny (1965), Voss and Hepburn (1968), that homicide victims are decidedly more likely to be black than white. Each city showed a majority of black homicide victims, yet there was a significant difference in the magnitude of the percentages. Nearly 86 percent (N = 583) of the homicide victims in Philadelphia were black, while in Dallas only 59.4 percent (N = 120) of the victims were black. Conversely, only

11.3 percent (N = 77) of the Philadelphia victims were white, while
33.2 percent (N = 67) of the Dallas victims were white. These city
differences were significant at beyond the .0001 level. Part of the
exhibited difference may be explained by the differing percentages of
blacks in each city's population. Census data from 1970 list a 34
percent black population in Philadelphia and a 25 percent black population in Dallas. It would seem, however, that the difference in
population base cannot explain the entire difference in the percentages
of black homicides in the two cities.

When comparing drug-using and nonusing victims by race, we
found that in Philadelphia a higher percentage of homicide victims
were black drug users than either white drug users, white nonusers,
or black nonusers. Both race and drug use seemed associated with
homicide victimization in Philadelphia. There was no such relationship in Dallas. Results are shown in Table 9.1.

TABLE 9.1

Philadelphia and Dallas Drug-Using and Nondrug-Using
Homicide Victims by Race

| | Race | | | |
	Caucasian	Black	Latin American, Puerto Rican, and Others	Total
Philadelphia				
Drug users				
Number	25	338	9	372
Percent	6.7	90.9	2.4	100.0
Nondrug users				
Number	52	245	10	307
Percent	16.8	79.8	3.3	100.0
Dallas				
Drug users				
Number	15	27	3	45
Percent	33.3	60.0	6.7	100.0
Nondrug users				
Number	52	93	12	157
Percent	33.2	59.2	7.6	100.0

Philadelphia: $X^2 = 196.7 \leq P$ .0001
Dallas: X^2 NS
Source: Compiled by the authors.

Marital Status and Homicide

This variable is especially interesting in that the relationship between marital status and homicide for each city is reversed. In Philadelphia, 54.6 percent (N = 371) of the victims of homicide were single, 33.7 percent (N = 229) were married, and 11.7 percent (N = 79) were separated, divorced, or widowed. In Dallas, only 31.1 percent (N = 59) of the homicide victims were single, while 46.3 percent (N = 88) were married, and 22.6 percent (N = 43) were either divorced, separated, or widowed. These findings were statistically significant (x^2 = 35.24 significant at the .0001 level) and may be a reflection of the somewhat older population of victims in Dallas. [7]

The drug and nondrug victim populations reflect the overall pattern of the respective cities in regard to marital status and homicide. In Philadelphia, in both the drug and nondrug categories, homicide victims were more likely to be single than married, divorced, separated, or widowed. As might be expected, among drug users the percentage of victims who were single was even higher than among the nonusing victims, 58.9 percent and 49.5 percent, respectively.

In Dallas, however, victims of homicide in both the drug and nondrug groups were more likely to be married than single. The difference was more pronounced in the nondrug category. Of additional interest is the fact that twice as many of the homicide victims in Dallas were divorced, separated, or widowed as in Philadelphia.

Characteristics of the Circumstances of Homicide

Drug-using and nonusing victims of the two cities taken together were compared on place of death, assailant, and circumstances surrounding the death. On these variables, it was expected that when a drug user was a victim his death would reflect participation in a drug-using world and transactional risks associated with drug use, including involvement in thefts, drug-related arguments, and the like.

Place of Death and Homicide

Data on place of death were grouped into died inside a commercial establishment (including bars, motels/hotels, stores, and so on), died inside a noncommercial place (at home or a friend's home), died outside on the street or in an empty lot, and other. Data indicated that there were significant differences in where

drug-using victims and nonusing victims died in Philadelphia; however, there were not such statistically significant differences in
Dallas. Drug-using victims in Philadelphia were most likely to die
outside on the street. Dallas drug users, similarly, were most likely to die on the street or in an empty lot. Nondrug-using victims in
both Dallas and Philadelphia were most likely to die at home followed
by death outside in the street or in an empty lot. These findings
changed somewhat when controlled for age in that in Philadelphia
younger victims, both drug and nondrug, were much more likely to
die on the street (over 40 percent of the victims in both drug and
nondrug groups were killed there). Other findings regarding place
of death are found in Table 9.2.

Assailant and Homicide

For both drug-using and nonusing victims there was a high percentage of cases in which the killer was unknown or the relationship
could not be determined from the records. Cases were coded where
the assailant was known. Categories which emerged included spouse
and other family member, friend, storekeeper/bartender/homeowner,
and police. There were significant differences in the known assailants of drug-using victims and nonusing victims in both Philadelphia
and Dallas (see Table 9.3).

In Philadelphia, a higher percentage of nonusing victims were
killed by a spouse (14.2 percent) or other family member (11.6 percent) than were drug-using victims (7.4 percent for spouse and 4.7
percent for other family member, respectively). Furthermore, for
both drug-using and nonusing victims a friend was likely to be the
assailant--47 percent of the drug-using victims and 64.5 percent of
the nonusing victims were killed by a friend. The police (on duty,
off duty, and private guards) were the assailants in 22.8 percent of
the cases of   drug-users' homicide but only 5.2 percent of the cases
of nonusers. Furthermore, drug users were killed by storekeepers,
bartenders, or homeowners in 18.1 percent of the cases in contrast
to nonusers who were killed by storekeepers, bartenders, or homeowners in only 4.5 percent of the cases. In all, drug-using victims
in Philadelphia were more likely than nonusing victims to be killed
by an officer of the law or a person presumably being attacked by
the decedent in some way.

In Dallas, the pattern was similar although with some notable
exceptions. As in Philadelphia, both drug-using and nonusing victims were most likely to be killed by a friend. Further, nonusers
were more likely to be killed by a spouse or other family member
than were drug users, although drug-using victims in Dallas were
more likely to be killed in marital or family relationships than were

TABLE 9.2

Philadelphia and Dallas Drug-Using and Nondrug-Using Homicide Victims by Place of Death

	Philadelphia				Dallas			
	Drug Users		Nondrug Users		Drug Users		Nondrug Users	
Place of Death	Number	Percent	Number	Percent	Number	Percent	Number	Percent
Inside a commercial establishment (bar, motel, store, etc.)	41	11.7	41	14.5	7	16.3	33	21.3
Inside a noncommercial establishment								
A. own home	41	11.7	100	35.3	11	25.6	49	31.6
B. friend's home	25	7.2	22	7.8	4	9.3	29	18.7
Outside (on the street or in an empty lot or house)	134	38.5	90	31.8	19	44.2	40	25.8
Other	108	30.9	30	10.6	2	4.7	4	2.6
Totals	349	100.0	283	100.0	43	100.1	155	100.0

$X^2 = 402.6$ P $\leq$ .0001 $\qquad$ $X^2 = 9.03$ NS

Source: Compiled by the authors.

TABLE 9.3

Philadelphia and Dallas Drug-Using and Nondrug-Using Homicide Victims by Known Assailant*

	Philadelphia				Dallas			
	Drug Users		Nondrug Users		Drug Users		Nondrug Users	
Known Assailant	Number	Precent	Number	Percent	Number	Percent	Number	Percent
Spouse	11	7.4	22	14.2	4	16.0	26	29.2
Other family member	7	4.7	18	11.6	2	8.0	12	13.5
Friend	70	47.0	100	64.5	11	44.0	37	41.6
Storekeeper, bartender, or homeowner	27	18.1	7	4.5	6	24.0	5	5.6
Police (on duty, off duty, or private)	34	22.8	8	5.2	2	8.0	9	10.1
Totals	149	100.0	155	100.0	25	100.0	89	100.0

$X^2 = 41.558$ P = .0001 $\qquad$ $X^2 = 8.725$ P = bet. .10 and .05

*This table lists only the cases where the assailant was positively known. Unknown and other categories have been eliminated.
Source: Compiled by the authors.

Philadelphia users. The notable exception between Philadelphia and Dallas occurred in the category of killed by the police. In Dallas, victims who were killed by the police were equally likely to be drug users or nonusers (8 percent of the drug-using victims were killed by police and 10 percent of the nonusing victims were) in contrast to Philadelphia where drug-using victims were much more likely to be killed by the police than were nonusing victims (see Table 9.3). In Dallas, however, storekeepers or bartenders or homeowners were the assailants in 24 percent of the drug-user cases, much higher than for Dallas nonusers (5.6 percent) and higher than for either users or nonusers in Philadelphia. In Dallas, then, it appears that informal mechanisms of control of crime committed by drug users are more widely used than formal (police) control. In either case, though, drug users are more likely to die in encounters with people they are presumably attacking in some way.

Data on decedents being killed while committing a felony further support this. Assessments of whether the decedent was killed while committing a felony were made from the records. For purposes of this study, a felony was considered to be a burglary or robbery attempt in which the offender was killed either by the intended victim or by a police officer or private security guard. In Philadelphia, 21.2 percent of the drug-using victims were killed while attempting to commit a felony; in Dallas, while the number was small, 23.5 percent of the drug-using victims were killed in this situation. By contrast, only 6.9 percent of Philadelphia's nonusing victims were killed while attempting a felony and 8.7 percent of Dallas' nonusing victims were so killed. Overall, while homicides of both drug-using and nonusing victims were generally not the result of their involvement in felonious activity, drug users were much more likely to be homicide victims in these situations than were nonusers. Furthermore, while the agent doing the killing was different in Philadelphia and Dallas, the overall pattern held in both cities.

Reason for Death and Homicide

While the variables already presented give a picture of circumstances surrounding the homicide event in drug-using and non-using populations, a fuller analysis is revealed by reviewing circumstances surrounding the event as described by participants in it. The records used in this study described the transaction between victims and offenders prior to the homicide act. In many cases the transaction was witnessed by a number of people and their descriptions of the event were transcribed into the records. Data of this type, of course, were not always available. Wherever the records indicated a clear description of the circumstances surrounding the

act, however, they were coded. Coded categories emerged from
the data and included victim of a robbery attempt, gang slaying,
drug-related argument, killed during a holdup, killed in other illegal
acts, accidental death, argument in a bar, domestic quarrel, other
reason, and unknown. Drug-related arguments, which were of
special importance here, were arguments where witnesses clearly
indicated that the decedent had been angry about a drug-related event
(for example, he had received "bad" drugs) or where the type of
killing indicated a strong likelihood that it was drug-related (for example, a slaying where two drug users were found bound and gagged
and shot in the head in an abandoned house). Evidence from subsequent interviews indicated prior heavy involvement of these two
users in the drug-selling market. This, plus other circumstances
of the case, indicated that the event was drug-related and the death
was so coded. Of the drug-using victims in Philadelphia and Dallas,
14.4 percent and 14.3 percent, respectively, were killed in such
arguments. While the percentage killed in drug arguments was almost identical in the two cities, it is important to note that they
were not of the same relative importance as a cause of homicide
death in the two cities. In Philadelphia, drug-related arguments
were of more importance--ranking third as the cause of homicide
death among drug-using victims. Killed during a holdup and killed
during other arguments preceded drug-related arguments as causes
of death in the drug victim population (see Table 9.4).

In Dallas, drug-related arguments equaled killed during holdup
as a circumstance of death and these circumstances were preceded
significantly by killed in a domestic quarrel, killed as a result of
other arguments, and killed in other illegal pursuits. As indicated
elsewhere in this chapter, drug-using victims in Dallas appear to
have been more involved in domestic pursuits than Philadelphia users
and their deaths reflect this. Furthermore, while transactional risks
were important as causes of homicide death among drug-using victims, they, taken together, did not represent the threat to life in
Dallas that they did in Philadelphia. In Philadelphia 44.3 percent
of drug-using homicide victims died in drug-related risk situations;
in Dallas 28.6 percent of the drug-using victims did. It seems that
drug-oriented life styles, while having similar risks attached, are
different depending on the city context within which the drug-using
group is located. Overall, drug-related risks and/or drug organization proves more lethal in the larger, Northeastern city studied than
in Dallas.

In contrast to drug-using victims, nonusing victims in Philadelphia were more likely to be homicide victims in domestic quarrels, arguments in a bar, and as victims of a robbery attempt. Similarly, nonusers in Dallas were more likely than the drug-using victim

TABLE 9.4

Philadelphia and Dallas Drug-Using and Nondrug-Using Homicide Victims by Reason for Death*

Reason for Death	Philadelphia				Dallas			
	Drug Users		Nondrug Users		Drug Users		Nondrug Users	
	Number	Percent	Number	Percent	Number	Percent	Number	Percent
Victim of robbery	9	3.3	31	12.9	1	2.9	21	15.0
Gang fight	20	7.4	23	9.6	0	0	0	0
Drug-related argument	39	14.4	1	.4	5	14.3	4	2.9
Killed during holdup	81	29.9	12	5.0	5	14.3	8	5.7
Killed as a result of other illegal pursuits	27	10.0	8	3.3	6	17.1	9	6.4
Accident	12	4.4	13	5.4	1	2.9	6	4.3
Argument in bar	12	4.4	27	11.3	2	5.7	6	4.3
Domestic quarrel	30	11.1	55	22.9	9	25.7	59	42.1
Other arguments	41	15.1	70	29.2	6	17.1	27	19.3
Totals	271	100.0	240	100.0	35	100.0	140	100.0

Philadelphia: $X^2 = 140.65$ $P \leq .0001$

Dallas: $X^2 = 19.19$ $P = .0076$

*This table lists only the cases where the events leading up to and surrounding the homicide event were definitely known.

Source: Compiled by the authors.

145

to be killed in these ways. There is, then, similarity in homicide circumstances of nonusing victims in the two cities. The major differences which occurred were in homicides during domestic quarrels and during gang fights. In Dallas, a full 42.1 percent of the nonusing victims were killed in domestic quarrels, while in Philadelphia, 22.9 percent of the nonusing victims were. Further, while there was not a single person killed in a gang fight in Dallas, nearly 10 percent of the nondrug-using victims in Philadelphia were victims in such situations. (Differences between Philadelphia and Dallas were significant at beyond the .0001 level.)

Overall, Table 9.4 reflects these two sets of significant differences: the difference which exists between drug-using and nonusing victims in both cities, and the differences which exist in circumstances precipitating homicide in the two cities. Drug-using victims in both cities were less likely than nonusing victims to die as a victim of a robbery attempt and in a domestic quarrel. They were much more likely than nonusers to be killed in a drug-related argument, killed during a holdup, and killed as a result of other illegal pursuits. Homicide among drug-using victims is more likely to be a result of involvement with drugs, attempts to secure them, or attempts to secure money for them. Drug use, then, is associated with circumstances of homicide death in both cities.

While this is true, data also showed that the context, that is, the city in which the homicide occurs, has a significant bearing on the circumstances under which one is likely to be such a victim. The two paramount differences in this regard were in death during domestic quarrels[8] and death during gang fights. There was not a single gang-related homicide in Dallas.[9] This was true for users and nonusers. In Philadelphia, on the other hand, 9.6 percent of the nonusing victims and 7.4 percent of the drug-using victims (total N = 43) were killed in gang-related ways. The significant difference between cities is further shown by the percent killed in domestic quarrels. Dallas victims, whether drug users or not, were more likely to be victims of homicide in domestic quarrels than victims in Philadelphia. As mentioned above, a full 42.1 percent of the nondrug-using Dallas victims were killed in this situation while 25 percent of the drug-using victims in that city were also killed in domestic quarrels. On the other hand, fewer Philadelphia victims were killed in this way: 22.9 percent of the nonusing victims were killed domestically as were 11.1 percent of the drug-using victims.

SUMMARY AND CONCLUSIONS

Reasons for these differences between cities can be only speculative at this point. Certainly variables such as size, density, degree of complexity, city type (manufacturing versus commercial, and so on), legal structure (for example, divorce laws) need to be examined in relation to these circumstances of death. It is our conclusion that illegal drug use does significantly affect the circumstances of death of those who are involved. The transactional risks associated with maintaining a drug supply and money for it often prove lethal. These risks, and presumably the organization of illicit drug markets, and of drug users' relations to social control agents, are somewhat affected by the city context in which they occur. It is to the city context and the multiple variables by which it may be described that fruitful investigation might now be directed. It seems that circumstances of death by homicide are affected by involvement in illegal drug use and associated subcultural life styles as well as by the overall city context in which such life occurs.

NOTES

1. Discussion of the transactional risks hypothesis and some data on Philadelphia were presented by Zahn and Bencivengo (1973b) at the American Society of Criminology meetings in New York.

2. Authors such as Agar (1973) and Waldorf (1973) have described the addict subculture in some detail. Their descriptions suggest the encompassing and compelling nature of this life style for those involved.

3. In Dallas, the Medical Examiner's Office is officially called the Southwest Institute of the Forensic Sciences.

4. Special thanks to Dr. James Garriott, Chief Toxicologist in Dallas, for his help in developing this list.

5. Ideally the universe of nonuser homicides would also have been used. However, time, limited numbers of personnel, and limited financial resources prevented our including the entire group.

6. Since the use of statistics such as chi square depends on a simple random sample and this study employed a disproportionate stratified sample, the assumptions underlying the use of such statistics are not met. Therefore, whenever they are used in this chapter they should be viewed only as a guide to interpretation.

7. Census data for 1970 show Philadelphia and Dallas with 58 percent and 63 percent overall married rates, respectively. Our control for age revealed expected results in that the younger victims tended to be single and older victims married or divorced, separated or widowed in both cities.

8. The pronounced difference in family killings may be accounted for by the differential availability of guns in Dallas and Philadelphia households. While we do not have adequate data to support such an interpretation, the following facts are suggestive:

The Southwest has a much more gun-oriented tradition than the East
(as noted by such authors as Harrington C. Brearley, John
MacDonald, Robert Sherrill, Carl Bakal, and the Presidential
Commission on the Study of Violence and Firearms in American
Life).
Firearms ownership is highest in the South (estimated 55 percent)
and lowest in the East (30 percent estimate). (Firearms and
Violence in American Life)
In Philadelphia, 48.2 percent of all killings in the home were ac-
complished with firearms; in Dallas, 70 percent of the killings in
the home occurred with guns.
    9. The investigators actually searched for instances of gang-
related deaths in Dallas upon realizing that none had shown up in the
sample. We were assured by investigative personnel--especially
Roger Smith, Chief Investigator--that there were no such cases in
Dallas.

REFERENCES

Agar, M.
    1973   Ripping and Running: A Formal Ethnography of Urban
           Heroin Addicts. New York: Seminar Press.

Beattie, R. H. , and J. P. Kenney
    1966   Aggressive crimes. Annals of the American Academy of
           Political and Social Science 364 (March): 73-85.

Blum, R. H.
    1967   Drugs, behavior and crime. Annals of the American
           Academy of Political and Social Science 374 (November):
           135-46.

Gastil, R. D.
    1971   Homicide and a regional culture of violence. American
           Sociological Review 36 (June): 412-27.

Hepburn, J. R. , and H. L. Voss
    1970   Patterns of criminal homicide: a comparison of Chicago
           and Philadelphia. Criminology 8 (May): 21-45.

Hogan, H. W.
    1969   Homicide in New Orleans. Human Mosaic 4 (Fall): 69-80.

Iskrant, A. P., and P. V. Joliet
  1968   Accidents and Homicide. Cambridge, Mass.: Harvard
          University Press.

Messinger, E.
  1965   Statistical study of criminal drug addicts. Crime and
          Delinquency 11 (July): 283-92.

Miller, W. B.
  1966   Violent crimes in city gangs. Annals of the American
          Academy of Political and Social Science 354 (March):
          96-112.

Moran, R.
  1971   Criminal homicide: external restraint and the subculture
          of violence. Criminology 8 (April): 357-74.

Pittman, D. J., and W. Handy
  1970   Patterns in criminal aggravated assault. In Crime in
          America, ed. B. J. Cohen. Itasca, Ill.

Pokorny, A. D.
  1965a   Human violence: a comparison of homicide, aggravated
          assault, suicide and attempted suicide. Journal of Crim-
          inal Law, Criminology and Police Science 56 (December):
          488-97.

  1965b   A comparison of homicides in two cities. Journal of
          Criminal Law, Criminology and Police Science 56
          (December): 479-87.

Van den Berghe, P. L.
  1974   Bringing beasts back in: toward a bio-social theory of
          aggression. American Sociological Review 39, no. 6
          (December): 777-88.

Voss, H. L., and J. R. Hepburn
  1968   Patterns in criminal homicide in Chicago. Journal of
          Criminal Law, Criminology and Police Science 59
          (December): 499-508.

Waldorf, D.
  1973   Careers in Dope. Englewood Cliffs, N.J.: Prentice-
          Hall.

Wolfgang, M. E., and F. Ferracuti
1967 The Subculture of Violence. Towards an Integrated Theory in Criminology. London: Tavistock Publications Ltd.

Zahn, M. A., and M. Bencivengo
1973a Murder in a drug using population. In Crime and Delinquency: Dimensions of Deviance, ed. M. Riedel and T. Thornberry. New York: Praeger.

1973b Violent death: a comparison between drug users and non-drug users. Addictive Diseases: An International Journal 1, no. 3: 283-96.

Zahn, M. A.
1975 The female homicide victim. Criminology 13, no. 3 (November): 400-15.

10

A STRUCTURAL ANALYSIS
OF FRAUD

Graeme R. Newman
Jean C. Jester
Donald J. Articolo

It is our aim in this chapter to attempt a sociological analysis of the basic components of fraud, with a view to establishing a structural framework for the understanding of the enormous variety of fraudulent techniques that have been identified in the literature. It is hoped that such a framework will bring much-needed coherence to the presently fragmented nature of research dealing with fraud from both a legal and a sociological point of view. It is understandable that work on fraud has to date been fragmented, since there appear to be an infinite variety of fraudulent techniques and strategies. Attempts to explain fraud usually have been confined to particular "types" (mostly legally defined) of fraudulent activities such as embezzlement, check forgery, price fixing, and many more (Cressey 1953; Lemert 1973; Geis 1968). It is not expected that the framework developed in this chapter will "explain" all fraud in the sense of uncovering "etiological" factors. The aim is rather to introduce coherence to the field so that future and past "etiological" research may be seen in clearer perspective. What is needed is a locus for interpretation, because at present it is extremely difficult to generalize from one study of fraud to another.

THE DEFINITION OF FRAUD

The problem of defining fraud is severely compounded when one realizes that it is a class of "illegal behavior" which is dealt with in civil codes as much as and probably more than in criminal codes. In fact, criminal codes and the common law generally have tended to confine themselves to such traditional crimes of forgery, counterfeiting, larceny by trick, false impersonation, and embezzlement as the main articles of fraud. For a general definition of fraud,

we must turn to civil codes. Perhaps the clearest definition is that
provided by the California Civil Code (Div. 3, Sec. 1710) which defines "deceit" (considered by that code to be the central element of
fraud) as:

1. The suggestion, as a fact, of that which is
    not true, by one who does not believe it to
    be true;
2. The assertion, as a fact, of that which is
    not true, by one who has no reasonable
    ground for believing it to be true;
3. The suppression of a fact, by one who is
    bound to disclose it, or who gives informa-
    tion of other facts which are likely to mis-
    lead for want of communication of that
    fact; or,
4. A promise, made without any intention of
    performing it.

However, it has been stated on at least two occasions in
California cases that fraud was a matter which necessarily depended
upon the pecularities of a particular case rather than upon bare
academic rules (Mead v. Smith 1951) and that it had no fixed, definite meaning (Anderson v. Board of Medical Examiners 1931).
Finally, it is clear that fraud involves misrepresentation of material
facts (Bretthauer v. Foley 1911) and the offender must be shown to
have knowingly done so (Nathanson v. Murphy 1955).
    We have constructed our own definition of fraud which, although
it assumes the elements of deceit described above, sets the act
clearly within a socioeconomic setting. Thus, the general definition
of fraud is as follows:

> A fraud occurs when, in an economic exchange,
> the offender deliberately misrepresents the basis
> of the exchange to the victim. An essential ele-
> ment of all fraud is the construction of a "false
> reality" by the offender.

Obviously, this is a very general definition and there are no
doubt many shades of grey ranging from what may clearly be criminal (for example, "big con") to the various forms of false advertising and simple exaggeration. Very few criminal codes have attempted to define fraud more specifically, and it is apparent that in
this area, more than any other, it is extremely difficult to predict
every situation, since the strategies for fraud are so varied, and

often creative. Our definition specifies that fraud occurs in an economic exchange. Although there may be a few minor exceptions to this[1] (for example, academic fraud when a researcher fakes his results), we consider the economic exchange a most useful starting point, for here we can analyze the basic components of the exchange and thus relate them to fraudulent strategies.

THE BASIC COMPONENTS OF FRAUDULENT EXCHANGE

There are six main components of fraudulent exchange that may be derived from a formal analysis of a "normal" business exchange or setting. These are:

The object of the exchange: whether manufactured goods, services, and so on.
The structural or largely unchangeable elements of economic activity.
The situational factors which may assist the offender to perpetrate his fraud.
The personal skills of the person attempting the fraud and the personal attributes of his victim.
The information which the offender is able either to gather or construct concerning the basis of the exchange with the victim. Information results, of course, from the above components.
The predominant external controls of the exchange.

The Object of the Exchange

Although, as we have seen, there are numerous definitions of fraud, when one considers fraud in terms of an exchange perspective, it is clear that fraud is essentially a perversion of the normal exchange process. Exchange properly conducted results in a condition which is mutually advantageous to both parties.[2] The concept of reciprocity governs the process throughout. In the case of fraud, however, reciprocity is bypassed and the benefits flow in one direction only. Hence the process is turned into a zero-sum game in which the victim is the sole loser. There are essentially three elements of the distorted process: exploiter, exploitee, and object of exchange or exploitation. While the process may be fruitfully analyzed from all three vantage points, employment of the latter--object of exchange--enables us to classify, in an admittedly rudimentary fashion, the numerous examples of fraud. While this classification cannot be considered a typology in any strict sense, nevertheless it does reduce the several hundred types of fraud which have been identified in the various criminal codes into a more manageable pattern.[3]

Generally, frauds can be divided into those in which the object of exchange is clearly evident and those in which it appears nebulous or difficult to identify. Paradoxically, it appears that those frauds which require the most elaborate organizational structure to be successful are those in which the object of exchange is more easily identified and in which the process of distortion is most evident. Thus in the typical con game, for example, the object of exchange is easily identified whether it be a preferred product such as a watch or the promise of huge returns on a relatively small investment. [4]

A second type of fraud in which the object of exchange is clearly identifiable is the commodity or futures fraud. This form of fraudulent activity is characterized by the promoter's efforts to capitalize on nonexistent merchandise. The transfer of warehouse receipts for these goods is an important element in this type of fraud. [5]

The securities fraud is the third case in which the process of distortion is fairly obvious. Securities frauds are characterized by an attempt to misrepresent the financial worth of a corporation or to suppress information which would, if made public, affect the value of the stock or a corporation. It involves conscious distortion of the true financial status of publicly held securities. Thus it is clear that the object of exchange is the securities certificates themselves, although one may argue that the security itself assumes its significance because of the element of speculation which goes with it. It is perhaps more accurate to state that the process of buying and selling the security is the object of exchange. [6]

Closely related to the securities fraud because of the nature of the object involved are frauds dealing with forms of negotiable paper such as credit cards, service vouchers, and other so-called new monies. Here, as in the securities fraud, one finds a conscious misrepresentation of the worth or ownership of these intangible assets. [7]

In addition to those already mentioned, there are several other types of fraud which may be easily identified in terms of their objectives of exchange. Service frauds practiced by skilled or allegedly skilled technicians or professionals such as doctors are predicated on the offer of a service (The Nation 1972). Real-estate fraud involves misrepresentation of the true worth of property to either buyer or subsidizing agency as occurs in mortgage frauds (The Progressive 1974).

Finally, one can identify frauds which involve misrepresentation in the area of true authorship as in the case of plagiarism[8] or art and literary hoaxes (Newsweek 1973), or which falsify in some way such things as research efforts or university degrees (Time 1974a; The New Republic 1973).

In each of these examples it is possible to point to some tangible or intangible asset or service which is the focus of the exchange process. There are, however, a number of frauds which cannot be easily classified in this manner, but which may, nevertheless, be analyzed within this framework. Among the frauds in this category are such activities as tax evasion, illegal collusion in restraint of trade, embezzlement, and forms of public victimization such as welfare cheating. Unlike the other frauds described, such activities are executed without the knowledge or cooperation of the victim. Hence, one finds in such cases not the perversion of the exchange process but rather its negation. The violated object in such cases is not a misrepresented service or product, but rather the relationship of trust which exists between victim and predator. This is clearly seen in the case of embezzlement of funds or information, but it also holds true for cases of tax frauds or other forms of deceit involving public agencies whose daily operations are organized around the assumption of honesty. The example of price fixing and other forms of collusion show this relationship less clearly but can, nevertheless, be viewed as a violation of the public trust in the operation of the free market.

Information in such types of fraud is not distorted but is completely withheld from the offended party. Paradoxically, this characteristic makes frauds of this type more vulnerable to detection since even a small amount of information regarding such activity is sufficient to destroy the structure of such frauds, and criminal intent--the distinguishing legal characteristic of fraud--is easier to prove in such cases than in cases of misrepresentation.

In terms of the evolution of fraudulent activity in modern societies, it is interesting to note that the earlier definition of fraud applied to actions of this sort (for example, The Carrier's Case). [9] However, the more modern, common meaning of fraud has come to apply to the types of fraud described earlier in which the victim takes an active part in his own exploitation, and which is very much a distortion of the exchange process on which modern societies rely.

The Structural Elements of Economic Exchange

Generally speaking, there are a number of structural components endemic to the exchange process of all modern industrial societies which may be considered expeditious in terms of fraud. Of primary importance is the imbalance of information between the two parties involved in the exchange process. In addition one must also consider such characteristics as the competitive nature of all modern exchange systems, the complexity and size of their institutions, the indirect quality of the business relations within such systems, and the bureaucratic organization of all business enterprises.

Information Imbalance

We have suggested that the basic element in every fraud involves an exchange of goods, services, or money between two or more parties, in which one party has greater information concerning either the basis or object of the exchange than the other. It will be recognized that this may be the basis of any kind of business or economic exchange: Each party exchanges his goods or services with a view to "profiting" from the exchange. For example, party A may purchase 100 cases of Chateau Mouton-Rothschild wine, 1966 vintage, from party B for $200 a case. Party B may have bought them for $150 and so, therefore, realizes a 33 percent profit. However, party A has a customer who will pay $400 a case because he knows that this particular wine is a very rare one. In this case, both parties profit, but party A profits much more, because he is in the more powerful position: He has more information concerning the object of exchange (that is, the rare vintage) and he is in organizational contact with a consumer. Thus, it can be seen that there are elements of information and organization endemic to the outcome of an economic exchange. B could not be considered a victim of dishonest trading by A since he also profited, and perhaps had he looked around for other buyers, he may have obtained the information A had. It is simply a situation of caveat vendor.

However, although one cannot claim that this was a dishonest business transaction, there is no doubt that there is an element of "false reality" involved, or, for want of a better word, "deception."[10] One should hasten to add that this is not a value judgment about the dishonesty of business, but rather it points to a situation of "false reality" that is endemic to the structure of business transaction: That is, there is no other alternative structure in an economy which relies upon buying and selling for profit (whether profit here means "money," "goods," "status," or merely meeting a turnover sales quota as may occur in a communist-based economy).[11]

It follows, therefore, that if differential information between two parties in án economic exchange is endemic to that exchange, then it must also be endemic to a fraudulent exchange. How, then, may we distinguish between a fraudulent and nonfraudulent exchange?

Although, as we have seen, the law has been able to differentiate fraud from nonfraud only on a case-by-case basis, we may suggest that a fraudulent exchange differs from the common business exchange in the following ways:

The offender falsifies the information concerning the true basis of the exchange. Thus, even though the victim may abide by the rule of caveat emptor, he is placed in a position in which he cannot acquire the true information. A false informational setting is constructed and capitalized on by the offender.

The offender constructs a reality for the victim which denies the victim any possibility, using the usual referents (for example, persons of authority and status) to establish the true basis of exchange. This technique is most graphically illustrated in the movie The Sting, in which offenders impersonated roles of high authority and status, even managing to "con" a person of authority (detective) to unwittingly play a part in their scheme.

This false reality is "tailor made" by the offender for the victim so as to capitalize on the victim's weaknesses, prejudices, needs, and so on. For example, the Homestake Oil Fraud took advantage of the need of high-income investors to shelter their income in tax-saving investments.[12]

It is obvious that the line between dishonesty and fraud may in some areas be very thin. In general, however, it seems reasonable to assume that the extent to which the offender uses his resources to falsify the information which the victim receives may be considered to be the key factor in discriminating between fraud and dishonesty. For instance, using our wine-vending example: Had the seller arranged for three leading wine experts to pronounce before the victim that bottles of vin ordinaire were products of Chateau Mouton-Rothschild and the victim naturally believed it, so paid an inflated price, this would be fraud. On the other hand, if there was only vin ordinaire in the bottles, but the vendor charged $15 a bottle not claiming them to be a rare vintage, this would not be fraud. Obviously, there is some difficulty in drawing a distinction between falsification and exaggeration, just as there is difficulty in drawing a distinction between falsification of information and falsification by withholding information. To come up with a clear rule to cover all possible situations is clearly not feasible.

Competitive Climate

All modern exchange systems are characterized by a spirit of competition among institutions. This surfaces in many cases in the personality patterns of the participants of the systems. An example of this was recently provided in the case of a respected research scientist at the Sloane Kettering Institute in New York who felt so pressured to produce publishable results that he resorted to fabricating data in his experiments.[13] One also finds examples of this in such fraudulent practices among students as purchasing term papers to meet course requirements.[14] A more direct effect of the pressures of competition can be found in the activities of business-men who engage in restraint-of-trade practices such as price fixing. An example of this type of fraud was recently reported among execu-tives of prestigious department stores in New York City.[15]

Complexity and Size

Normal business activity in modern industrial societies re-quires the participants to deal in large quantities, often so large that they cannot be conceived of in other than abstract terms. The effect of trading in such amounts is the creation of a psychological climate of unreality which lends itself to fraudulent manipulation. In addi-tion, because of the impossibility of physically transferring large quantities of goods, it becomes necessary to rely on such devices as warehouse receipts, bills of exchange, letters of credit, and so on. While these may represent real property in the eyes of the law, they are, in effect, quite intangible assets whose net worth is calculated in terms of "paper profits" or marketplace potential. Consequently it is somewhat easier to dupe the unsuspecting victim in fraudulent schemes involving these intangible assets.

We find a good example of this in the celebrated case of the salad oil swindle. Thousands of gallons of salad oil were purchased by the brokerage firm Ira Haupt, Inc. in a deal involving more than $5 million (The New Yorker 1964). Warehouse receipts, which were later proved to be forged, were accepted as proof of ownership of the oil which, in fact, never existed.

Billy Sol Estes engaged in a similar charade when he sold hundreds of tanks of anhydrous ammonia which existed only on paper (Business Week 1962). Because the world of high finance literally runs on the transfer of negotiable paper as a substitute for large quantities of merchandise, there is inherent in the situation a poten-tial for manipulation which would not be possible were one to deal in the actual commodity.

A feature related to size is the complex network of rules and traditions which have emerged to govern transactions of tangible assets. One sees the negative effects of this in the now famous ac-counts of the Bank of Sark scandal (Business Week 1971). The suc-cess of this operation rested on the manipulation of such things as letters of credit, international bank drafts, negotiable bonds, and government bills. Without such devices this and other "big cons" would not be possible; however, it is also true that such devices are, in fact, the mainstay of international high finance and without them the world of high finance would not be possible.

In this light, the numerous examples of tax fraud which surface
regularly can be seen as an outgrowth of the complex rules of taxation. The claiming of illegitimate deductions, for example, is simply
the inevitable distortion of provisions of the tax law which must nevertheless exist if the law of taxation is to function effectively and
fairly.

Indirectness

Homans (1961) has noted what he refers to as the "increasing
roundaboutness" of the exchange process of industrialized societies.
This condition is evidenced by the increased dependence on middle-
men in the transactions between buyers and sellers. The indirect
nature of business transactions creates a situation in which potential
for fraud is heightened since the degree of control which can be ex-
ercised over a process is inversely proportional to the number of
people involved at various stages of the process. In addition, the
psychological distance created by layers of agents and representatives appears to negate the uncomfortable effect of dishonest dealing.
The real estate industry with its traditionally high rate of fraudulent
dealing is perhaps the best example of this situation. The proliferation of agents and brokers in the field has created an extremely
hazardous market from the buyer's point of view.[16]

Bureaucratic Organization

The benefits of the economic structure which are provided by
bureaucratic organization are well-documented. However, the dys-
functional aspects of it with regard to the possibilities for fraud
which such organization affords have been given less attention.
Smigel and Ross (1970) have pointed out a number of features of all
bureaucracies which they feel make them likely victims of crime:
large size, impersonality, and formality of rules and regulations.
The problems caused by the last characteristic are particularly evident in such fraudulent acts as the submitting of false insurance
claims. In such cases the more-or-less inflexible process of bureaucratic decision making is manipulated to the advantage of the false
claimant. Perhaps the best arena for this type of fraud is the welfare state which has evolved to deal with the casualities of modern
exchange systems.[17]

The Special Case of Securities Fraud

The securities market is probably the most complex of economic markets (save, perhaps, the mysterious sphere of the world

market and foreign exchange). We suggest that there are five structural components in the securities market which may facilitate the perpetrator of fraud:

The unavoidable delay in the exchange process between the buyer and the seller. (Only mutual funds and similarly powerful investment groups are able to insist on delivery of stock certificates at the time of purchase.) Small investors generally must bide their time, having handed over their money, until the seller delivers his securities to his broker, who delivers the securities to the buyer's broker. Furthermore, it is common practice (and legitimate) for brokers to use their client's securities as collateral to finance their operations. Of course, especially when the market is booming, it may be in the best interests of the client to have his certificate held by his broker. In fact, many investors prefer this arrangement. It is apparent, however, that the time which elapses between buying and selling, and the distance that the investor is from the floor of the exchange or the seller of the securities, results in a "securities no-man's land." Such a situation creates a setting for the easy appropriation or "loss" of securities. Indeed, over $100 million in securities are reported "lost or stolen" each year.[18] In recognition of this problem, laws have been introduced to control the "hypothecation" of securities.[19]

The necessity, because of these time and space difficulties, for a complicated system of "go-betweens."[20] It may be worth noting here that the common-law origin of fraud began with the Carrier's Case--the first case involving a go-between in an economic exchange (Hall 1952).

Thus, there are compounded difficulties of the dissemination of information on an equal basis to all investors, leaving open the possibility of "insider" information. In the securities market this is crucial, since there are so many potential victims involved who could be at the mercy of one person in possession of special information. The dissemination of information therefore takes on supreme importance, and the recognition of this is evidenced by the various laws and rules requiring accurate representation of assets in financial prospectuses, the requirements of immediate notification of the Securities and Exchange Commission (SEC) and stock exchange if fraud is suspected or if there is other information which could radically affect the price of stock.[21]

Because of the complex system of marketing and the immense amount of paper work involved, the difficulty of keeping accurate records or even estimates of assets of brokerage houses is very great. Thus, the falsification of information may more easily be achieved, especially by those occupying positions of trust.

The difficulty of attaching a "true value" to any stock. For example, it might be argued, depending on how one wishes to interpret the economy as a whole, that in a time of economic boom, all prices of stock are inflated far beyond their "true value." Market analysts are forever arguing about the true value of a stock. Thus, in the case of the Equity Funding fraud, although it may be said that the stock was inflated far above its "true value," since the company's activities were misrepresented in its annual reports, it may often be a matter of judgment as to whether a share price reflects the "true value" of the stock. It may simply reflect the confidence buyers have in a booming economy. We may hypothesize, therefore, that frauds similar to Equity Funding, which rely heavily upon an inflated share price, may be more likely to be perpetrated during economic boom and, conversely, will be "found out" during economic recession.

In conclusion, it should be pointed out that these are structural elements which we see as largely unchangeable aspects of economic life. It is not to suggest that all economic activity is fraudulent, or that Wall Street is "crooked." In fact, most activity in the securities market has been rated as "honest" or "fair" business by a number of quite critical securities experts (for example, Hurd). It is only a small portion of economic activity which becomes fraudulent. It becomes fraudulent because the persons involved are sufficiently sophisticated to capitalize upon the structural elements of exchange to convert them into fraud. Furthermore, as a mode of explanation, it makes a great deal of sense to begin with legitimate economic activity as a means of explaining illegitimate economic activity, since most economic activity is legitimate and nonfraudulent. In other words, one is on safer ground trying to explain the "pathological" by means of the "normal," rather than, as often happens in the study of crime, the "pathological" by the "pathological."

Situational Factors

Organization

Most economic activity occurs within an organized setting. Banks or corporations are organized along hierarchical lines, with key positions of trust as part of that organized setting. A person in such a position of trust, therefore, is in a powerful position to convert that trust into information. For example, a trusted branch manager may falsify his sales records to inflate his business success. The result may be an inflated representation of financial gains in the company's prospectus.[22] It is apparent that one's position of trust in an organizational setting may also encourage embezzlement, as Cressey (1953) has pointed out. The line between embezzlement and fraud may, therefore, be difficult to draw. However, one need not even "abuse" the position of trust to construct a fraud. It may be that merely being in contact or part of an established organization may facilitate the construction of false information. For example, a respectable accountant may unwittingly underwrite a corporate stock of a "paper" company, thus giving it an air of legitimacy and respectability.

Access to Communications Media

It goes without saying that access to communications media would be an enormous resource of power for one who wished to construct a false informational setting. Of course, money to purchase advertising would make for greater access as would close contacts with journalists, announcers, newspaper editors, and so on. False advertising is perhaps the most common "crime" which results from access to the communication media. Mail-order frauds also fall into this category.

Access to Technology

Again, money would no doubt make access to technology more easy. Perhaps the most important aspect of technology today as far as fraud is concerned is the computer. However, to use a computer for massive fraud requires a great deal of money, so one may be more likely to see such frauds occur only in large companies. Computers, of course, offer the greatest possibility for elaborate falsification of records which could be extremely difficult to unscramble.

Sphere of Economic Activity

The old stereotype of the crooked used-car salesman suggests the possibility of fraud in a simple buying-selling exchange. However, unless the crooked used-car salesman extends his business activities into a complex organizational network of marketing, there are limitations on how far he can go. In contrast, in the securities market, the possibilities are almost infinite. There is potentially an enormous mass market of investors, because of the aspect of speculation upon which the stock exchange relies so heavily for its activity. Thus, the spheres of economic activity where there is a mass market, where speculation or some other "weakness" of the victim is readily tapped, are more likely to be converted into massive frauds.

We may also note that it is likely that the opportunity for fraud occurs during a period of prosperity in the economy, when money is "free," and people don't watch it so closely. Further, because of the usual complexity of securities frauds, they can continue during periods of prosperity, provided credit can be readily obtained to cover necessary payments, or to cover falsified assets, and so on. However, during times of economic recession, when credit is limited, such as now and in 1929, stress is placed upon all economic activity. Money is tight, people check their records, frauds which depend on "cover-up" payments are suddenly discovered, since there is no credit to cover them. In addition, it is likely that those "feeling the pinch" in an economic recession are more likely to risk a little money for a "fast buck" since they have little to lose.

Personal Skills

Personality

The most notorious frauds are usually those which were perpetrated by one or two highly personable and persuasive persons. The "Ponzi" scheme is perhaps the most famous American example, where a Mr. Ponzi, in 1929, sold stock in a fictitious company, paying off old clients with the money from new clients. He enticed victims through his most persuasive salesmanship and by offering 40 percent return on investment. There have been many cases in which the offender used only his personality to pull it off.

The force of personality is particularly important in the "con game" and other high-level maneuvers such as commodities swindles and securities frauds. This fact is made very clear in such cases as the Bank of Sark swindle mentioned earlier. The operators in this scheme were successful because their appearance and contacts bespoke wealth and breeding. Very often they managed to interpose themselves in the social circles of their victims, which further enhanced their credibility. A similar situation was found in the Homestake Oil swindle also referred to earlier. In this case, the victims, many of whom were theatrical celebrities, reported that they considered the promoter's obvious friendly relations with their fellow professionals as proof of his credibility. Personality factors were paramount, as well, in the Billy Sol Estes case. Indeed, it is generally understood that Sol Estes was successful only because he was able to cash in on the prestige of his family and his political contacts. Even in con games of a less-elaborate nature, such as the common case of the travel agent who absconds with his clients' payments while they are en route, one sees that the ability to impress and inspire confidence is a crucial element of a successful deception.[23] The recent report of prisoners of war who were duped out of their back pay in a phony investment scheme seems to turn on the fact that the contact man was able to pass himself off as a former prisoner of war himself (The Wall Street Journal 1974).

Use of Status

In addition to personal magnetism, professional status is often a necessary adjunct to fraud. In the case of medical shams, the relationship between professional status and fraud is obvious. However, influential positions within financial organizations such as banks or brokerage houses are also an essential element in most securities-related frauds. The ability to manipulate such publications as pink sheets, brokerage reports, and corporate financial statements is related to one's professional status within the respective organizations. Careful examination of accounts such as the Baptists Foundation of America ruse reported in the Wall Street Journal several years ago clearly reveals the necessity of inside contacts in banks and brokerage firms.[24]

Status is also a factor in forms of plagiarism and falsified research data. Fraudulent efforts of this type are possible only if the perpetrators have already achieved a degree of success or recognition in their respective endeavors to establish their veracity.

Finally, status or position in a particular organization can be the precipitating factor in one's involvement in fraudulent activity. In the case of price-fixing, for example, the participants are operating simply as representatives of their company. Personal gain is not a factor. Hence their criminal behavior is, in effect, simply an occupational hazard which accompanies a position of high status in an organization predisposed to this type of activity.

Organizational and Managerial Skills

Many massive frauds require all the skills of a top executive to organize and manage an enormous staff. The top executives of the Equity Funding fraud, for example, had an enormous insurance sales operation (approximately 3,000 salesmen) to manage, as well as the difficult task of juggling the company's financial activities. It is clear, then, that we should expect perpetrators of massive frauds to be sophisticated, well-trained, or educated in their special field (whether securities, land promotion, or whatever).

Technological Expertise and Other Skills

Allied to the above is the technological expertise of the offender. The early image of fraud (still of many legal codes today)
was check forgery and various other types of forgery which took
varying degrees of skill. Today, however, a new technology is at
hand which makes possible all kinds of fraud: the computer. Thus,
the Equity Funding fraud was highly facilitated by the falsification of
records on the computer. And this was made possible only by the
performance of a highly trained and skilled technician.

In addition to technological skills, there are certain types of
frauds such as art or literary hoaxes which require special talents.
A news magazine has reported, for example, that the recent interest in pre-Columbian art has encouraged talented sculptors and even
professional archaeologists to manufacture primitive artifacts which
are virtually indistinguishable from the originals (Newsweek 1973).

Information

Depending on the admixture of all the above components of the
fraudulent exchange, the offender is able to establish himself as having a great deal of information concerning the true basis of the exchange. He not only constructs a false informational setting, but he
also acquires an often-intimate knowledge of the victim's attributes.
He may apprise himself of the victim's special needs or motivations.
For example, the recently reported fraud concerning the selling of
worthless municipal bonds to returned Vietnam war prisoners took
advantage of the ex-POW's naturally maladjusted state after several
years' imprisonment. Securities fraud relies upon the investors'
preparedness to speculate to some degree, plus the investors' necessary reliance upon brokers and others in authority who recommend
and underwrite stock. The offender is also apprised of the victim's
economic and social status. The Homestake Oil scheme took advantage of rich persons looking for tax breaks, as we noted earlier.

In general, in a well-perpetrated fraud, the offender is apprised of all exigencies or complications which may arise from the
exchange. It also follows that if the offender is as sophisticated as
we suggest he is, he is also going to be thoroughly apprised of the
workings of the law and law enforcement in regard to his activities.

One sees quite clearly the role which differential access to information plays in the numerous examples of fraud involving "technical experts" such as doctors or other skilled technicians. Although
early written accounts seem to describe frauds of this type, the

increasingly influential position of the technocrat in modern industrial societies has amplified the importance and scope of this type
of fraudulent activity. The very nature of the expert-client relationship, dealing as it does with such intangibles as skills, knowledge,
and judgments, creates a situation conducive to abuse. In the case
of medical treatment, for example, the inability of the patient to
authoritatively challenge the medical practitioner's advice and treatment often prevents the victims from even realizing that they have
been victimized.

The ease with which a respected professional can engage in
this type of fraudulent activity plus the profits which are to be made
when undertaken on a large scale, such as in the case of billing the
government for fictitious Medicare services, makes the field of medicine a prime contributor to frauds of this type (DeWolf 1972). However, technical experts in other fields such as auto or electronic
specialists are equally well-positioned to use their clients' relative
ignorance to their advantage (Crother and Winehouse 1966). Indeed,
one may say that in all situations in which the ultimate worth of the
profferred commodity or service is dependent upon the "expert
opinion" of the seller, the prospective buyer is at an informational
disadvantage and totally dependent on the good will of the seller,
such as it may be.

Predominant External Controls

The fact that external controls are either absent or minimal
in the exchange process has been an important determinant in the
direction of fraudulent activity. It is a fact that controls are much
more effective in discouraging relatively minor fraudulent activity,
such as the small-time cons involving fraudulent mail-order businesses, than in elaborate schemes such as the Bank of Sark swindle,
which because of its complexity was virtually unprosecutable. Weak
controls also appear to encourage participation where it would otherwise be precluded by fear of apprehension. For example, a report
on the rise of fraudulent use of credit cards emphasizes that because
these articles can be used as money but are not subject to the same
type of controls as legal tender, they have become a preferred activity among dishonest people in both the underworld and upperworld of
crime.[25]

Aside from the general tendency to assume a laissez-faire
stance regarding business activity, the nature of the object of ex-
change--often intangibles such as information regarding corporate
plans, and so on--makes traditional controls inapplicable.[26]

Nor can one discount the reluctance with which professionals from one field (law, for example) approach the correction of fellow professionals (doctors, for example). A report of a Medicare-defrauding doctor who had earned $80,000 from his dishonest practice and was then fined $10,000 when brought before the court is a good example of the problems which arise in this area (The Nation 1972).

In the case of such frauds as the art hoax noted earlier, there is often a failure to prosecute because the victim is embarrassed to admit his own lack of judgment. This is also true of swindles involving figures in the world of finance. In the Homestake Oil case, for example, it is doubtful if the case would have been broken at all were it not for the fact that the victims, mostly entertainment personalities, were not averse to publicity. The financial notables, however, who were also victimized by the scheme felt that their professional status was threatened by revelation and have been extremely reluctant to participate in the prosecution (Time 1974b).

Although the U.S. tradition has always preferred the least amount of government regulation of the marketplace as possible, over the years various forms of government controls have been introduced.[27] However, these exterior controls have been minimal and stand in stark contrast to the controls which are exerted in relation to traditional crime, where the assumption commonly is that people are not self-regulatory, that without criminal law anarchy and destruction would follow. Not so, for example, in the securities marketplace. Emphasis is placed upon self-regulation (thus the New York Stock Exchange and other exchanges have their own rules of trading), and enforcement is achieved through various regulatory bodies such as the SEC or the Securities Investor Protection Corporation, which are not seen as criminal prosecutory agencies. The role of these agencies becomes, in fact, the subject of considerable debate and argument. We should note, however, that regulatory agencies were set up as a result of various crises in the stock market. They were not set up with a view to "catching" the few who perpetrated fraud. Nor has it ever been shown that increased regulation of the market has reduced fraudulent activity.[28]

The question of the effectiveness or even necessity of external regulation has been the subject of very heated debate among economists and securities analysts since the Great Depression. The well-known paper by Stigler (1964), for example, sought to demonstrate that investors fare no better today than they did in 1933. What may be noted for the moment, however, is that many of these regulations and laws were leveled against speculation, a sphere of economic activity which is usually viewed by economists as functional to society. Economists rarely address themselves to the effects of law enforcement upon fraudulent activity itself.

CONCLUSIONS

An attempt has been made to develop a largely descriptive framework within which to view all types of fraud. Having developed this structured context, a number of crucial questions may now be raised as to the directions that future research might take, especially in regard to the basic concepts used in the present analysis. The most crucial question to be answered is the comparative extent to which the structure of economic and marketing relations in society contribute to fraudulent activity as against the behavior of individuals. It is apparent that definite personality and technical skills are necessary to bring off many kinds of fraud. On the other hand, if the socioeconomic structure of society were different, many frauds would not be possible (for example, if economic exchange were not a central feature of societal functioning). We suggest, however, that it is difficult to imagine a society in which economic exchange were not a central feature. Indeed, it would seem to be a foundation stone of social order.[29] The extent to which the various structural arrangements of economic activity are or are not changeable would be a very productive area of future research.

It is also apparent that the study of the personality and personal skills of the offender would be worthwhile, since it is very often his skill, and his skill alone (sometimes with the help of some friends), by which the "normal" structure of economic activity is perverted into a pathological or illegitimate activity. It is interesting that in the study of white-collar criminals, attempts have not been made to compare such persons to nonwhite-collar criminals in the way that the neopositivists have compared delinquents to nondelinquents. Why not? Since as far as we can tell the majority of top executives and businessmen do not commit wholesale fraud, yet they operate within the same structural framework as the white-collar criminals, then one might surely argue that there is something special about white-collar criminals that sets them apart from other executives and businessmen. One may, of course, argue that all businessmen are crooks and it is only the unlucky ones who get caught. But this argument is easily recognized as a radical prejudice in the sense that if one applied the same paradigm to the statistics on blacks and crime, one would have to assume that all blacks are crooks and only the unlucky ones get caught. The same question which subculture theorists of delinquency have faced must also be asked of fraudulent businessmen: Why do only some (a clear minority) commit fraud even though it is argued that socioeconomic structure of society is an important contributor to the deviant behavior? In the present case, we are arguing that the socioeconomic structure makes fraud of various kinds possible but that it takes the independent actions of individuals to convert those possibilities into realities.

A third area of research must also concern the victims of fraud, since the successful completion of a fraud often relies upon thorough knowledge of the needs, perceptions, and other traits of the victim. It may be most productive to study the victim, not only as a losing participant and contributor to the exchange process but also as a consumer to whom fraudulent products and schemes are marketed. Identification of those most likely to be susceptible to such marketing of fraud might be a useful undertaking.

Finally, research on the relationship between law enforcement and fraud would be especially provocative. Strong arguments can be made that economic activity is largely self-regulatory. Thus, to superimpose a law enforcement upon such self-regulation would be an extremely complex undertaking, for how could one enforce laws without interfering with self-regulation of the market? It follows that the only kind of enforcement can be that which acts as a "receiving house." It would deal only with instances of fraud, rather than have any serious effects upon the economic structure which makes fraud possible. That is, its role must be reactive rather than preventive. Indeed, it is extremely rare to hear of a fraud that was prevented before it happened. And since a central element of fraud is its nondetectable quality, then the chances of law enforcement fulfilling any effective preventive function would seem to be extremely unlikely. Near-total surveillance would be necessary, and business could not be conducted under such circumstances. It would therefore be more productive for future research to concentrate upon developing new self-regulatory strategies for the marketplace.

NOTES

1. It has also been argued that this element of exchange underlies all social relationships: See P. Blau, Exchange and Power in Social Life (New York: Wiley, 1964). Thus, the possibility that some types of fraud are not related to economic exchange, but to social exchange, is not a serious exception to our scheme.

2. We do not suggest that the exchange be equally advantageous, only that it be advantageous in some degree to both parties.

3. This observation is based upon a perusal of the Florida, Massachusetts, California, and U.S. Criminal Codes. If one were also to consider the civil codes, these kinds of fraud would be in the hundreds.

4. For examples of the several different types of con games possible, see the following: Changing Times, September 1973, "Gyps Aimed at Older People"; Time, November 24, 1967, "Inheritances"; U.S. News and World Report, June 3, 1974, "Bunko"; Popular Science, December 1971, "Counterfeit Watches"; Time,

June 2, 1972, "Counterfeit Prescriptions"; Time, May 25, 1962, "Hawaiian Fairy Tale"; Business Week, July 19, 1971, "A multi-national swindle. . . ."

5. The two most blatant examples of this type of fraud are the "great salad oil swindle" of 1964 which is described in The New Yorker, November 14, 1964, "Making the Customers Whole"; and the Billy Sol Estes scandal, which is described in Business Week, April 17, 1962, "Finance Companies Fleeced."

6. In addition to Equity Funding, there have been a number of notable securities frauds since 1972: Time, March 15, 1962, "The $5 Million Swindle"; Newsweek, February 23, 1972, "The Money Machine"; Newsweek, December 11, 1972, "The I.O.S. Saga"; Newsweek, May 21, 1973, "Problems at Paragon"; Newsweek, August 20, 1973, "The Arnholt Smith Affair"; Time, January 7, 1974, "Indicting Hughes."

7. Frauds involving illegal manipulation of negotiable paper are described in Aviation Week and Space Technology, March 23, 1964, "Airline Ticket Swindle"; and Time, November 24, 1967, "Charge."

8. Recent examples include a plagiarized speech delivered by a member of the House of Representatives, New York Times, October 12, 1974.

9. The Carrier's Case was decided in 1473. A man was hired to carry bales to Southampton. Instead he broke open the bales and took the contents. It was argued that the defendant had not committed a felony since he had possession "by a bailing and delivery lawfully." (The Carrier's Case Y.B. 13 Edw.IV.f.9.pl.5)

10. Indeed, it is commonly argued by social theorists that all people "misrepresent" themselves to others in social relationships in that they present only their "public self," when in fact there is a "private self." In other words, persons selectively present information about themselves to others on social occasions, just as do businessmen selectively present information to their clients on business occasions. See E. Goffman, The Presentation of Self in Everyday Life (New York: Doubleday, 1959).

11. After all, the Greek god Hermes, originally the god of thieves, who obtained his father's cattle by trickery, became the god of merchants. He later became Mercury, the Roman god of the marketplace and merchants: a fast mover and a slick talker. See N. Brown, Hermes (New York: Grove Press, 1956).

12. For the several accounts of this fraud, see Wall Street Journal, June 26, 1974. It has even been suggested that a number of these investors, by the time they write off their losses as income tax deduction, will come out ahead (see Fortune, September 1974).

13. The scandal involved a staff researcher who admitted to painting the bodies of laboratory animals to make it appear they had been the successful recipients of skin transplants.

14. An article in the New Republic, June 2, 1973, entitled "Academic Business," explains that this has become so common that companies have been formed to hire graduate students and even professors to ghost-write material for a fee.

15. This case of collusion involved Bergdorf Goodman, Saks Fifth Avenue, and other stores. Representatives of these firms had made an agreement to maintain artificially high prices on items of clothing.

16. For a very comprehensive overview of the corrupt practices in the real estate industry, see The Progressive, May 1974, "This Land Is Whose Land?"

17. We have already mentioned the abuses with regard to such welfare systems as Medicare. In addition, there is considerable documentation regarding the so-called welfare cheat in Newsweek, January 23, 1972, "Welfare Fraud: The Backlash."

18. See "Organized Crime--Stolen Securities," Hearings before the Permanent Subcommittee on Investigations, Senate Committee on Government Operations, 92nd Cong., 1st sess. (1971), Vols. 1-5. Also Second Series, 93rd Cong., 1st sess., 1973, Vols. 1-4.

19. See, for example, the Code of the New York General Business Law, Article 21-A, Sec. 339. It is interesting to note, however, that the punishments for these "crimes" were no longer specified after 1965 and that all acts under this section were reduced from "felonies" to "misdemeanors."

20. See H. Baruch, Wall Street (Baltimore: Penguin, 1973), for a detailed account of these problems of exchange.

21. Thus Dirks, the broker who "disclosed" the Equity Funding scandal, was suspended from the New York Stock Exchange because he notified his best clients first, thus giving them "inside" information.

22. An example of this occurred recently in the Chase Manhattan Bank, where a manager of one of the bank's trust departments deliberately overstated the value of the assets in his trust by over $30 million. This had the effect of artificially inflating Chase Manhattan's earnings, and its exposure required a reduction in the company's previously reported earnings, resulting in a decline in the bank's common stock. See New York Times, September-October 1974.

23. This type of con game is described in Newsweek, June 3, 1974, "Have Agency, Will Travel."

24. Michael Gartner, ed., Crime and Business (New York: Dow Jones Books, 1971), pp. 51-61. The history of the development

of the swindle makes it clear that cooperative bankers and brokers were needed to look the other way when necessary and to accept questionable assertions.

25. This point is made in an article in Time, November 24, 1967, "Charge."

26. The problem of executives who sell corporate secrets is discussed in Duns Review 90, no. 6 (December 1967), "The Case of the Disloyal Executive."

27. See note 19 above.

28. See G. J. Stigler, "Public Regulation of the Securities Market," 37 J. Bus. U. Chicago, 117 (1964) and R. A. Posner, Economic Analysis of Law (Boston: Little, Brown, 1974), who presents the standard economist's opposition to law enforcement in the securities market.

29. See, for example, B. Malinowski, Crime and Custom in Savage Society (Paterson, N.J.: Littlefield Adams, 1964), for the clearest statement of the role of economic exchange in relation to social order.

REFERENCES

Anderson v. Board of Medical Examiners
    1931   3, P. 2d, 344, 117 C.A. 113.

Bretthauer v. Foley
    1911   113 P. 256, 15 C.A. 19.

Business Week
    1962   April 17.

    1971   July 10.

Cressey, D.
    1953   Other People's Money. New York: The Free Press.

Crother, S., and I. Winehouse
    1966   Highway Robbery. New York: Stein and Day.

DeWolf, R.
    1972   Medicare: the easy swindle. The Nation, November 6, pp. 429–31.

Geis, G.
    1968   White Collar Criminal. New York: Atherton.

Hall, J.
1952 Theft, Law and Society. New York: Bobbs-Merrill.

Homans, G. C.
1961 Social Behavior. New York: Harcourt, Brace.

Lemert, E.
1973 Human Deviance, Social Problems and Social Control.
Englewood Cliffs, N.J.: Prentice-Hall.

Mead v. Smith
1951 234, P. 2d, 705, 106 C.A. 2d, 1.

Nathanson v. Murphy
1955 282 P. 2d, 174, 132 C.A. 2d, 363.

The New Republic
1973 Academic Business. June 2.

Newsweek
1973 Time of the Forgers. April 13.

The New Yorker
1964 November 14.

The Progressive
1974 This Land Is Whose Land? May.

Smigel, E., and H. L. Ross
1970 Crimes against Bureaucracy. New York: Van Nostrand
Reinhold.

Stigler, G. J.
1964 Public regulation of the securities market. Journal of
Business 37, no. 117. University of Chicago.

Time
1974a The S.K.I. Affair. April 29.

1974b A Star Spangled Swindle. July 8.

The Wall Street Journal
1974 October 7.

Victimology is the scientific study of victims, the process, etiology, and consequences of victimization. As such, it is not a new discipline but a relatively new conceptualization for organized knowledge and systematic, scientific analysis. Victimology has its roots in many disciplines, for example, criminology, law, social psychology, medicine, social work, and psychology, to name a few, and it is still in a developmental stage. The relative newness of the subject helps explain the absence of unified theories and the general paucity of hypotheses. The need, therefore, is great for an integrated approach to the role of the victim in society in general and in the criminal justice system in particular. But whether an integrated theory of victimology is possible at all remains an open question at this time, in view of the fact that none of its parent disciplines possess a unified theory either.

Whereas early work in victimology revolved around the individual victim of crime, there is now a shift of focus among some scholars to the study of victimization resulting from structural sources in society. Utilizing such a perspective, social institutions become victimizers and victims become specific groups. Jews as victims of genocide, racial and religious minorities suffering discrimination at the hands of racially or religiously different majorities, displaced persons and other war refugees, these are examples of specific groups who have received the brunt of the inhumanity of man's social institutions. Another relatively neglected but potentially fertile category of victimization may well test to the limit the various features of victimology as a scientific enterprise. In corporate victimization, noncrimes or quasi crimes rather than true statutory violations are frequent hallmarks of the "criminal" relation between the victim and the offender. It is therefore appropriate to ask whether victimology should remain confined to a subdiscipline of criminology or sociology of deviance, or whether it should become a discipline of its own right. If victimology remains a part of criminology, quasi crimes or regulatory violations committed by businesses and corporations would fall outside the scope of true victimology. The same would be true if victimology includes the consideration of unintended harm, such as injuries resulting from medical malpractice, or if the harm that befalls the lawbreaker in the very act of his lawbreaking, as when exploitative acts are inflicted upon such groups as alien immigrants. Expansions such as these of the scope of victimology pose serious questions for this field of study, in terms of its future.

Regardless of whether or not victimology will eventually
emerge as a generally recognized and separate discipline, there is
no doubt as to its considerable impact to date on the state of knowledge concerning victim/offender relationships, on the role of the
victim in society, on the assessment of the extent of victimization
in society, and on the law profession. Victimology has also had a
major influence on many procedural aspects of the criminal justice
system and has helped to improve the administration of justice--at
least to some extent. However, much remains to be done. Current sketching of major theoretical perspectives must continue in
the hope of eventually building a cohesive theory of victimology. A
major task in this respect will be to seek an overall approach to the
problem of victimization in society rather than to continue to look
for ad hoc solutions to the multitude of theoretical and methodological
problems facing victimology.

The following chapters by Weis, Meade, Richard and Mary
Knudten, Holmstrom, and Burgess are not only thought-provoking
but also will make a significant contribution to both the conceptual
development and scope of victimology and the substantive knowledge
in this field. Kurt Weis provides a fascinating and most-challenging
examination of the theory and politics of victimology. Looking at
victimization as a social process, the author notes with considerable chagrin the outright "antivictimological" perspective of many
victimologists. There can be no question that a considerable
amount of criminological writing to date tends to identify with
offenders, reflects occasionally a deep sympathy for criminals and
other underdogs in society, and is mostly offender- and "guilt-"
oriented. While such obviously biased approaches may be easier
to understand by some as far as criminology is concerned, it is
distressing indeed when victimological writings share the existing
cultural dislike for victims and engage in the subtle art of "blaming
the victim." Evoking Howard S. Becker's famous query to criminologists ten years ago, Weis asks today's victimologists, "Whose
side are we on?" Had criminology dealt with crime instead of
criminals, and had it been less preoccupied with the criminal as an
individual, it would not have lost sight of the victim or the sociological knowledge concerning societal responsibility for the conditions in which crime arises.

Weis also clears up some widespread myths concerning the
work of Hans von Hentig. Von Hentig is frequently identified in
U.S. victimological literature as the father of the concept of blaming the victim. Contrary to these assumptions, von Hentig apparently did not stress the victim's guilt but emphasized instead the
vicious cycle of the relationship between offender and victim. Weis
goes on to lament the tendency of certain scholars to oversimplify

and to follow the modish line of shifting the blame from the offender
to the victim. He thus provides a timely warning for victimology
not to become imbalanced in its perspective. Victims do not always
want or ask for their own victimization. And people do not become
criminals because there are victims. An example of such tenden-
tious reasoning (and one frequently heard at victimological discussions and on campuses) is the view that stealing, looting, robbery,
and burglary are merely forms of "recycling" or redistributing
goods, which minimize the effects of inequality in unjust societies.
These crimes are viewed as the direct result of the affluence of
those who own the material goods worth stealing. Such victimizations are furthermore seen as benefiting the entire social system,
since they are thought to syphon off and channel the anger of the
poor, which would otherwise build up unimpeded by the operation
of an unequal social system. The same point of view also sees
crime-control measures as counterproductive, since they would
merely raise the tariff due to improved counterstrategies undertaken by those bent on stealth and violence. As a result, it is
reasoned that social systems might be better off simply tolerating
economic crime increases and arrange to have the cost borne by
the propertied in the form of a "tariff," or by the entire social group
through such mechanisms as public compensation or public insurance programs, pegged at rates all persons can afford. Such
reasoning, which blames the victim for his own victimization, is
quite clearly flawed. The possession of material goods may not
always be a reflection of unequal social systems but may also result from unequal effort. This view also disregards callously the
fact that the poor and the economically deprived are usually the
primary victims of such economic crimes. Also, physical harm is
often inflicted in such crimes as robbery and during lootings, which
further aggravates victimization. Finally, the view totally ignores
the concept of corporate and other white-collar crime, the magnitude of which exceeds economic "street" crimes immeasurably. As
a result, the so-called tariff to be leveled against the properties
would in reality be borne by those who can least afford to pay it.
Weis concludes his discussion by identifying social approval of
victimization as one of the biggest problems for victimology to
solve. Such approval serves to internalize the norms and values
of those who follow ideologies best characterized by social Darwinism and the spirit of the Protestant ethic, which emphasize material
possessions and success at all cost and which, more importantly,
have no compassion or understanding for victims.

The chapter by Anthony Meade, Mary Knudten, and Richard
Knudten takes the position that diversion, as a form of decriminalization, may not be as beneficial as many criminologists and criminal

justice practitioners assume. While diversion is an operative policy in most judicial jurisdictions and helps decrease the workload of
criminal justice agencies, the concept lacks systematic evaluation
as to its effectiveness and equity for all concerned. Whether diversion serves the interests of defendants is debatable since the
implementation of this practice may lead to a substantial extension
of social control over many citizens accompanied by a remarkable
lack of due process safeguards. The authors caution that before
diversion is implemented more extensively than it is at present, it
would be prudent to scrutinize the position of other parties to the
criminal process, namely that of victims and witnesses. On the
basis of an extensive victim/witness study, the authors found strong
approval of the concept of penal retribution and confidence in the
deterrent effect of punishment on the part of those questioned. Even
though respondents showed some tolerance for alternatives to traditional criminal justice dispositions, the authors caution that more
extensive use of more lenient options might seriously erode public
confidence in criminal justice and significantly reduce the willingness of witnesses to cooperate with the legal system. Since the
lack of a cooperative and alienated citizenry is recognized today as
a major obstacle to progress in impeding crime, it would be wise
to proceed with caution when expanding the use of diversion, especially when it involves offenders accused of serious crimes. The
same advice applies if there are to be any improvements in witness
cooperation and management in the field.

The chapter by Mary Knudten, Richard Knudten, and Anthony
Meade is complementary to the previously discussed study. The
authors examine empirically the effect of criminal justice system
experiences on the intentions of witnesses to report and cooperate
with government officials. In essence, the study finds a significant
association between the experiences of serious problems on the
part of witnesses (such as lost time, transportation, and perception of district attorney efforts in prosecuting cases) and a less
favorable assessment of officials, which in turn tends to lead to a
decline in intention to report crime. The authors go on to note
that approximately one-fourth of their respondents had been victimized before. And since current victims are more likely to be
future victims, they are precisely those who should be reporting
other, new crimes. Yet, if there is an attrition in reporting, such
persons would simply join the already intolerably large pool of
persons who do not now cooperate with criminal justice officials.
It is therefore reasonable to assume that there may have been a
gradual eroding of cooperation because of previous difficulties and
disappointments with the system. As a result, the nurturing of
existing victim assistance programs, as well as their expansion

and development, will be necessary in order to assure that there will continue to be those who are willing to testify.

The chapter by Lynda Holmstrom and Ann Burgess on rape is, once again, most timely. Consonant with previous chapters, it is noted that the scholarly and professional literature on sexual offenses, and most notably rape, has traditionally overlooked the victim. Sociological and criminological literature in particular has tended to analyze rape victims through use of the victim precipitation concept, or at least victim participation. But it is worth noting here that the use of the offender's perception of his victim has recently left the world of ivory-tower discussions and invaded judicial decisions. For example, in one recent notorious case, a Minnesota judge ruled that a young secondary school student's dress style had invited and provoked her own rape. And a recent California State Court of Appeals reversed a rape conviction by a lower court stating that lone female hitchhikers "advertise" that they have less concern for the consequences (read sexual assault) than the average female. Such decisions clearly pave the way for men to rape, molest, and otherwise harm women at any time, knowing that they will surely be exonerated under a criminal justice system that consistently places the onus of responsibility on the victim. While judicial decisions such as those discussed above remain firmly wedded to Paleolithic times, the field of research has moved on to look at societal processes, such as the creation and function of victims, institutional responses to rape victims, and at the victim's experience of rape and its aftermath. Holmstrom and Burgess go on to identify several critical areas for future research, such as the need to explore further the social definition of rape, the concept of victim outrage and perception of the crime of rape, the phenomenon of false accusations, and the function of rape in terms of social control. A particularly fertile area of research identified by the authors would be comparative work within sociopolitical and economic contexts. There appear to be significant differences in the incidence of sexual crimes, as well as organized and street crime, between capitalist and socialist countries, with the latter experiencing fewer such crimes. It would be interesting indeed to empirically test these apparent differences through comparative cross-national research.

11

ON THEORY AND POLITICS OF VICTIMOLOGY AND GENERAL ASPECTS OF THE PROCESS OF VICTIMIZATION
Kurt Weis

VICTIMOLOGY'S LACK OF A THEORETICAL BACKGROUND

Oftentimes, when a new discipline has just seen the light of day and lived through the naming ceremonies, its promoters and disciples want to endow it not only with new books and new congresses but also with a theory and a method of its own. This is particularly difficult if the newborn is interdisciplinary in nature and godfathered by a variety of independent disciplines. Victimology is a case in point. With its roots in (to name but a few and strictly follow alphabetical order) criminology, law, medicine, psychology, social psychology, and sociology, victimology will never enjoy a theory of its own, simply because there is no single theory of sociology, social psychology, or the other separate disciplines.

The real problem with victimology is that not even its subject matter has been clearly defined. Elsewhere we have outlined an open-systems approach to studies in the field of victimology (Smith and Weis 1976). One of the purposes of this approach was to identify areas of victimological work and concern without limiting the field or, in other words, to tackle the problem of definition by circumventing it. "Science and study of victims" is a meaningless translation of this artificial Graeco-Latin compound "victimology," as long as neither the term victim nor the sources and processes for becoming a victim have been defined, nor the groups or institutions have been identified that enjoy the definitorial power for labeling someone a victim and for providing for consequences of such label. These problems are not necessarily encountered to the same extent in otherwise similarly new and interdisciplinary branches of the social sciences. For example, suicidology, dealing

with suicidal and self-destructive behavior and its genesis and prevention, much more self-evidently outlines the scope and tasks of
this new science.

Yet, the lack of a theoretical background for victimology may
be more apparent than real. Victimology is primarily a matter of
perspective and concern. To a large extent, the basic theoretical
work has been done in the respective godfather disciplines. Sometimes it seems that there is a certain correlation between an author's apparent lack of knowledge of the literature in the neighbor-
ing fields of a supposedly interdisciplinary victimology and the
energy with which he calls for a new science of victimology. Instead of stressing the need for something new, perhaps we should
ask for the application of something old. If victimology is a matter
of perspective and concern, where is the victimologist who rewrites
Howard Becker's famous address "Whose Side Are We On?" in
victimological terms? If an achievement-oriented society is very
hard on losers and victims of all sorts, where is the victimologist
who integrates or even cites the works and analyses of the so-called
counterculture or antiachievement movements a decade ago?

DEFINING VICTIMS AND VICTIMIZING PROCESSES

This lack of a clearly defined field and target group of victimology leads us to some policy statements about the scope and
goals of victimology. Defining the scope of victimology, the science
of victims and of losing in life means first of all to identify those
who are labeled victims. The decision of whether or not to apply
this label to a person or a group of persons is the political task of
the victimologist. But he is not the only one engaged in this task of
labeling others. Apart from victimologically minded scholars, the
label "victim" is used in legal terminology and in everyday (common-
sense) terminology.

The legal definition refers to the most clearly defined target
group of victimology, "victims of crime." It is here that for criminologists the science of victimology takes its starting point to become a sub- or sister-discipline to criminology. Of classic concern
is the victim-offender relationship, the victim's contribution to the
crime, his or her compensation for the injury suffered, and, more
generally speaking, his or her treatment by the criminal justice
system. In general, common-sense definitions include the legal
definition but widen the scope to cover persons and groups that were
harmed in incidents that need not be defined as illegal. They may
actually be the victims of certain laws and regulations as well as of
accidents or an unfortunate economic situation or development.

Behavioral and social scientists and legal scholars may eventually wish to go even beyond the scope of everyday definitions and include certain target groups otherwise not yet defined as victims. This can be shown by Figure 11.1. The victimological definition is broader than and inclusive of the common-sense definition, and the latter is broader than and inclusive of the legal definition.

FIGURE 11.1

Recognition of a Process as Victimizing
and of a Person as a Victim

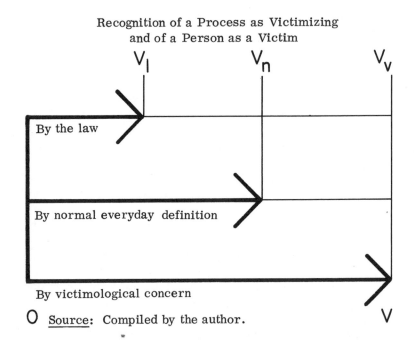

Source: Compiled by the author.

With regard to awakening and increasing social consciousness and promoting social and legal response, it is one of the policy goals and strategic objectives of many victimologists to move the definitions of victims and victimizing events from the level of their own definitorial power up to the level of everyday acceptance and further up to the level of legal recognition. In other words, the goal of victimological politics is to introduce victimological concern into areas of legal and everyday neglect of victimological problems. State compensation for victims of violent crimes is a successful outcome of these endeavors. The case of pollution and its victims may serve as another example of this development. Originally not deemed harmful and suspected only in esoteric circles, the impact of pollution on the human and natural environment became a matter of public concern and finally legal action was taken to improve the fate of victims of polluted air and waters.

The order of recognition of a process as victimizing and of a person as a victim as indicated above is reversed only in rare instances of attempted or ongoing social change. In such instances, the law may express more social concern than the people. This can be the case in a racist society in which the letter of the law and the application of the law grant the oppressed groups more civil rights and protection by criminal law than the dominating classes are willing to allow. Another example of this reversed order may be encountered in scholarly victimological studies that find victims responsible for their victimization and try to dissuade everyday understanding as well as the law from granting them full status and recognition as victims. (These processes are dealt with below under the headings "The Antivictimological Perspective" and "Social Approval of Victimization".)

THE ANTIVICTIMOLOGICAL PERSPECTIVE

Ten years ago, in his famous presidential address to the Society for the Study of Social Problems, Howard S. Becker asked, "Whose side are we on?" Arguing that it is not possible to do research that is uncontaminated by personal and political sympathies, he found the question of whether we should take sides an idle one. Instead he realized that, especially in the fields of deviance and social problems "and for who knows what private reasons, we fall into deep sympathy with the people we are studying, so that while the rest of the society views them as unfit in one or another respect for the deference ordinarily accorded to a fellow citizen, we believe that they are at least as good as anyone else, more sinned against than sinning" (Becker 1967: 240).

This is not the place to indulge in the eternal discussion of whether value-free work is possible in sociology or related fields. However different from sociology, criminology, and the like, victimology has never claimed to be neutral in perspective. It is meant to provide "a new focus" as the title of the five-volume series on victimology edited by Drapkin and Viano (1974) suggests. Victimology does not only provide a new focus, but should also provide a new perspective. Becker left his question, "Whose side are we on?" unanswered, although he indicated the difficulties and importance of, as well as his preference for, taking the perspective of the subordinate group. In victimology there cannot be any ambiguity with regard to the perspective to take--it has to be the perspective of victim. We can study prison problems through the eyes of the administration, the guards, or the inmates. We should utilize all three perspectives, but we should keep them apart. In order to understand the situation and problems of prisoners our primary perspective has to be that of inmates. The same holds true for victimology and a victimological perspective. As long as we can assume conflicting perspectives, it would be a strange science that would turn to the criminal in order to obtain a victimological perspective on the crime victim. (Ours is a strange science indeed.)

Many victimologists, however, seem to live happily with an antivictimological perspective. For victimology, in some circles, has become the art of blaming the victim. It should be the social scientific explanation and analysis of the victim's situation, as well as of the art of blaming the victim for his fate. But it should not be the scientific application of this perfidious art.

If a supposedly victimological study shares the general cultural dislike and disregard for victims and finds that victims of crime "asked for it" and "got what they deserved" and that they contributed to the crime like an unselfish accessory to the crime, then we deal with the usual attitude of criminal perpetrators and an offender- and guilt-oriented criminology. (For an example see the victimological and methodological critique of Amir's famous rape study by Weis and Borges [1976]). Criminology's recent rediscovery of the victims of crime as partners in crime does not turn this criminology into victimology, just like the postmortem examination of a murdered person remains in the realm of criminalistics and does not turn the investigation into applied thanatology, the science of dying.

Some authors (they seem to come from all five continents but shall remain anonymous here), and sometimes especially those who do not miss any chance to stress the importance of victimology as a new discipline, and who do not fail to reassure their readers of the victimological nature of their work, take such an antivictim perspective that whatever the merits of their work, it can be labeled only antivictimological in nature. They frequently refer to the late von Hentig as godfather of their victim-blaming attitude. This reference is doubly mistaken: von Hentig stressed the vicious cycle in the relationship between offender and victim, rather than the victim's guilt, and von Hentig very clearly abstained from calling his work victimological. It should be noted that von Hentig, although always listed among the pioneers of victimology, never used this term in English or German.

Not everything that is done to a victim, like calling him a victim, investigating his social background, feeding him, or beating him, is victimological. For someone who cannot identify with or understand a victim's fate, it may be plainly impossible to become a victimologist. A lawyer who supports a legal move of a prisoner or a crime victim is certainly not yet a victimologist, although there are lawyers who believe they are.

In many instances truly victimological work is not a problem of lawyers and criminologists whose orientation toward power and establishment has often been commented upon, but rather the type of problem that is frequently encountered by social workers. Social workers in their daily work on the borderline between agencies of informal and formal social control are much closer to the political implications of the victimological perspective and of the simple question: Whose side are we on? Being a victimologist is a task, and a difficult one, and I wonder whether most of us--and those who are so much on the sunny side of the road to academic success that they can meet in Jerusalem in 1973, in Bellagio, Italy, in 1975, and in bicentennial Boston in 1976 to promote the science of victims --have the moral fiber to feel more at east in true victimological work than in happily joining the self-enhancing chorus of self-styled victimologists.

CRIMINOLOGY: VICTOROLOGY PLUS VICTIMOLOGY?

Some criminologists with a background in law find criminological aspects such a daring extension of their legal reference points that they are usually not inclined to widen this perspective even further but tend to consider victimology only an interesting and important shift of focus inside the old criminolegal framework. For them victimology, at best, would be a subdiscipline to criminology. Elsewhere (Weis 1972: 175ff), the implications of the suggestion that victimology should be a subdiscipline of criminology were taken seriously. It was argued that if "victims" warrant "victimology," offenders should claim the same right and should be entitled to a science of their own based on the well-known Christian name Victor, thus "victorology." It was deplored that criminology and criminologists, in general, have not dealt with crime, as the discipline's name would suggest, but with criminals, preferably criminals in the arms of the law. Had this discipline truly dealt with crime, it would have come across the unhappy or crime-provoking victim much earlier. This discovery, however, was left to scholars like von Hentig (1940; 1948: 383-450; 1961: v). Unfortunately, most criminology since Lombroso has been "victorology," which may be termed a well-describing insult since, like in detective novels, it reflects more interest in the winners (Latin, victores) than in the losers of criminal activities. For it points to the preoccupation with the criminal as an individual, the mobilization of public and police forces to fight criminals rather than crime, and thus loses sight of victims and of sociological findings and theories on societal responsibility for the conditions in which crime arises. Only with the parallel notion of "victorology" in mind can "victimology" be accepted as one of the two major subdisciplines of criminology.

In the aftermath of von Hentig's pioneering chapter on "The Contribution of the Victim to the Genesis of Crime" (1948: 383–450) some authors in a certain oversimplification followed the modish line of shifting the blame from the offender to the victim. This seemed to be up to date and progressive in two ways: First, it followed the trend of understanding rather than blaming the criminal; and second, it showed the writer abreast with the newly emerging discipline of victimology.

The shift of the criminological focus from a "personal cult of the offender" to a new "personal cult of the victim" resulted in a necessary broadening of our perspective, but not in a new discipline. It is like playing with a coin and shifting emphasis from head to tails: it is still the same coin, as it is still the same criminology. Likewise, if a botanist shifts emphasis from watching the plants grow to stressing the importance of good and fertile soil, he becomes neither an ecologist nor a geologist. A criminologist who suddenly discovers the victim in criminal encounters remains a criminologist no matter how many nice or nasty things he says about victims (see Cornil 1959; Nagel 1963). Victimology, I submit, is first of all a matter of a particular concern and a particular perspective rather than of renamed concepts with old contents.

On the other hand, criminologists with a background in and an orientation toward social sciences are more inclined to consider their field of work part of the sociology of deviance or the psychology of being different. In this instance, victimology, too, can be accepted as adding new light to old problems and is therefore most easily compartmentalized as a subfield of social problems. In other words, rather than becoming a metadiscipline and bridging the gap between law and (other) social sciences, victimology is occupied and subdued by the respective established disciplines. This need not necessarily be disadvantageous, since victimology, nevertheless, provides just another vehicle of bringing scholars and practitioners of different training and conceptions together in order to jointly and from different angles approach problems that concern all of us.

MENDELSOHN'S CONCEPTS OF VICTIMOLOGY AND VICTIMITY

For the last 30 years the most definite and vigorous endeavors to launch victimology as a true metadiscipline and science of its own have been undertaken by the lawyer Mendelsohn (1946; 1956; 1959; 1974; 1976). As indicated above, one should agree with his statements that "one cannot use the term 'victimology' for the study of victims of crime. . . . This carelessness should be stopped" (Mendelsohn 1976: 21). The concepts should not be confused (p. 26) because the criminal and the victim as his accessory belong to the same field: criminology (p. 9).

Unfortunately, since Mendelsohn demanded something new rather than just a shift of focus inside old established tracks, his perceptions and concepts did not fall upon very fertile soil. If one were to follow the suggestion stated below that the sociology of deviance so far is the best-developed subdiscipline or branch of victimology, then one might as well include the general area of social problems and further widen the scope to accept Mendelsohn's concept of what he terms "victimity." "Victimity," according to Mendelsohn (1976: 12), "is the foundation of victimology and led to the creation of this branch of science." Victimity is said to be "the most important" notion in the new field (1974: 25). Nowhere clearly defined ("a vast sphere"), victimity seems to match criminality as a concept or phenomenon. Both are seen as contrary phenomena, although victimity is held to be broader and more general (1974: 25; 1976: 14). Sometimes it appears as if victimity is meant to be a metaconcept even to criminality and criminology. The confusion is widespread, which we see when criminology is correctly observed and incorrectly defined as being "concerned with the personality of the criminal and with the problems of crime" (1974: 27). Victimity and victimology are notions that cannot be subcategorized to respective notions in the criminal sciences, since criminal behavior is only one source of suffering and victimization. In terms of victimological politics, however, the programmatically all-embracing and consequently vague working definitions are clear: The essential goal of victimology is the reduction of the number of victims in all sectors of society to the extent that society is concerned with this problem (1976: 8), and victimity is defined as "the whole of the socio-psychological characteristics, common to all victims in general, which society wishes to prevent and fight, no matter what their determinants are (criminals or others)" (1974: 27). In any case, victimology should be understood as a science of social concern for the victim.

PROCESSES OF VICTIMIZATION

It may be true that a theory of victimology cannot be stated and the subject matter of victimology cannot be neatly defined, if only because it has to be so broad not to exclude anything or anyone at this early stage of victimological work. Nevertheless, there are many theoretical issues of prime victimological concern. One is the function of victims and processes of victimization in an achievement-oriented society. An even more fundamental task is to outline general aspects of processes of victimization. The following discussion will emphasize some societal aspects and therefore will be limited to the social sciences.

Processes of victimization may be observed in many settings. Victimization is generally understood as unhappy deviation from the normal. Deviance, on the other hand, refers only to those that are looked down upon by others who are united in conformity. Books on "deviance and social control" and on the "sociology of deviance" do not deal with those few who deviate by being on top of the power structure. Instead, they are preferably dealt with under the heading "elite." Status and role of the deviant are granted only to those marginal people who are believed to be different in terms of being criminal, mentally sick, suicidal, without presentable domicile, of forbidding poverty, or of other characteristics or misfortunes that are culturally disapproved. In some sense, they are all outcasts of society. They are said to create social problems and societal services are generated which are supposed to take care of these problems. Police, courts, and prisons serve the criminals; mental institutions serve the mentally ill; suicide prevention centers serve the potential suicides; and many welfare organizations have important tasks of making the lives of the unhappy and unlucky worthwhile. Experience shows and the sociology of organizations tries to explain that all of these services are unsuccessful insofar as they do not prevent the problems. Prisons, mental hospitals, suicide prevention and crisis intervention centers, welfare institutions, and houses of refuge do not close for lack of occupants or callers. Rather, at least in some instances, the "problem" is perpetuated by these services creating and maintaining their own dependent clientele. This in turn results in a good case for expanding these services since their target and problem groups seem to expand.

As soon as society reacts negatively to deviation the deviant becomes a victim. This reaction may range from purposeful neglect to compulsive "treatment." Social reaction is one of the basic concerns of the labeling and, more generally speaking, of the societal reaction approach to the understanding of deviance and criminality. When society becomes threatened by something that has been termed a social problem, it tends to fight back by blaming, isolating, criminalizing, and perpetually victimizing rather than helping the persons selected as "problematic." In other words, as our textbooks show, the process of becoming different and deviant is a case of being victimized. With this starting point in mind, it seems safe to argue that a good deal of theory and application of victimology has already been dealt with under the heading of deviance, when the processes of becoming deviant and the societal reaction to deviancy are described. Victimology, after all, may not remain a subdiscipline of criminology, but the sociology of deviance is already the best-developed subdiscipline or branch of victimology.

Even if there is no general agreement on the theoretical localization of victimology, guidelines for the study of elements that influence processes of victimization can be given. One attempt of an all-inclusive descriptive definition of "successful" victimization reads as follows: Both the term and the concept of victimization refer to societal processes that before, during, and after the event simultaneously render the victim defenseless and even partly responsible for it. Victimization includes the preparation of the victim for the event (often a crime), his or her experience during the event, and treatment and responses he or she will encounter as part of the aftermath of the event.[1]

Out of a lengthy checklist of possible items for victimological investigation, in a certain simplification at least four major ingredients should be stated that contribute to the process of victimization and mark, like cornerstones, the boundaries of escalation and interplay: the immediate source of victimization or the victimizer, the victim, the situation and social surround, and society's reaction to the original victimization. It is submitted that by studying these four rather obvious elements and comparing them in different cases of victimization, victimological knowledge for theory and practice is enhanced. However, when we deal with victims of social processes rather than with victims of accidents, and so on, we should guard against attempts to identify the source of victimization in a monocausal manner. Social processes are products of the social structure, and the identification of causal factors usually turns out to be too narrow and one-sided.

To some extent, I believe, the processes of victimization can be compared with or are part of the processes of social control. Social control is characterized by processes and mechanisms that are used by society to motivate or force people to adhere to norms and patterns of behavior that are held to be important to the smooth functioning of society. However, as conformity presupposes needs, and therefore creates a certain amount of deviance and some deviants (criminals) who are sacrificed (imprisoned, stigmatized, and so on) for the common good, other social values, in order to prove their importance, may also demand some unhappy individuals who are sacrificed as a result of negative social control. This type of victimization may be pathologically widespread in an achievement-oriented society. Agents of social control are victim-producing

pressure groups. From a victimological point of view it might be
worthwhile to compare the harm done to individuals and the production of victims affected by agents of formal social control (for example, state, police, prisons), agents of informal social control
(primary groups; for example, family, friends, colleagues), and
the individual self (the superego that in cases of moral rigidity may
lead to self-punishment and suicidal behavior).

When informal social control is replaced by agents of formal
social control, this frequently results in a lowering of social status
of the controlled person and a dehumanization of the individual.
These obviously inevitable processes have been outlined and analyzed
as degradation ceremonies (Garfinkel 1956) and as procedures of
personal defacement and disidentification (Goffmamn 1961: 21), but
they apparently were not integrated into any victimological perspective or theory.

From a macroscopic perspective, society, law, nature, and
the environment may be found among the sources of victimization.
In a more microscopic view the actually victimizing agent may be
another person or the victim himself. In the latter case it is frequently society's subsequent reaction that constitutes the victimization and thus provides for an external victimizer. (Sometimes,
however, society's negative reaction is fully anticipated and internalized so that the individual agent at the same time can become
source and victim of an uninterrupted internal interaction.)

The victim can be a person or a group, class, race, or even
a people as in the case of genocide.

Generally speaking, it seems that the victimizer, when compared to the victim, is of higher status. This superiority by status
may be ascribed or achieved or only situational. Corresponding to
the victimizer's superiority is the victim's inferiority with regard
to the ability and chances to defend against victimization in a given
situation. The actual moment, situation, and social surroundings
of the victimization have to be taken into account to understand the
ongoing dynamics. The analysis of this situation includes the interaction between the victimizer and the victim, as well as the victim's anticipation of society's reaction to the victimization (for example, the feeling of helplessness and the fear of relating the experience). There seems to exist a general tendency to define
situations in terms of normality. Very often, the victim initially
or even over an extended period of time tends to deny the reality of
what is happening. The stronger this inclination for denial, the
longer will be the period of inaction before the victim starts with
actions toward effective defense. This holds especially true for
all situations in which the victim gets "taken" through a violation of
trust anticipated and offered by the victim.

In criminology this interaction is most often dealt with under the headings of "the victim-offender relationship" or "the victim's contribution to the commission of the crime." Here the victim is treated almost as an accessory to the crime. This concept became best known as "victim-precipitation." This leads to the next major aspect to be discussed, society's reaction to victimization.

SOCIAL APPROVAL OF VICTIMIZATION

One of the biggest problems of victimization is social approval. It is social approval of victimization that makes victimization possible as a never-ending dynamic process. Social approval often appears as an instance of "scapegoating" and may be explained by psychoanalytic theory. Furthermore, in societies whose ruling ideologies are largely characterized by social Darwinism and the Protestant ethic with an overriding emphasis on material possession, success, health, and beauty, social approval of victimization serves to internalize the norms and values of those not victimized and of those who obey the ideology of the former. Well-known patterns of argumentation are developed to rationalize victimizing behavior and to neutralize the outcome. In their famous "Techniques of Neutralization: A Theory of Delinquency" Sykes and Matza (1957: 664-70) describe procedures for establishing a deserving victim as a technique learned by some juveniles as they become delinquents. Those five techniques of argumentation--the denial of responsibility, the denial of injury, the denial of the victim, the condemnation of the condemners, and the appeal to higher loyalties--may not necessarily provide for a learning theory of delinquency, but they reflect well established thinking patterns of an aggressive, achievement-oriented society.

These techniques are general patterns of argumentation that can be applied to neutralize moral guilt feelings. Especially the first three can be seen to operate in an offender's and society's reaction to victims. The basic dynamic is to shift the blame from the source of victimization to the victim himself, emphasizing the victim's deserving characteristics. These dynamics are outlined in social psychology textbooks under the heading of "reduction of cognitive dissonance." Unfortunately, the same dynamics and techniques are applied, but not detected, in many self-styled victimological studies that deal with victims of some sort and analyze the victim's contribution to their fate. If the victims are found responsible, cognitive dissonance is reduced, the world is more just, better than we thought, and victimology has contributed to this feeling.

This social approval of victimization is not necessarily openly admitted. Often, it is cloaked in humanitarian kindness and deep concern for the victim. Sometimes called the art of blaming the victim, it is an attitude usually not openly admitted (or realized) by "sympathetic social scientists with social consciences in good working order, by liberal politicians with a genuine commitment to reform" (Ryan 1971: 6), or by other victimologists, for that matter. The following passage (Ryan 1971: 7) is taken from the same book that was written to expose this ideology and to make the reader "turn his attention away from fruitless tinkering with the victim and fix his sight on the real targets" (Ryan 1971: 277).

> Blaming the Victim is, of course, quite different from old-fashioned conservative ideologies. The latter simply dismissed victims as inferior, genetically defective, or morally unfit; the emphasis is on the intrinsic, even hereditary, defect. The former (scil. the above stated "humanitarian" or "liberal" ideology) shifts its emphasis to the environmental causation. The old-fashioned conservative could hold firmly to the belief that the oppressed and the victimized were born that way--"that way" being defective or inadequate in character or ability. The new ideology attributes defect and inadequacy to the malignant nature of poverty, injustice, slum life, and racial difficulties. The stigma that marks the victim and accounts for his victimization is an acquired stigma, a stigma of social, rather than genetic, origin. But the stigma, the defect, the fatal difference--though derived in the past from environmental forces--is still located within the victim, inside his skin. With such an elegant formulation, the humanitarian can have it both ways. He can, all at the same time, concentrate his charitable interest on the defects of the victim, condemn the vague social and environmental stresses that produced the defect (some time ago), and ignore the continuing effect of victimizing social forces (right now). It is a brilliant ideology for justifying a perverse form of social action designed to change, not society, as one might expect, but rather society's victim.

THE CONCEPT OF SECONDARY VICTIMIZATION

The type of treatment outlined in the quote taken from Ryan can result only in secondary victimization, if we may introduce this concept to the field of victimology which, of course, is borrowed from Lemert's concept of secondary deviance. Lemert, in cautioning against confusing original causes or antecedents of deviance with its effective causes, introduced the concept of primary and secondary deviation. Deviant behavior is not significant until there is severe societal reaction which changes the role and self-perception of the deviator and assigns a new status to him (Lemert 1951: 75ff). The deviant act itself, the primary deviation, which may originate from any cause or motive that influences human behavior, is of only minor importance if it does not affect the social status and psychic structure of the person involved. It is the secondary deviation that matters, brought about as a change of said status and personality structure in response to a strong deviation (Lemert 1972). This societal reaction may depend on the severity and on its visibility, as well as on the previous status of the deviator (Lemert 1972: ix):

> The concept of secondary deviance is a logical extension of the formulation of deviance as problems of social control. It proposes that changes in psychic structure accompany transition to degraded status, during which the meaning of deviance changes qualitatively, as well as in its outward expressions. Deviance is established in social roles and is perpetuated by the very forces directed to its elimination or control. This, of course, has to be understood as a process of meaningful social interaction.

To see the overlap of the sociology of deviance and the sociology of victimization in the above quote by Lemert the reader is asked to replace "deviance" by "victimization." The text following below is likewise based on Lemert's (1972: 62-63) analysis of secondary deviation and applied to the concept of victimization.

Primary victimization, as contrasted with secondary, may result from an unlimited number of sources. The notion of secondary victimization is introduced to distinguish between original and effective causes of victimizing events and actions. While it may be socially recognized and even defined as undesirable, primary victimization has only marginal implications for the status and psychic structure of the person concerned. Resultant problems are dealt with reciprocally in the context of established status relationships. This is done either through normalization of the situation, in which the victimization is perceived as normal variation--a problem of everyday life--or through management and some help, both of which do not seriously impede basic accommodations people make to get along with each other.

Secondary victimization is the product of society's reaction to and interaction with primary victimization. If it results in stressing the fact of victimization, then from the sociology of deviance and social control the related concepts of "deviation amplification" (Wilkins 1964: 85) and "dramatization of evil" (Tannenbaum 1938: 19ff., 477) may likewise be borrowed, renamed, applied as concepts of "victimization amplification" and "dramatization of victimization," and integrated into a theory of victimization. In his reproach against the "dramatization of evil," society's most self-defeating device for dealing with the deviant, Tannenbaum (1938: 19ff., 477) described how, in the "process of tagging, defining, identifying, segregating, describing, emphasizing, making conscious and self-conscious," the person becomes the thing he is complained of as, or warned of, being. All these analyses agree on the fact that social reaction to deviation and victimization is at least as important a factor for perpetuating (and thereby re-creating the problem of) deviance and victimization as is the original cause. We shall close with a passage from Lemert (1972: 62-63):

> Secondary deviation [victimization] refers to a
> special class of socially defined responses
> which people make to problems created by the
> societal reaction to their deviance [victimiza-
> tion]. These problems are essentially moral
> problems which revolve around stigmatization,
> punishment, segregation, and social control.
> Their general effect is to differentiate the sym-
> bolic and interactional environment to which the
> person responds, so that early or adult socializa-
> tion is categorically affected. They become cen-
> tral facts of existence for those experiencing
> them, altering psychic structure, producing
> specialized organization of social roles and
> self-regarding attitudes. Actions which have
> these roles and self attitudes as their referents
> make up secondary deviance [victimization].
> The secondary deviant [victim] as opposed to his
> actions, is a person whose life and identity are
> organized around the facts of deviance [victimiza-
> tion].

THE END OF VICTIMIZATION

In this chapter, processes of victimization were primarily understood as social processes. Social processes can be stated only in general terms and predicted on the basis of probabilities, not, however, with regard to an individual outcome. There are, of course, many individuals who are in a position that would qualify them to be subjected to a victimization process who never become victimized and who do not end up at the lowest end of the downward spiral. For those unhappy who do, the process of victimization is ideally completed if the victim accepts the blame, is ashamed, does not find anyone to whom he or she can complain about or relate the victimization, or does not dare to share the experience with anyone at all. The victim then may perish, end up in a mental hospital, or commit suicide.

NOTE

1. This definition was originally given in a paper on victimization which "deals with victimization as the process of making a person a victim and utilizes rape as the most extreme example." The definition continued: "If these processes of victimization are successful with regard to rape, the raped woman is a 'legitimate' or 'safe' victim who will not be dangerous to the rapist, since she is unable to relate her experience to others or to effectively direct blame and accusation against the person who raped her" (Weis and Borges 1973: 71, 72). The whole paper by Weis and Borges may be seen as an attempt to apply the model of the process of total victimization to a particular problem and a linè of social events in (American) life.

REFERENCES

Becker, Howard S.
    1967   Whose side are we on? Social Problems 14 (Winter):239-47.

Cornil, P.
    1959   Contribution de la victimologie aux sciences criminolo-
            giques. Revue de Droit Pénal et de Criminologie:
            587-600.

Garfinkel, H.
    1956   Conditions of successful degradation ceremonies. Amer-
            ican Journal of Sociology 61: 420-24.

Goffmann, E.
    1961   Asylums. Garden City, N.Y.: Doubleday.

von Hentig, H.
   1940   Remarks on the interaction of perpetrator and victim.
           Journal of Criminal Law and Criminology 31: 303-09.

   1948   The Criminal and His Victim: Studies in the Sociobiology
           of Crime. New Haven, Conn.: Yale University Press.

   1961   Das Verbrechen, Band I, Der kriminelle Mensch im
           Kraftespiel von Zeit und Raum. Berlin-Gottingen-
           Heidelberg.

Lemert, E. M.
   1951   Social Pathology: A Systematic Approach to the Theory of
           Sociopathic Behavior. New York: McGraw-Hill.

   1972   Human Deviance: Social Problems, and Social Control,
           2nd ed. Englewood Cliffs, N.J.: Prentice-Hall.

Mendelsohn, B.
   1946   New bio-psycho-social horizons: victimology. A manu-
           script distributed in Bucharest.

   1956   Une nouvelle branche de science bio-psychosociale. La
           victimologie. Revue Internationale de Criminologie et de
           Police Technique 10: 95-109.

   1959   La victimologie: science actuelle. Revue de Droit Pénal
           et de Criminologie: 619-27.

   1974   Victimology and the technical and social sciences: a call
           for the establishment of victimological clinics. In Vic-
           timology: A New Focus, ed. I. Drapkin and E. Viano.
           Vol. I. Lexington, Mass.: D. C. Heath, pp. 25-35.

   1976   Victimology and contemporary society's trends. Victimol-
           ogy: An International Journal 1, no. 1: 8-28.

Nagel, W. H.
   1963   The notion of victimology in criminology. Excerpta
           Criminologica (Abstracts on Criminology and Penology) 3:
           245-47.

Ryan, W.
   1971   Blaming the Victim. New York: Random House.

Smith, D. L., and K. Weis
1976   Toward an open-systems approach to the study of vic-
       timology. In Victims, Criminals, and Society, ed.
       E. Viano. Leiden, Holland: A. W. Sijthoff International
       Publishing Co.

Sykes, G. M., and D. Matza
1957   Techniques of neutralization: a theory of delinquency.
       American Sociological Review 22: 664-70.

Tannenbaum, F.
1938   Crime and the Community. New York: Columbia Uni-
       versity Press.

Weis, K.
1972   Viktimologie und viktorologie in der kriminologie.
       Monatsschrift für Kriminologie und Strafrechtsreform
       55: 170-80.

Weis, K., and S. S. Borges
1973   Victimology and rape: the case of the legitimate victim.
       Issues in Criminology 8: 71-115. (Reprinted in L. G.
       Schultz, ed. Rape Victimology. Springfield, Ill.:
       Charles C. Thomas, 1975, pp. 91-141.)

1976   Rape as a crime without victims and offenders? a
       methodological critique. In Victims and Society, ed. E.
       Viano. Washington, D.C.: Visage Press, pp. 230-54.

Wilkins, L. T.
1964   Social Deviance: Social Policy, Action, and Research.
       London: Tavistock.

CHAPTER

12

DECRIMINALIZATION
AND THE VICTIM
Mary S. Knudten
Richard D. Knudten

Decriminalization is an inclusive concept. It refers, on the
one hand, to legislative action in the form of criminal statute repeal
and misdemeanorization and, on the other, to charge dismissal policies in criminal cases conditional upon the performance of specified obligations. Direct restitution to the victim by the offender,
voluntary submission by the offender to extralegal supervision, or
good behavior agreements or enrollment in outside treatment and
training programs are common examples.

Diversion, as a form of decriminalization, refers to the disposition of a criminal complaint short of full prosecution. Nimmer
(1974) refers to the existence of a "dispositional dilemma" as a
major determinant of the diversion decision. He maintains that
this dilemma is largely a function of two perceptual factors. First
is the low seriousness of the criminal act, and second is the marginal criminality of the offender. The notion of diversion ranks very
high among present topics of criminological interest and discussion.
A hopelessly overcrowded criminal justice system and the popularity
presently enjoyed by labeling theory among academicians and justice system officials alike account for the conspicuous concern with
diversion.

THE BASES AND SHORTCOMINGS OF THE
DIVERSION CONCEPT

Diversion is primarily an accommodation to the interests of
justice system officials and defendants. It is justified on the bases
that it decreases the workloads of justice system officials; lowers
the financial costs of justice administration; avoids the stigmatization of defendants; lessens the disruptive potential of the justice

system upon the lives of defendants; and serves as a rehabilitative alternative for the basically ineffective penal incarceration experience.

Diversion is an operative policy in the contemporary United States. It has already moved significantly beyond an exclusive concern with victimless crime, petty property offenses, or intrafamily assaults to an inclusion of most felony charges short of homicide. There is no shortage of confidence in the potential of diversion as a progressive alternative to the more formal, traditional process of justice administration and correction. Indeed, the only issue seems to be that of deciding how quickly to expand the scope of diversion. Nimmer (1974) takes the position that rarely has such a degree of certainty been expressed in the face of so little evidence. We concur. We are not taking a stand in opposition to diversion, but merely pointing out that conclusive support based upon controlled evaluation of existing programs is lacking in this area.

This premature enthusiasm is not surprising in light of diversion's close ties to labeling theory. Recidivism is increasingly coming to be interpreted as a result of the negative social and psychological effects upon an offender of official adjudication and disposition. Poor self-concepts and/or hostility toward the legal system on the part of the law-violators are expected to result from official handling of cases. These psychological responses along with demeaning behavior on the part of those who become aware of the offender's record are, in turn, supposed to bring about further criminal acts. However, not only has there been a failure to adequately test the major propositions of labeling theory in the area of criminology, but several of the central concepts of the theory have even defied valid empirical measurement (Meade 1974). The most damaging case that can be made against labeling theory is the fact that not all officially defined defendants become "secondary" offenders. It has been the lack of progress in spelling out the contingencies which might influence susceptibility to the negative effects of official labeling which is most apparent to critics of the labeling perspective. This approach also consistently ignores any deterring effect which formal procedures might have (Zimring 1971).

To the question of financial costs and system workloads, it certainly should be expected that as diversion expands, the new programs and facilities will become more expensive and overcrowded. As a prototype the juvenile court would serve as a good example. Similarly, as was the case with the juvenile court, the policies and objectives of new diversion programs will undoubtedly have to be defended in reference to the spirit of due process. Already, suggestions that the right to counsel be guaranteed at referral and revocation hearings and that more rigid standards for determining the sufficiency of criminal evidence in such cases be established

before the individual's decision to accept the terms of diversion can
approach voluntariness (Balch 1974). Any attempt to assure such
protections will most likely be resisted by program administrators
and, if implemented, would require additional funding. Finally,
even if use of diversion were doubled, it would serve as an alternative in no more than 15 to 20 percent of the present criminal case
load. If this resulted in a more efficient and prompt processing of
citizen complaints, the long-term result would probably be an increase in officially filed complaints on the part of the citizenry.
Indeed, the citizen-victim population in this country is presently
functioning as our primary diversion agency in that only about one-
half of all serious crimes are even being reported in the first place.
Morris (1974) has warned that diversionary techniques may even
"lead to substantial extension of social control by official state
processes rather than to a reduction." In support of this statement,
Morris (1974) points out that while California's Probation Subsidy
Program and Community Treatment Project have decreased the
severity of official control over offenders, they have increased the
numbers under control.

As stated earlier, diversion, and decriminalization in general, primarily accommodate the interests of system officials and
defendants. It has also been suggested here that the extent to which
such procedures are entirely consistent with defendants' interests
is debatable. Furthermore, before such "progressive action" is
fully implemented, it would be wise to scrutinize carefully the position of other parties to the criminal justice interaction structure.
We are referring here to the citizen-victim or citizen-witness.
These persons are either the recipients of criminal harm or con-
tributors of information regarding the factual dimensions of the
case. Their confidence in and cooperation with justice system personnel are critical to the successful prosecution of criminal cases.

PILOT STUDIES ON THE ATTITUDES
OF VICTIMS AND WITNESSES

In preparation for a 12-month victim-witness study, the Center for Criminal Justice and Social Policy at Marquette University
carried out several pilot runs of research instruments and techniques with actual citizen-victims and citizen-witnesses of crime in
a large metropolitan court system. The data results presented
herein involve three different time periods. Saturation samples of
294, 78, and 184 respondents were examined. The same court
system was used in each survey. The first pilot run was carried
out in March 1974. The second pilot run gathered data in September-

October 1974, while the third pilot run was carried out in October-November 1974. Interview results from these pilot runs shed some interesting light on several dimensions of victim and witness orientations. A strong approval of penal retribution and confidence in the deterring effect of punishment is apparent from the interview results. In the third pilot run, for example, 85 percent of the 184 respondents agreed with the statement: It is only fair that a criminal receive some kind of punishment for his offense. Sixty-seven percent agreed that: The best way to prevent crime is to make sure offenders are punished so that an example is set for others. Forty-eight percent of the respondents agreed with the statement: If an individual offender receives a stiff penalty for a crime, he will be less likely to commit another offense. Forty-eight percent disagreed with the statement: It makes more sense to give criminals social and psychiatric help than to punish them.

Respondents were also asked to indicate how they felt the offender or offenders in each case should be dealt with. Some kind of official action ranging from probation through execution, in one case, was suggested for 69 percent of the offenders in crime against the person. The comparative figure for nonpersonal offenders was 52 percent. Fines were recommended for 10 and 17 percent of the offender types, respectively. In the first pilot run, 46 percent of 294 victim and witness interviewees felt that the offender had been dealt with in a lenient manner. Thus, while it appears that there exists an area of tolerance for alternatives to traditional, official dispositions, an increase in the use of such alternatives could result in an increase in victim and witness perceptions of leniency on the part of system officials.

In the second pilot run, 78 victims and witnesses ranked the seriousness of the offense in which they were involved on a ten-point scale. When responses were broken down into three seriousness categories, the results showed that the more serious the offense is perceived, the more likely is the feeling that the offender was dealt with in a lenient manner. While 33 percent of those indicating the lowest seriousness scores felt the offender was dealt with in a lenient manner, the percentage figure for the highest seriousness category was 51. Recent studies of perceived offense seriousness demonstrate a tendency on the part of subjects to clearly discriminate along a continuum. These studies, however, are not exclusively of criminal justice victim and witness participants. Significant here is the fact that in the second pilot run, which also employed a ten-point seriousness scale, the mean score was 7.1. In the third pilot run, a four-point Likert scale was used. Ninety-three percent of the respondents perceived the offense as very serious or serious. It should be recalled here that low seriousness serves as a major criterion in the diversion decision. Obviously, any proposed expansion of the use of diversion should be sensitive to the perceptions of citizen-victims and witnesses regarding offense seriousness. With respect to the marginality criteria, in the second pilot run 58 percent of the offenders were perceived as either mentally ill, careless, or irresponsible. Only 23 percent were perceived as intrinsically bad. It appears, then, that victims and witnesses are able to distinguish among specific offenders in terms of degree of intent.

THE FUTURE OF DIVERSION

How far can diversion go in terms of expanding its boundaries to different types of offenders and offenses? Its ultimate fate will depend upon at least six developments:

The degree to which overcrowding remains a characteristic of formalistic procedures within the criminal justice system;
The ability of the concept to hold up against due process challenges;
The extent to which valid and reliable evidence of the negative effects of official labeling becomes available;
The extent to which societal and victim confidence in the deterrent effect of punitive sanctions decreases;
The extent to which societal and victim support of the retributive function of punitive sanctions decreases, or the extent to which parallel forms of retribution can be integrated with diversion programs;
The performance of available diversion alternatives.

Victim compensation programs present a relevant parallel retribution form. Eighty-one percent of the second pilot run respondents were in favor of a law which would permit payment to injured victims of crimes for medical expenses. Eighty-one percent also were in favor of such a law which allowed compensation for loss of earnings. Sixty-two percent even favored compensation for physical pain and suffering. In each case, more than 60 percent of those favoring such a law were willing to pay an increase in their taxes to help finance it. Victim compensation legislation and victim advocacy units within prosecutor offices could be effective means of softening possible citizen resistance to diversion programs.

SUMMARY AND CONCLUSION

The orientation of crime victims and witnesses to the social-control apparatus is a complex one. On the one hand, our data indicate that victims and witnesses are favorable toward retributive and deterrent functions of the criminal law. On the other hand, there appears to be some degree of tolerance for nonofficial dispositions. This may be related to our finding that while victims and witnesses are more likely to perceive their crime as a serious one, at the same time they tend to perceive their criminal as more irresponsible or careless than intrinsically bad. Our preliminary results, however, do show that as perceived seriousness of an offense increases, the percentage of respondents who feel that the handling of their offender was too lenient also increases. It is likely that perceptions of leniency will increase among the less-serious offenses should the less-severe sanctions of diversion be implemented on a broader scale.

We see the immediate future of diversion to be filled with controversy. The programs will push forward due to system crunch and the labeling hysteria. Due process challenges are inevitable on the legal front as a result of the concept's high abuse-potential. Within the social control fraternity itself, conflict is a likely result. First-line enforcers, that is, the police, are likely to view justice system diversion programs as just one more example of criminal coddling. This perception is likely to be shared by citizen-victims unless there develops a simultaneous concern, within the justice system, with their attitudes, problems, and needs. As long as diversion is approached solely as a means of lightening prosecutor overload and court backlogs, or of shielding the offender from the criminal sanction, it must run the risk of public resistance. Only by establishing an equilibrium of benefits, which includes victims and witnesses, can the full potential of justice system programs such as diversion be realized.

REFERENCES

Balch, R. W.
  1974   Deferred prosecution: the juvenilization of the criminal
          justice system. Federal Probation 38, no. 2 (June).

Meade, A. C.
  1974   The labeling approach to delinquency: state of the theory
          as a function of method. Social Forces 53, no. 1 (Sep-
          tember).

Morris, N.
  1974   The Future of Imprisonment. Chicago: University of
          Chicago Press.

Nimmer, R. T.
    1974   Diversion: The Search for Alternative Forms of Prose-
            cution. Chicago: American Bar Foundation.

Rossi, P. H., E. Waite, C. E. Bose, and R. E. Berk
    1974   The seriousness of crimes: normative structure and
            individual differences. American Sociological Review
            39, no. 2 (April).

U.S. Department of Justice, Law Enforcement Assistance Administration
    1974   Crime in Eight American Cities. Washington, D.C.:
            U.S. Government Printing Office.

Zimring, F. E.
    1971   Perspectives on Deterrence. Washington, D.C.: U.S.
            Government Printing Office.

13

WILL ANYONE BE LEFT TO TESTIFY? DISENCHANTMENT WITH THE CRIMINAL JUSTICE SYSTEM

Mary S. Knudten
Richard D. Knudten
Anthony C. Meade

INTRODUCTION

As interest in victimization (von Hentig 1948) has been renewed (Schafer 1968, 1970, 1975) and bills for victim compensation
have been proposed (Edelhertz and Geis 1974), a serious effort has
also been undertaken to understand the scope of citizen victimization. The victimization surveys initiated in the late 1960s (Ennis
1967a, 1967b) and continued into the 1970s by the Law Enforcement
Assistance Administration's sponsored Criminal Victimization Surveys (NCJISS 1974a, 1974b, 1974c, 1976a, 1976b) all have examined
the nonreporting problem. While some variation occurs from city
to city, these surveys have generally found that approximately one-
half of the crimes known to victims were actually reported to the
police.

While it is evident from these studies that victimization is
far greater than once believed (Biderman et al. 1967), of potentially
even greater consequence is the potential of victim (and witness)
noncooperation due to the costs incurred upon entrance into the
criminal justice system (Ash 1972; 1973; and Umano 1972).

Most of the literature focusing on the experiences of victims
and witnesses within the criminal justice system suggests that both

Prepared under Grant No. 75-N1-99-0018 from the National
Institute of Law Enforcement and Criminal Justice, Law Enforcement
Assistance Administration, U.S. Department of Justice. Points of
view or opinions stated in this document are those of the authors and
do not necessarily represent the official position of the U.S. Department of Justice.

groups generally receive little satisfaction when confronted with a
criminal act and the need to process a case through the criminal
justice system (Bodemer 1970; Andrew 1964; Ennis 1967a, 1967b;
M. Knudten 1974; Morris 1966; Mansfield 1974; and Glaser 1970).
In order to partially rectify this problem, a number of states have
recently sought to develop compensation plans to provide a more
positive means by which to compensate victims (Schafer 1970;
Brooks 1975; Floyd 1972; Lamborn 1970; and R. Knudten 1968).
While such programs and proposals are justified on the grounds of
social welfare considerations, fairness, the need to encourage the
reporting of crime, and the belief that such programs preserve
citizen confidence in the processes of government, there are those
who ask whether this method really faces the question at issue.
Those who do step forward and enter the criminal justice system as
victim-witnesses or nonvictim-witnesses face sufficient hurdles
and obstacles to militate against their being likely to cooperate in a
similar fashion in the future (Ash 1972, 1973). While a major
reason for not reporting cited by respondents in the NCJISS Survey
(1974b) was that nothing could be done, there was no attempt made
to determine whether this opinion resulted from previous experience
with the criminal justice system. With an increasing emphasis in
sentencing upon probation and diversion, an ever-increasing number
of victims may feel cheated unless alternative forms of satisfaction
are made available to the victim or to his or her family.

This chapter attempts to examine the effect of criminal justice
system experiences on intentions of reporting or cooperation. The
thrust of the analysis is on the problems victims and witnesses experience in the criminal justice system, the assessments they make
regarding the performance of personnel in the system, and the relationships of these two factors to stated intentions of future
cooperation.

METHODOLOGY

The data presented here were gathered by a team from
Marquette University from respondents interviewed within the Milwaukee County (Wisconsin) court system during 1974. The report
discusses some of the findings supplied by a respondent sample of
214 persons provided at an early stage of project interviewing.
More detailed results of the later interviewing is reported elsewhere
(R. Knudten 1976; Doerner 1976; Meade et al. 1976; M. Knudten
1977). Each respondent was queried at one of four criminal justice
system locations (district attorney's charging conference, preliminary hearing, misdemeanor trial, or felony trial) during the

interviewing period of mid-October through November 1974. An interview schedule including both fixed-answer and open-ended items was administered to respondents as they were present in the court setting. The schedule asked respondents to indicate whether they experienced certain problems, how serious they regarded that experience to be, the nature of the victimization, the seriousness of the victimization, their assessment of district attorney and judge effort and effectiveness or fairness, and their likelihood of reporting crime in the future. The respondents represent a nonrandom sample; therefore, significance tests will not be reported.

FINDINGS

As Table 13.1 indicates, there is a considerable range in the percent of respondents who regard certain experiences within the criminal justice system as a problem. While lost time and having to pay for transportation and/or parking are thought to be a problem by 70 to 76 percent of the respondents, only 10 percent had difficulty getting transportation and 14 percent found the need for child care to be a concern. Among those who experience problems, the perceived seriousness also varies considerably with lost pay and exposure to threatening persons being regarded by the greatest number (82 and 81 percent) as a serious experience.

Relationship of Problems and Seriousness, Offense, and Postponements

In order to determine if there was any association among experiencing problems and such factors as the perceived seriousness of the event, the type of offense, or the number of case postponements, the problem dimensions were cross-tabulated with factor indicators.

Seriousness

While there is some tendency for those respondents who perceive their victimization in serious or very serious terms also to perceive their problem experiences as more serious, the pattern is not consistent. In fact, an association is evident for only the four problems reported in Table 13.2. However, simply having experienced a problem is associated in several cases with perceiving the victimization in more serious terms. These relationships are reported in Table 13.3.

TABLE 13.1

Respondents Indicating Problems Experienced by Level of Perceived Seriousness

	Percent Experiencing Problem	Percent Who Experienced Problem and Regard It as	
		Serious	Not Serious
Inconvenience			
Unnecessary trips	37	69	31
Lost time	70	76	24
Lost pay	42	82	18
Long wait	66	73	27
Difficulties with location and getting there			
Transportation	10	59	41
Parking	28	57	43
Cost of transportation and parking	76	38	62
Finding correct location	22	44	56
Finding out what to do	20	52	47
Waiting conditions	35	63	37
Exposed to threatening persons	17	81	19
Personal difficulties			
Need for child care	14	68	32
Property kept as evidence	22	57	43

Source: Compiled by the authors.

TABLE 13.2

Respondents Considering Experienced Problem as Serious by Perceived Seriousness of Victimization
(in percent)

Problem Experienced and Considered Serious	Seriousness of Victimization		
	Very Serious	Serious	Not Too Serious
Lost time	79	73	64
Difficulty getting transportation	85	25	0
Difficulty finding parking	68	53	0
Waiting conditions	76	55	33

Source: Compiled by the authors.

TABLE 13.3

Respondents Experiencing Problems by Perceived
Seriousness of Victimization
(in percent)

Experienced Problem	Seriousness of Victimization		
	Very Serious	Serious	Not Too Serious
Lost pay	47	41	33
Long wait	70	68	50
Property kept as evidence	31	19	15
Difficulty getting transportation	13	9	0
Cost of transportation and parking	80	77	50
Threatening persons	22	14	11

Source: Compiled by the authors.

In spite of the fact that some associations exist between experiencing problems and perceiving the victimization in more serious terms, the strength of these associations (as measured by gamma) is minimal. Thus, we can conclude that the respondent's perception of the seriousness of the victimization is not related to the experiencing of problems within the criminal justice system.

Offense

Examination of the relationship of type of offense either to experienced problems or to their perceived level of seriousness reveals virtually no association. While there is some tendency of respondents to view personal offenses as more serious than property offenses, with victims taking this view to a greater extent than witnesses (see Table 13.4), whatever assocations exist between perceived seriousness of the victimization and experienced problems do not carry over to the type of offense.

Postponements

It is only logical that the experiencing of problems would increase among those respondents who also experienced multiple postponements. This is particularly true of the types of problems

generally classified as inconveniences (see Table 13.5). Those who
had their case postponed did indeed make more unnecessary trips
(28 to 75 percent), had more long waits (66 to 77 percent), and lost
more time (70 to 77 percent) and income (37 to 59 percent). While
there was variation in the extent to which these problems were regarded as serious, in all cases almost 80 percent or more of those
experiencing two or more postponements regarded this problem as
serious or very serious. From 60 to 76 percent of those with no
postponements held this view.

TABLE 13.4

Perceived Seriousness of the Victimization
by Type of Offense
(in percent)

	Personal	Serious Property	Offense Less Serious Property	Other
All respondents				
Very serious	59	41	29	56
Serious	34	48	65	33
Not too serious	7	11	6	11
Victims				
Very serious	63	47	23	67
Serious	30	41	69	33
Not too serious	7	12	8	0
Witnesses				
Very serious	55	25	50	40
Serious	39	65	50	40
Not too serious	6	10	0	20

Source: Compiled by the authors.

Measures of the strength of the association used to test these
relationships revealed only one strong association, that between
postponements and making unnecessary trips (see Table 13.6).
Such a finding is so expected that it hardly deserves mention: however, it is important that of the various control factors examined,
this is the single relationship which is this strong. The importance
of this finding is that the effect of experiencing problems on future

intentions of reporting, which is examined below, cannot be explained away as occurring only among those who perceive their victimization to be more serious, those who suffer a particular type of offense, or those whose cases are adjourned frequently. Experiencing difficulties within the criminal justice system occurs across the board among victims and witnesses with all levels of victimization and offense.

TABLE 13.5

Experienced Problems with Level of Seriousness
by Number of Postponements

	Number of Postponements			Percent Serious			Percent Not Serious		
	0	1	2 or More	0	1	2 or More	0	1	2 or More
Unnecessary trips	28	36	75	60	69	79	40	31	21
Long wait	66	69	77	76	68	82	24	32	18
Lost time	70	75	77	71	67	88	29	33	12
Lost pay	37	44	59	73	75	88	27	25	12

Source: Compiled by the authors.

TABLE 13.6

Experiencing Unnecessary Trips by Postponement
(in percent)

Experienced Unnecessary Trips	Number of Postponements		
	0	1	2 or More
Yes, serious	17	25	59
Yes, not serious	11	11	16
No	72	64	25

$\gamma = -.548$
Source: Compiled by the authors.

Assessment of Criminal Justice Personnel

While the literature would suggest that many persons in the population distrust or are dissatisfied with the performance of criminal justice personnel (Johnson and Gregory 1971; Jacob 1970; Hahn 1971; Block 1970), when one examines the viewpoints of cooperating victims and witnesses this is not as clearly evident. As Table 13.7 indicates, between 60 and 77 percent of the respondents in this study assess the performance of these officials as good or excellent. The assessment made, however, is associated with the experiencing of certain problems. Whether they are literally regarded as responsible or not, both the district attorneys and judges are thought to expend less effort by a greater proportion of victims and witnesses who experience difficulties with the system. Table 13.8 reveals that the respondents evaluating district attorney effort as "excellent" decreases from 50 percent or more for those who do not experience the problem to 31 percent or less among those who regard their problem as serious.

TABLE 13.7

Assessment of District Attorney's and
Judge's Performance
(in percent)

	Assessment of Performance				
	Excellent	Good	Fair	Poor	No Opinion
District attorney effectiveness	39	31	15	8	7
District attorney effort	45	32	12	6	4
Judge effort	31	31	14	7	17
Judge fairness	34	26	13	8	19

Source: Compiled by the authors.

The strongest association between problems experienced and assessment of judge effort exists in relation to finding out what one is supposed to do. This relationship, while not as strong as the similar one for district attorney effort (gamma = -.264), is nevertheless evident.

TABLE 13.8

Assessment of District Attorney Effort
by Experienced Problems
(in percent)

Problems	Assessment of District Attorney Effort			
	Excellent	Good	Fair	Poor
Babysitting[a]				
Yes, serious	15	35	35	15
Yes, not serious	67	22	11	0
No	50	35	10	5
What supposed to do[b]				
Yes, serious	26	13	39	22
Yes, not serious	45	35	20	0
No	50	37	8	5
Waiting conditions[c]				
Yes, serious	31	33	23	13
Yes, not serious	42	35	15	8
No	54	34	8	4

[a] $\gamma = -.403$
[b] $\gamma = -.394$
[c] $\gamma = -.355$
Source: Compiled by the authors.

While several problems are strongly associated with the perception of official's effort, there are no significant associations with
assessment of judge fairness and only one factor is associated even
moderately with the assessment of district attorney effectiveness.
This is whether or not the respondent had a long wait (see Table
13.9). The increase in the percentage of respondents who assess
the district attorney's effectiveness less favorably is clearly evident here.

Relationships of Experiencing Problems and
Assessment of Officials with Intentions
of Future Reporting

The respondents in this study were asked about their intentions
of reporting any future violent personal or nonviolent property crime
victimizations. As a group, these respondents intend to be remarkably

cooperative, especially in view of the reporting data available from victimization surveys.

TABLE 13.9

Assessment of District Attorney Effectiveness
by Experiencing a Long Wait
(in percent)

Assessment of District Attorney Effectiveness	Yes, Serious	Yes, Not Serious	No
Excellent	31	60	49
Good	34	23	38
Fair	22	14	6
Poor	13	3	6

$\gamma = -.323$.
Source: Compiled by the authors.

As Table 13.10 reveals, about three-fourths of the respondents indicate they are extremely likely to report future crime. When one examines this finding more closely, however, a somewhat less optimistic picture emerges. While the data are not completely consistent, there is an association between the experiencing of problems, especially when they are regarded as serious, and a less-favorable assessment of officials in the system which leads to a lessened intention of reporting. Table 13.11 reports these findings for those problems and assessments in which the likelihood of reporting decreases.

TABLE 13.10

Expectation of Reporting Crime in the Future
(in percent)

	Extremely Likely	Likely	Not Likely	No Opinion
Violent crime	77.6	16.8	5.8	
Property crime	72.9	22.4	3.7	1.0

Source: Compiled by the authors.

TABLE 13.11

Expectation of Future Crime Reporting by Experienced
Problems and Assessment of Officials
(in percent)

Experienced Problems and Assessment of Officials	Violent Crime Extremely Likely	Violent Crime Not Too Likely	Property Crime Extremely Likely	Property Crime Not Too Likely
Inconvenience problems				
Unnecessary trips				
No	78	4	79	2
Yes, not serious	84	4	71	4
Yes, serious	73	5	62	9
Long wait				
No	80	0	75	2
Yes, not serious	87	8	80	3
Yes, serious	72	7	71	6
Lost time				
No	81	6	71	2
Yes, not serious	76	3	77	6
Yes, serious	76	4	74	4
Time waiting				
0–60 minutes	83	3	74	3
61–120 minutes	79	4	83	0
121+ minutes	70	7	65	6
Difficulties with location and getting there				
Transportation				
No	80	4	75	3
Yes, not serious	44	11	67	11
Yes, serious	69	15	62	8
Finding correct location				
No	76	5	75	4
Yes, not serious	88	4	69	4
Yes, serious	75	5	63	0
Personal difficulties				
Need for child care				
No	79	5	73	4
Yes, not serious	80	0	80	0
Yes, serious	67	5	71	5
Property kept as evidence				
No	81	4	76	4
Yes, not serious	94	0	88	0
Yes, serious	67	5	67	0
District attorney effort				
Excellent	84	1	80	1
Good	72	10	65	6
Fair	73	8	76	8
Poor	62	0	77	8
District attorney effectiveness				
Excellent	80	2	78	1
Good	82	4	71	2
Fair	64	13	58	16
Poor	67	6	83	6

Source: Compiled by the authors.

217

Not only does the percentage of respondents who say they will be extremely likely to report decrease, but the number who say they are not too likely to report increases in many instances. In other words, the respondents do not just decrease their intentions from "extremely likely" to "likely," they actually indicate they are "not too likely" to report.

CONCLUSIONS AND IMPLICATIONS

The problems victims and witnesses experience because they must come to court to testify are associated with both their assessment of personnel in the system (district attorneys and judges) and their stated intentions of future cooperation. Whether these relationships exist in a linear pattern or in triangular form is difficult to determine (see Figure 13.1).

FIGURE 13.1

Victim-Witness Relationships to the Court System

Source: Compiled by the authors.

For these respondents the experiencing of problems is prior in a time-order to their being asked to make assessments or indicate intentions. While experiencing some problems is associated with a lesser assessment of officials' effort or effectiveness and the latter is associated, in turn, with decreased intention to cooperate in the future, the data are of such a nature that no firm conclusions regarding a "causal" pattern can be drawn. Nevertheless, the final result with which the criminal justice system and the public is interested--that is, encouraging cooperation and the reporting of crime--is affected by the experiences victims and witnesses have in the system.

While this group of respondents generally intend to cooperate in the future, 73 to 78 percent indicating they would be extremely likely to report, any decline in future reporting tendencies by those who are now reporters has important ramifications.

First of all, there seems to be a tendency for some persons to be victimized and revictimized. Although this finding is not directly relevant to the issues examined in this chapter, approximately one-fourth of the respondents in this study report that they had been additionally victimized within the preceding year. In other words, current victims are somewhat more likely to be future victims and they are the individuals who should be reporting other crimes. If a certain portion of these individuals do not report other victimizations, they are simply adding to the already existing group of nonreporters.

In the second place, if this pattern has operated in the past, the present lack of cooperation by at least half of the victimized population possibly may be attributed to the experiences of previous victims. There may have been a gradual eroding away of cooperation because of difficulties reporting victims had in the past within the criminal justice system. If this is the case, then it is especially important that the cycle be broken, that new factors be introduced to alleviate the kinds of problems victims experience. In recent years there has been a proliferation of victim assistance programs developed to deal with these issues. This is an important development because if the cycle continues and there is consistently a small group of reporters who determine not to report in the future, will anyone be left to testify?

REFERENCES

Andrew, C. J.
   1964   The reluctant witness for the prosecution. Journal of Criminal Law, Criminology and Police Science 55 (March): 1-15.

Ash, M.
   1972   On witnesses: a radical critique of criminal court procedures. Notre Dame Lawyer 48 (December): 386-425.

   1973   Court delay, crime control, and neglect of the interests of witnesses. Reducing Court Delay. Washington, D.C.: U.S. Department of Justice, Law Enforcement Assistance Administration, pp. 1-34.

Biderman, A. D., L. A. Johnson, J. McIntyre, and A. W. Weis
   1967   Report on a Pilot Study in the District of Columbia on Victimization and Attitudes Toward Law Enforcement: Field Surveys I, Washington, D.C.: U.S. Government Printing Office, p. 146.

Block, R. L.
1970   Police action, support for police and support for civil
        liberties. Paper delivered at the American Sociological
        Association Meetings (September).

Bodemer, O. A.
1970   The expert witness hassle. American Psychologist 25
        (September): 882.

Brooks, J.
1975   How well are criminal injury compensation programs
        performing? Crime and Delinquency 21 (January): 50-56.

Doerner, W., R. D. Knudten, A. C. Meade, and M. S. Knudten
1976   Correspondence between crime victim needs and available
        public services. The Social Services Review 50 (September): 482-90.

Edelhertz, H., and G. Geis
1974   Public Compensation to Victims of Crime. New York:
        Praeger.

Ennis, P.
1967a   Crimes, victims and the police. Transaction 4 (June):
        36-44.

1967b   Criminal Victimization in the United States: A Report of
        a National Survey: Field Surveys II of the President's
        Commission on Law Enforcement and the Administration
        of Justice. Washington, D.C.

Floyd, G.
1972   Victim compensation: a comparative study." Trial 8
        (1972): 14.

Glaser, D.
1970   Victim survey research: theoretical implications. In
        Criminal Behavior and Social Systems, ed. A. I. Guenther.
        Chicago: Rand McNally, pp. 136-48.

Hahn, H.
1971   Ghetto assessment of police protection and authority.
        Law and Society Review 6:183.

von Hentig, H.
1948   The Criminal and His Victim, Studies in the Sociology of
       Crime. New Haven, Conn.: Yale University Press,
       Chapter 12.

Jacob, B. R.
1970   Reparation or restitution by the criminal offender to his
       victim. Journal of Criminal Law, Criminology and Police
       Science 61 (June): 154.

Johnson, D., and R. J. Gregory
1971   Police-community relations in the United States: a re-
       view of recent literature and projects. Journal of Criminal
       Law, Criminology and Police Science 62: 94-103.

Knudten, M. S.
1974   Influences on prosecutors' decisions. Ph.D. dissertation,
       University of Chicago, Department of Sociology.

1977   The victims' role in crime prevention. In Theory and
       Practice of Criminal Justice, ed. R. Rich. Washington,
       D.C.: University Press of America.

Knudten, R. D.
1968   Criminological Controversies. New York: Appleton-
       Century-Crofts, pp. 307-33.

1976   The Victim in the administration of criminal justice:
       problems and perceptions. In Criminal Justice and the
       Victim, ed. Wm. F. McDonald. Beverly Hills: Sage
       Publications, pp. 115-46.

Lamborn, L.
1970   Remedies for victims of crime. Southern California Law
       Review 43 (1970): 22-53.

Mansfield, M.
1974   Justice for the victims of crime. Case and Comment 77
       (March-April): 22.

Meade, A. C., M. S. Knudten, W. G. Doerner, and R. D. Knudten
1976   Discovery of a forgotten party: trends in American victim
       compensation legislation. Victimology: An International
       Journal 1 (Fall): 421-33.

Morris, A.
  1966   What about the victims of crime? Correctional Research,
          United Prison Association of Massachusetts, Bulletin
          No. 16.

National Criminal Justice Information and Statistics Service (NCJISS)
  1974a   Crime in Eight American Cities. Washington, D.C.: U.S.
          Department of Justice.

  1974b   Crime in the Nation's Five Largest Cities. Washington,
          D.C.: U.S. Department of Justice.

  1974c   Crimes and Victims: A Report of the Dayton-San Jose
          Pilot Survey of Victimization. Washington, D.C.: U.S.
          Department of Justice.

  1976a   Crime in the Nation's Five Largest Cities: A Comparison
          of 1972 and 1974 Findings. Washington, D.C.: U.S.
          Department of Justice.

  1976b   Crime Victimization Surveys in Eight American Cities:
          A Comparison of 1971/72 and 1974/75 Findings. Wash-
          ington, D.C.: U.S. Department of Justice.

Schafer, S.
  1968   The Victim and His Criminal. New York: Random House.

  1970   Compensation and Restitution to Victims of Crime.
          Montclair, N.J.: Patterson Smith.

  1975   The proper role of a victim-compensation system. Crime
          and Delinquency 21 (January): 45-49.

Umano, M.
  1972   Victims of Crime. Washington, D.C.: U.S. Government
          Printing Office.

14

RAPE VICTIMOLOGY: PAST, PRESENT, AND FUTURE RESEARCH

Lynda Lytle Holmstrom
Ann Wolbert Burgess

The scholarly and professional literature on sexual offenses, including rape, is voluminous. But traditionally it has overlooked the victim. When rape victims were even considered, they were conceptualized only in certain limited ways. This chapter reviews some of the main ways victims have been portrayed in criminology, victimology, and sociology; looks at some of the newer themes that are emerging; and makes suggestions for future research.

THE TRADITIONAL VIEW

One of the most pervasive ways of analyzing rape victims in the criminological and sociological literature has been through use of the concept of victim precipitation or victim participation.[1] This conceptualization was promoted not only for rape victims but also for victims of crime in general by people such as von Hentig, Mendelsohn, Wolfgang, and Schafer who were important figures in the development and expansion of the field of victimology.

Von Hentig (1940: 303) suggested that the victim is one of the causes of a crime. We can often see, von Hentig says, "a real mutuality in the connexion of perpetrator and victim, killer and killed, duper and dupe." "In a sense the victim shapes and moulds the criminal. . . . To know one we must be acquainted with the

This chapter is a revised and abridged version of a paper presented at the American Association for the Advancement of Science Annual Meeting, session on "Crime: What We Know and What We Need to Know." Boston, February 23, 1976.

complementary partner" (von Hentig 1948: 384-85). He thus suggests that the relationship between perpetrator and victim may be more complicated than our criminal law with its facile and definite classifications would indicate. The complexity that does exist is expressed, he suggests, in the title of Werfel's novel Der Ermordete ist Schuld (The Murdered One is Guilty). Mendelsohn (1963: 239-41) wrote of the bio-psycho-social personality of the accused and "parallelly" the personality of victims. He was interested in various types of crimes, including crimes passionnels. He began to elaborate the doctrine of victimology while preparing for the trial of Stephan Codreanu who, had it not been for "the perversity of his former wife," would never have been guilty of murdering her and her lover. Wolfgang (1958: 252) has utilized the concept of victim-precipitation in his well-known studies of criminal homicide, applying it to those cases in which the "role of the victim is characterized by his having been the first in the homicide drama to use physical force directed against his subsequent slayer." An example is the husband who attacked his wife with a milk bottle, a brick, and a piece of concrete block while she was making breakfast and, having a butcherknife in her hand, she in turn stabbed him. And Schafer, in more recent years, writes of the functional responsibility of and for the victim. In his volume The Victim and His Criminal Schafer (1968: 152) concludes: "It is far from true that all crimes 'happen' to be committed; often the victim's negligence, precipitative action, or provocation contributes to the genesis or performance of a crime."

Amir (1967; 1971),who has carried out some of the most frequently discussed research on rape, has continued to utilize the concept of victim precipitation.[2] Amir has departed, however, from Wolfgang's definition of the concept. Wolfgang talks of the behavior of the victim, whereas Amir talks of the offender's interpretation of the behavior of the victim. Because Amir's recent book, Patterns in Forcible Rape (1971: 260-61) is so often mentioned both in scholarly and popular circles, it is worth quoting him here at some length:

> Theoretically, victim precipitation of rape means that in a particular situation the behavior of the victim is interpreted by the offender either as a direct invitation for sexual relations or as a sign that she will be available for sexual contact if he will persist in demanding it. . . .
> Victim behavior consists of acts of commission (e.g., she agreed to drink or ride with a stranger) and omission (e.g., she failed to react strongly enough to sexual suggestions and overtures). . . .
> (Emphasis added.)

Amir's revision of the concept has important ramifications: It means that although he indicates he is studying victims, he is in fact using offenders' perceptions to study victims. He has had his critics in this regard.[3] Weis and Borges (1973: 80), commenting on the above-quoted pages of Amir, state: "A leading study on forcible rape, after initially setting up distinct analytical categories for victim-precipitated rape, collapses all these categories so that the only ingredient necessary for constituting a victim-precipitated rape is the offender's imagination."

CONTEMPORARY VIEW

In the last few years, researchers have begun to reconceptualize rape. They have questioned assumptions in the rape literature and as a result new perspectives are beginning to emerge. Rather than continue to do what Ryan (1971) calls "blaming the victim," they are beginning to look at the connection between social processes and victims, the experience of the victim, and the institutional response to victims. In addition, there is a continuing interest in rapists, but sometimes now with a focus on aspects that have particular relevance for victims. These topics are ones that a focus on victim precipitation tends to obscure.[4]

Societal Processes: The Creation and Function of Victims

In looking at social processes as related to victims, recent analysts have dealt with at least two main issues: How do certain categories of people get transformed into "legitimate" victims-- people who are considered fair game--and what is the function for the society of having such victims.[5]

Weis and Borges (1973: 72) analyze "the societal creation of 'legitimate' victims." They use the concept of victimization to refer to societal processes that include preparation of the victim for the crime, the victim's experience during the crime, and the responses that will be encountered as the aftermath of the crime. "If these processes of victimization are successful with regard to rape, the raped woman is a 'legitimate' or 'safe' victim who will not be dangerous to the rapist since she is unable to relate her experience to others or to effectively direct blame and accusation against the person who raped her."

They state, furthermore, that victims and offenders are socialized for their respective roles. Women are molded into victims by being trained to think of themselves as passive, weak, and dependent. Likewise, men are molded into being offenders by being trained to think they must appear strong, active, and independent and to believe that manliness is associated with aggression, including sexual aggression.

What is the function of having women singled out as legitimate victims ? Increasingly analysts are coming to the conclusion that defining women as appropriate victims for rape serves the function of social control: It keeps women "in their place" (Weis and Borges 1973: 94; Reynolds 1974; Russell 1973: 15). Rape--and, equally, important, the fear of rape--controls women since it limits their ability to move about freely and makes it difficult for them to participate in many activities on an equal footing with men. It thus helps keep them in a subordinate position.

Reynolds (1974: 63-65) has emphasized the theme of rape as social control. She argues that in practice, laws against rape act "primarily to punish those men who do not rape appropriately." The question then is what kind of woman can be appropriately raped. She concludes that a plausible thesis is that "rape is viewed as a legitimate punishment for women who give the appearance of violating traditional female role expectations." Under these conditions, the woman can be raped and the man who rapes her will be supported by the cultural values.[6]

The Victim's Experience of Rape

The experience of the victim has recently gained the attention of researchers. What is her view of rape, what does she experience, what happens to her after the rape? In the past this aspect has been obscured by too exclusive a focus on victim-precipitation. If the researcher views the victim as to blame, then she deserved what she got and there is less motivation to understand how she perceives the event.

The victim's experience has been studied either by obtaining information from the victims themselves and/or studying those people and institutions with whom the victim comes into contact. Holmstrom and Burgess (1973, 1975, 1976, and forthcoming) combined both approaches in their interdisciplinary research. They interviewed rape victims at the time of admission to the emergency ward and also did follow-up interviews to obtain data on the subjective experiences of victims during the attack and its aftermath. To complement these data they used participant-observation with regard to police, hospital, and court to obtain firsthand data on the institutional response to rape victims. Russell (1975: 14) has also interviewed victims in depth and has published a set of these case

histories in an attempt "to educate people about rape from the victim's perspective." Bart (1975: 36) read and analyzed questionnaire
accounts of 1,070 women who had been raped. Her report includes
information on the consequences of rape, including the subsequent
loss of trust in male-female relationships, negative effect on sexuality, hostility to men, fear of men, and loss of self-respect. In conclusion she states that her most important finding is "the seriousness of the effect of the rape." These studies document the enormity
of the victim's suffering not only during the attack but afterward
during encounters with family, friends, and officials.[7]

Researchers interested in the victim's experience increasingly
have come to conceptualize rape as an act of violence and power
rather than primarily a sexual act. They have made statements
such as the following:[8] "It became clear in our conversations with
rape victims, that from their point of view, rape is an act initiated
by the assailant, and it is not primarily a sexual act, but an act of
violence" (Burgess and Holmstrom, 1974b: 4). "Rape is a power
trip--an act of aggression and an act of contempt--and in most cases
is only secondarily sexual" (Schwendinger and Schwendinger 1974:
20). "Psychiatrists say a gun is a substitute phallus. After reading
and analyzing the stories of these 1,070 women who have been raped,
I find the reverse to be true. A PHALLUS IS A SUBSTITUTE GUN.
Rape is a power trip, not a passion trip" (Bart 1975: 2).[9]

The Institutional Response to Victims

Researchers also are increasingly aware of the importance
of the institutional response to rape victims. Chappell (1975: 93)
states, for example, that "probably no factor is more crucial to the
outcome of rape proceedings than the way the victim is treated by
the police." He suggests, furthermore, that attitudes toward victims are changing in criminal justice agencies (1976: 18). Holmstrom and Burgess (1973 and forthcoming)--as previously men-
tioned--observed police, medical personnel, district attorneys,
and defense lawyers as they interacted with rape victims; they have
made policy recommendations for such professionals based on that
data. Sanders (1976 and forthcoming) has been studying police investigations of rape; he accompanied detectives during their investigations, thus observing all phases of the investigation process.
Williams (1976) has been studying the problems of prosecution in
sexual assault cases by comparing the conviction rates for five
major types of crimes: sexual assaults, murder and manslaughter,
aggravated assault, robbery, and burglary. Battelle Law and
Justice Study Center (1977), under Chappell's direction, has carried

out a national survey of the responses of police to rape. And, in
collaboration with the National Legal Data Center, they have done a
similar survey of prosecutors (1977). These studies looked at such
things as factors involved in decision making and recent innovations
in handling rape cases (for example, special training programs in
the handling of rape). Zonderman (1975) has approached the response
to victims from a different angle. Her study of volunteer counselors
shows how difficult it can be for people to work with rape victims.
Some of the volunteers developed several symptoms that rape victims usually develop. A small minority of the volunteers developed
five to seven such symptoms, and Zonderman called this phenomenon
the "rape counselor syndrome." Clark (1976) has studied the response of the Canadian criminal justice system to rape victims.

Summary

Traditionally, the criminological and sociological literature
looked at rape victims from the point of view of victim precipitation.
In recent years, researchers instead have been looking at the societal processes such as the creation and function of victims, the
victim's experience of the rape and its aftermath, and the institutional response to rape victims.

SUGGESTIONS FOR FUTURE RESEARCH

Victim Provocation or Victim Outrage:
the Social Definition of Rape

There is an increasing amount of information available on both
the victim's experience and the rapist's experience--that is, information from in-depth studies that look at both the victim's and
the rapist's perceptions. If we wish to understand the interaction
of people in different roles, then our theories should incorporate
the perceptions of both of the actors. Thus, it would seem useful
for researchers to integrate more fully than they have these two
bodies of knowledge. In some cases, we may find a convergence of
perceptions. For example, data from both victims and rapists suggest that rape is an act of violence--that victims experience it as
violence and that rapists (or at least certain types of rapists) intend
it as such. In other areas we may find a divergence of perceptions.
For example, the offender may be honestly expressing his perception of the interaction when he says, "She really was asking for it,"
just as the victim may be honestly expressing her perception and

outrage when she says, "I certainly wasn't looking to get raped."
There is, after all, a tremendous amount of ambiguity in human
relations and, therefore, numerous opportunities for competing
definitions of those relations.

A related idea is the notion of doing research more generally
on the social definition of rape. Rather than taking the definition of
rape as a given, it would seem worthwhile to do research on how
various groups of people in the population (not just victims and
rapists) define rape. The work of Klemmack and Klemmack (1976:
135-47) shows us, for example, that what is clearly a rape to one
person is not necessarily seen as a rape by another person. Research by Russell (1975: 71-81) and Gelles (1977) raises the issue
of marital rape. If a husband forces sexual acts upon his wife
against her will, is it rape? Will it be perceived as rape?

False Accusation

The issue of false accusation by women (through either lying
or fantasizing) has had such a dominant place in the literature and
has such an impact in the institutions that deal with rape that perhaps it would be worthwhile to confront it directly: that is, by doing
research on cases of false accusation. There are, of course,
enormous difficulties in doing this research--the main problem
being who gets to define what is and is not a false accusation. (See
the previous section on the social definition of rape.) Nevertheless,
such a study might make several contributions. First, it would increase our understanding of what happens in such cases (why do
women do it, what is their motivation, how far do such cases get in
the system, do they in fact lead to the conviction of the person accused). Second, it might put these cases into perspective and
perhaps in the long run might remove the disproportionate amount
of attention given to them.

Function of "Blaming the Victim": Social Control

Researchers have begun to look at the function of rape and to
see it in terms of social control. Researchers also might find it
useful to analyze the function of blaming the victim. It would seem
that here too the function is that of social control. Ryan (1971: 5)
has noted, critically, that "the generic process of Blaming the Victim is applied to almost every American problem." Giving an example of how the ideology works in the economic sphere, he states
(1971: 28) that "if one comes to believe that the culture of poverty

produces persons <u>fated</u> to be poor, who can find any fault with our
corporation-dominated economy?" Paraphrasing Ryan, one might
say, if one comes to believe that rape is the woman's fault, then
who can find any fault with our male-dominated society? The ideology of blaming-the-victim in the academic literature on rape may
have the function of keeping women in their place, too.

The Collective Experience of Victims

Rape victims' collective experience and revolt merit further
study. One particularly interesting aspect of rape victims is that
recently--in contrast to victims of most types of crimes--they have
organized to fight back on a group level. Victims and potential
victims have joined together to declare a "war against rape." This
war started in connection with the broader women's movement and
began with such activities as consciousness-raising sessions, the
1971 Speak Out On Rape, and small protest groups that formed
throughout the country (Largen 1976: 69). This war was not pre-
dicted--least of all by men. As Brownmiller (1975: 397), speaking
of the antirape movement, notes:

> The wonder of all this female activity, decen-
> tralized grass-roots organizations and programs
> that sprung up independently in places like
> Seattle, Indianapolis, Ann Arbor, Toronto, and
> Boulder, Colorado, is that none of it had been
> predicted, encouraged, or faintly suggested by
> men anywhere in their stern rules of caution,
> their friendly advice, their fatherly solicitude
> in more than five thousand years of written
> history. That women should <u>organize</u> to combat
> rape was a women's movement invention.

Studies of rape victims' experiences so far primarily have looked at
victims who are isolated from each other and have not yet looked as
closely at victims who have bonded together to form an organized
group. This collective phenomenon deserves further study, and an
analysis of it could well make important contributions both to
criminology and the sociology of social movements.

Rape Prevention

Rape prevention is a topic of great discussion today, especially
among those concerned with victims. Suggestions currently being

made for prevention run a wide gamut. Some focus on the woman:
she should be more careful and take precautions to avoid an attack,
if attacked she should fight back, if attacked she should not fight
back, she should engage in activities that will expose her to more
risk (for example, walk alone on the streets) in order to change the
image of women in the society, she should organize with other women
to fight rape collectively. Some suggestions focus on doing things
either to and/or for the offender: increased efforts should be made
to treat rapists or to convict rapists. And, as noted in a separate
section, some suggestions focus on changing the entire socioeconomic
structure of the society. It would seem worthwhile to analyze these
proposals for rape prevention from at least three points of view.
First, increased attention should be given to the distinction between
preventing rape of particular individual women and preventing rape
in general. It is quite possible that efforts by individual women do
prevent their own rape, but not rape in general: the rapist simply
finds another victim. Second, what is effective? What, if anything,
does prevent rape either at the individual level or in general? Examples of recent research at the individual level include a study
which, among other things, asked rapists what would deter them
(S. Brodsky 1976: 75-90) and a study asking rapists about their
modus operandi and their likely response to a variety of rape prevention methods (Chappell and James 1976). Other research at the
individual level focuses on victims: comparing victims of rape
versus attempted rape, or resisters versus nonresisters (Queen's
Bench Foundation 1976; Bart 1976; McIntyre 1977). Third, where
is the burden for prevention being placed? Are women expected to
be responsible for rape prevention, and if so, at what social and
psychological cost? For example, are the measures that many
suggest women should take so confining that they are victimized not
only by rape, but by rape prevention?

Rape as Defective or as Normal Behavior

A controversy exists as to whether rape is more usefully
viewed as "defective" or "normal" behavior. This controversy
exists both on the victim's side and on the rapist's side. There are
those who say that certain women are victim-prone (often because
of a personality defect) and others who say that women as a group
in our society are socialized into becoming easy victims. A recent
relevant study is that by Javorek and Lyon (1976). California
Psychological Inventories for attempted and completed rape victims
were factor analyzed. They found victims of completed rapes to be
virtually indistinguishable from three comparison groups, but victims of attempted rapes were dramatically different. With regard

to rapists, there are those who see the rapist's behavior as an
aberration (often the result of a personality defect) and those who
say that men as a group in our society are socialized into becoming
rapists and potential rapists. One study relevant to the issue of
whether there are cultural supports for the rapist is Smith's (1976)
work on pornography. His content analysis of 428 "adults only"
fiction paperbacks showed that in this literature rape is portrayed
as an almost normal part of male-female sex relations and both
attackers and victims are described as usually profiting from the
encounter. Other relevant research is Curtis's (1974; 1975) work
utilizing cultural variables to interpret forcible rape by American
blacks. He notes (1974: 35-37) critically that the psychiatric
literature describes criminal violence using the language of pathology and he asks "whether there are any absolute standards by which
to measure normalcy." The controversy over whether rape is
deviant versus normative behavior would seem to lend itself to future research for various reasons, one being that the answer to
this question has implications for the approach one might take for
rape prevention.

Comparative Research: Homosexual Rape of Males

     Most of the current theoretical and empirical work on rape
has dealt with male assailants and female victims. It would seem
useful to do systematic comparative work on male assailants and
male victims. Some similarities have been reported. Schwendinger
and Schwendinger (1974: 25) who emphasize power and dominance
as factors in the rape of women, note that Davis' (1968: 15) work
suggests that these also appear in the homosexual rape of men in
prisons. "It appears that need for sexual release is not the primary
motive of a sexual aggressor. . . . A primary goal of the sexual
aggressor, it is clear, is the conquest and degradation of his victim." Burgess and Holmstrom (1974b: 257-68) report similarities
in the psychological reactions of female and male victims of rape.
The frequent occurrence of rape in the prison setting has been mentioned by several authors. Drapkin (1976), for example, reviewed
numerous books on prison life written by inmates, as well as reports written by special commissions; one of the common themes in
these works is that of sexual abuse, including the violation of young
newcomers. It would seem useful to systematically explore both
similarities and differences between the rape of females and of
males, whether in prison or not. Not only would study of the male
homosexual rape be of interest in and of itself, but incorporation
of the male case into our thinking might force us to alter some of
our theoretical interpretations of rape.

Comparative Research: The Socio-political-
economic Context

Controversy exists as to whether the victimization of women—-
including their victimization through rape--varies depending upon
whether the society is capitalist or socialist. One of the strongest
statements in this regard is by Schwendinger and Schwendinger
(1974: 25):

> Crimes of violence as we know them today have
> been produced by capitalism; and the contradic-
> tions of capitalism will continue to feed the hatred
> and contempt of certain men toward women. To
> resolve the contradictions, and the expression in
> rape of the social psychological effects of these
> contradictions, is to change a class system of
> oppression in America today to a socialist polit-
> ical economy and a relatively crime-free to-
> morrow.

They state that their conclusion is not utopian. "Regarding nations
that are now socialist, comparisons between pre- and post-
revolutionary periods show enormous differences in the incidence
of 'organized crime' and 'crime in the streets' which include sexual
crimes" (1974: 25). It would seem worthwhile to test propositions
such as these empirically through comparative cross-national research. Heiple and Jankovic's (1976) analysis of Yugoslavian data
is a step in this direction.

NOTES

1. For discussion of the theme of victim participation in the
literature on child victims of sexual assault, see Gagnon (1965) and
Schultz (1975). For a summary of Japanese research on rape victims see Miyazawa (1976); considerable emphasis is placed on concepts of "culpability of the victim," "victimal receptivity," "victim
negligence," "less guilty versus not guilty victims," and "inviting
an attack."

2. In his study of several hundred forcible rapes in Philadelphia, he concludes that 19 percent were victim-precipitated.

3. For other important criticisms, both methodological and
theoretical, see Lotz (1975) and Reiss (1974).

4. For more popular literature in which writers have been
rethinking rape, see Griffin (1971), Greer (1975), and Brownmiller
(1975).

5. It should be emphasized that the term "legitimate victim" is used in this chapter to mean someone who social conventions define as legitimate to victimize; it is considered justifiable to victimize the person. One will also hear the term "legitimate victim" used--for example, by emergency-ward personnel--to mean the exact opposite; namely a victim who in their view was "really raped" and who, therefore, according to social conventions, has a legitimate complaint to make.

6. For another approach, much of which could be incorporated into an analysis of the social creation of victims, see Collins (1971: 7). He sees females as the subordinate class in a sexual stratification system. After presenting two propositions--that humans possess strong sexual and aggressive drives, and that males are physically dominant over females--he then argues that "the element of coercion is thus potentially present in every sexual encounter, and this shapes the fundamental features of the woman's role." However, variations in sexual stratification do occur. These, he argues, result from the forms of social organization affecting the use of force and the market positions of males and females.

7. There is also a new trend to focus on the victim's experience in the psychiatric literature on rape victims (Sutherland and Scherl 1970; Werner 1972; Burgess and Holmstrom 1974a, 1976a, 1976b; Notman and Nadelson 1976; Metzger 1976; C. Brodsky 1976; Hilberman 1976).

8. The data base for making these statements varies. They may cite data from victims, or rapists, or both. Some are not explicit in this regard.

9. In the 1970s clinicians and researchers studying rapists also talk of rape as violence inflicted by the assailant on the victim. Cohen et al.(1971: 311) note that "descriptively, the act of rape involves both an aggressive and a sexual component." Groth (1973) has stated that "rape is primarily an aggressive act, not a sexual one. It is a way to humiliate the victim. Sex is the way to express the aggression." Groth, Burgess, and Holmstrom (1977) have analyzed the power, anger,and sexual components in the motivation to rape.

REFERENCES

Amir, M.
  1967   Victim precipitated forcible rape. Journal of Criminal Law, Criminology and Police Science 58: 493-502.

  1971   Patterns in Forcible Rape. Chicago: University of Chicago Press.

Bart, P. B.
1975   Rape doesn't end with a kiss.   Unpublished manuscript,
        Department of Psychiatry, Abraham Lincoln School of
        Medicine, University of Illinois, Chicago. Published in
        abridged version in Viva, June 1975.

1976   Private communication.

Battelle Law and Justice Study Center (Duncan Chappell, Project
Director)
1977   Forcible Rape: A National Survey of the Response by
        Police (Police Volume I). Project Report, National In-
        stitute of Law Enforcement and Criminal Justice, Law
        Enforcement Assistance Administration, U.S. Depart-
        ment of Justice. Washington, D.C.: U.S. Government
        Printing Office.

Battelle Law and Justice Study Center and National Legal Data
Center (Duncan Chappell, Project Director)
1977   Forcible Rape: A National Survey of the Response by
        Prosecutors (Prosecutors' Volume I). Project Report,
        National Institute of Law Enforcement and Criminal Jus-
        tice, Law Enforcement Assistance Administration, U.S.
        Department of Justice. Washington, D.C.: U.S. Gov-
        ernment Printing Office.

Brodsky, C. M.
1976   Rape at work. In Sexual Assault: The Victim and the
        Rapist, ed. M. J. Walker and S. L. Brodsky. Lexington,
        Mass.: Lexington Books, D. C. Heath, pp. 35-51.

Brodsky, S. L.
1976   Prevention of rape: deterrence by the potential victim."
        In Sexual Assault: The Victim and the Rapist, ed. M. J.
        Walker and S. L. Brodsky. Lexington, Mass.: Lexington
        Books, D. C. Heath.

Brownmiller, S.
1975   Against Our Will: Men, Women and Rape. New York:
        Simon and Schuster.

Burgess, A. W., and L. L. Holmstrom
1974a   Rape trauma syndrome. American Journal of Psychiatry
        131 (September): 981-86.

1974b   Rape: Victims of Crisis. Bowie, Md.: Robert J. Brady.

1976a   Coping behavior of the rape victim. American Journal
        of Psychiatry 133 (April): 413-18.

1976b   Rape: its effect on task performance at varying stages in
        the life cycle. In Sexual Assault: The Victim and the
        Rapist, ed. M. J. Walker and S. L. Brodsky. Lexington,
        Mass.: Lexington Books, D. C. Heath, pp. 23-33.

Chappell, D.
1975   Forcible rape and the American system of criminal justice.
        In Violence and Criminal Justice, ed. D. Chappell and
        J. Monahan. Lexington, Mass.: Lexington Books, D. C.
        Heath.

1976   Forcible rape and the criminal justice system: surveying
        present practices and projecting future trends. In Sexual
        Assault: The Victim and the Rapist, ed. M. J. Walker
        and S. L. Brodsky. Lexington, Mass.: Lexington Books,
        D. C. Heath.

Chappell, D., and J. James
1976   Victim selection and apprehension from the rapist's per-
        spective: a preliminary investigation. Paper presented
        at the Second International Symposium on Victimology.

Clark, L.
1976   The treatment of rape and rape victims within the Canadian
        criminal justice system: failure, facts, and theory.
        Paper presented at the Conference, Research on Women:
        Current Projects and Future Directions.

Cohen, M. L., R. Garofalo, R. Boucher, and T. Seghorn
1971   The psychology of rapists. Seminars in Psychiatry 3
        (August): 307-27.

Collins, R.
1971   A conflict theory of sexual stratification. Social Prob-
        lems 19 (Summer): 3-21.

Curtis, L. A.
1974   Toward a cultural interpretation of forcible rape by Amer-
        ican blacks. Paper presented at the Eighth World So-
        ciology Congress.

1975   Violence, Race, and Culture. Lexington, Mass.: Lex-
        ington Books, D. C. Heath.

Davis, A. J.
  1968   Sexual assaults in the Philadelphia prison system and
          sheriff's vans. Trans-action (December): 8-16.

Drapkin, I.
  1976   The prison inmate as victim. Victimology 1 (Spring): 103.

Gagnon, J. H.
  1965   Female child victims of sex offenses. Social Problems
          13 (Fall): 176-92.

Gelles, R. J.
  1977   Power, sex, and violence: the case of marital rape.
          The Family Coordinator 26 (October): 339-47.

Greer, G.
  1975   Seduction is a four-letter word. In Rape Victimology, ed.
          L. G. Schultz. Springfield, Ill.: Charles C. Thomas.
          (First published in Playboy.)

Griffin, S.
  1971   Rape: the all-American crime. Ramparts 10 (Septem-
          ber): 26-35.

Groth, A. N.
  1973   Talk given to Central Massachusetts Family Planning
          Council, Inc. Worcester Chapter. Meeting held in
          Shrewsbury, Mass., June 29, 1973.

Groth, A. N., A. W. Burgess, and L. L. Holmstrom
  1977   Rape: power, anger, and sexuality. American Journal
          of Psychiatry 134 (November): 1239-43.

Heiple, P., and I. Jankovic
  1976   Rape in Yugoslavia. Paper presented at the American
          Sociological Association annual meeting.

von Hentig, H.
  1940 Remarks on the interaction of perpetrator and victim.
          Journal of Criminal Law and Criminology 31 (September-
          October): 303-09.

  1948   The Criminal and His Victim. New Haven, Conn.: Yale
          University Press.

Hilberman, E.
    1976   The Rape Victim. Washington, D.C.: American Psy-
            chiatric Association.

Holmstrom, L. L., and A. W. Burgess
    1973   Rape: the victim goes on trial. Paper read at the annual
            meeting of the American Sociological Association.

    1975   Rape: the victim and the criminal justice system. Inter-
            national Journal of Criminology and Penology 3: 101-10.

    1976   Delays in the criminal justice system: the impact on the
            rape victim. Paper presented at the Second International
            Symposium on Victimology.

    Forthcoming   The Victim of Rape: Institutional Reactions.
            New York: Wiley-Interscience.

Javorek, F. J., and L. Lyon
    1976   Personality characteristics which differentiate among
            victims of attempted rape, completed rape, and general
            populations of women: a multivariate approach. Paper
            presented at the Second International Symposium on
            Victimology. Abstracts: 93.

Klemmack, S. H., and D. L. Klemmack
    1976   The social definition of rape. In Sexual Assault: The
            Victim and the Rapist, ed. M. J. Walker and S. L.
            Brodsky. Lexington, Mass.: Lexington Books, D. C.
            Heath.

Largen, M. A.
    1976   History of women's movement in changing attitudes, laws,
            and treatment toward rape victims. In Sexual Assault:
            The Victim and the Rapist, ed. M. J. Walker and S. L.
            Brodsky. Lexington, Mass.: Lexington Books, D. C.
            Heath.

Lotz, R.
    1975   Review of Menachem Amir: patterns in forcible rape.
            Contemporary Sociology: A Journal of Reviews 4 (July):
            381-82.

McIntyre, J. J.
    1977   Private communication.

Mendelsohn, B.
  1963   The origin of the doctrine of victimology. Excerpta
          criminologica 3: 239-44.

Metzger, D.
  1976   It is always the woman who is raped. American Journal
          of Psychiatry 133 (April): 405-08.

Miyazawa, K.
  1976   Victimological studies of sexual crimes in Japan. Vic-
          timology 1 (Spring): 107-29.

Notman, M., and C. C. Nadelson
  1976   The rape victim: psychodynamic considerations. Amer-
          ican Journal of Psychiatry 133 (April): 408-13.

Queen's Bench Foundation
  1976   Rape: Prevention and Resistance. San Francisco:
          Queen's Bench.

Reiss, A. J., Jr.
  1974   Review of Menachem Amir: patterns in forcible rape.
          American Journal of Sociology 80 (November): 785-90.

Reynolds, J. M.
  1974   Rape as social control. Catalyst (Winter): 62-67.

Russell, D. E. H.
  1973   Rape and the masculine mystique. Paper presented at
          the annual meetings of the American Sociological Asso-
          ciation.

  1975   The Politics of Rape: The Victim's Perspective. New
          York: Stein and Day.

Ryan, W.
  1971   Blaming the Victim. New York: Random House.

Sanders, W. B.
  1976   Rape investigations. Paper presented at the American
          Sociological Association annual meeting.

  Forthcoming. Detective Work: A Study of Criminal Investiga-
          gations. New York: Free Press.

Schafer, S.
    1968   The Victim and His Criminal: A Study in Functional Re-
            sponsibility. New York: Random House.

Schultz, L. G.
    1975   The child as a sex victim: socio-legal perspectives. In
            Rape Victimology, ed. L. Schultz. Springfield, Ill.:
            Charles C. Thomas.

Schwendinger, J. R., and H. Schwendinger
    1974   Rape myths: in legal, theoretical, and everyday practice.
            Crime and Social Justice: A Journal of Radical Criminol-
            ogy 1 (Spring-Summer): 18-26.

Smith, D. D.
    1976   Sexual aggression in American pornography: the stereo-
            type of rape. Paper presented at the American Sociologi-
            cal Association annual meeting.

Sutherland, S., and D. J. Scherl
    1970   Patterns of response among victims of rape. American
            Journal of Orthopsychiatry 40 (April): 503-11.

Weis, K., and S. S. Borges
    1973   Victimology and rape: the case of the legitimate victim.
            Issues in Criminology 8 (Fall): 71-115.

Werner, A.
    1972   Rape: interruption of the therapeutic process by external
            stress. Psychotherapy: Theory, Research and Practice
            9 (Winter): 349-51.

Williams, K. M.
    1976   Sexual assaults and the law: the problem of prosecution.
            Paper presented at the American Sociological Association
            annual meeting.

Wolfgang, M. E.
    1958   Patterns in Criminal Homicide. Philadelphia: Univer-
            sity of Pennsylvania.

Zonderman, S. R.
    1975   Rape crisis counselors--stress factors and coping strate-
            gies. Unpublished manuscript based on Master's Thesis,
            School for Social Work, Smith College.

INTRODUCTION TO PART VII

Today, the U.S. criminal justice system is buffeted by strong winds of public discontent and in great turmoil concerning its purposes, objectives, and methods. Changes in crime-control policy are now being advocated which distinctively reflect a "hard-line" philosophy as far as societal response to the offender is concerned. There are calls for increased police effectiveness, in view of the fact that the majority of offenders who commit crimes against persons and property escape apprehension. There are efforts to reform the judiciary through the imposition of mandatory sentencing and the reduction or removal of the judges' discretionary powers by means of legislative fiat. Concomitantly, there is a drive to reduce the use of alternatives to incarceration, such as probation or the imposition of fines, in favor of prison sentences designed to lock more offenders away than ever before and for longer periods of time.

The impact of these efforts and changes has been to reverse a trend in criminal justice during which a greater selectivity and sophistication in the use of crime-control and correctional methods was advocated. This trend probably reached its zenith with the publication of the report of the National Advisory Commission on Criminal Justice Standards and Goals which stressed that the great powers of the criminal justice system be reserved for controlling those persons who seriously threaten the safety of others, and which viewed the criminal justice system as the agency of last resort for social problems and the correctional institution as the last resort of correctional problems. Since the publication of that report, many court systems in the United States have assumed a more standardized and punitive function, judicial discretion has frequently been subjected to restraints, and the widespread use of alternatives to incarceration of the past has been supplanted by extended prison and jail terms. The highest prison population in the history of this country occurred in 1976. The growth of prison and jail populations has now reached crisis proportion, and states are reopening old institutions that had been deemed unsuitable for human habitation at an earlier

Portions of the following discussion were first developed by Dr. Flynn in 1977 and are reprinted from "The Correctional Facility: The Environment Today and in the Future," Library Trends 26 (Summer 1977): 8-12, by permission of the publishers. Urbana: University of Illinois.

day. Tents, trailers, airport hangars, and even old battleships are now being used to accommodate the onslaught of prisoners. Across the nation, inmates are reported to be crammed into every conceivable space, and prison conditions are deteriorating fast.

The reasons for this far-reaching trend reversal are many: Philosophically, the return to the simplicities of punitive action against the criminal is politically attractive and has been hastened by the writings of such conservative academicians as James Q. Wilson and Ernest van den Haag. There are many within and without the criminal justice system who prefer the uncomplicated processes of retribution to the discretionary latitude of social-welfare-oriented decisions. From a practical perspective, it is incontestable that the criminal justice system has been incapable of stemming the spiraling crime rate. Recidivism rates--the rates at which prisoners return to institutions because of new convictions--are unacceptably and notoriously high. There is widespread disenchantment with the rehabilitation model used by most correctional institutions because of its inherent coercive nature and its failure to achieve an acceptable degree of success. As a result, such liberals as David Fogel, Robert Martinson, and Andrew von Hirsch have joined in the call for the swift and certain punishment of criminals to deter crime and for viewing punishment itself as intrinsically just and beneficial.

What lies behind the failure of criminal justice and this general state of discontent? Unquestionably, the inability of criminal justice to reduce crime and the failure of corrections to correct have been due in part to public neglect in providing the system with sufficient financial and manpower resources. But more significant in inhibiting change toward greater effectiveness has been the way criminal justice has perceived its task and mission. The definition of corrections as society's official reaction to convicted adult and adjudicated juvenile offenders neither states nor implies what corrections should try to achieve. This is critical if realism is to replace current ideology and rhetoric in this troubled field. Corrections has many purposes, of which rehabilitation is only one. It could be argued that if correctional processes were truly rehabilitative, they should be extended to all who need them and not be restricted to the convicted adult or adjudicated juvenile. Corrections is limited to the convicted and adjudicated offender because there are other justifications for coercively intervening in their lives in addition to helping them. Among these justifications are the protection of the community from the depredations of those who cannot otherwise be controlled, special and general deterrence, the upholding and confirmation of the validity of society's laws, and the punishment of offenders who deliberately break the law. Clearly, correctional purposes must differ for various types of offenders. When a person is sentenced for murder, corrections serves a punitive and deterrent function. When a socially deprived, undereducated, vocationally incompetent youth is adjudicated delinquent, corrections should seek to rehabilitate and reintegrate that youngster into the mainstream of society.

There is no doubt that corrections can contribute more than it does to the reduction of crime. To the extent that recidivist crime contributes significantly to all crime, corrections should be able to reduce crime. But it should be abundantly clear at this point that the pursuit of a single purpose for corrections--whether it be rehabilitation or punishment--is doomed to failure. Yesteryear's exclusive focus on the rehabilitation of offenders has failed incontestably. Insofar as the word "rehabilitation" suggests compulsory treatment or coercive programs, there is a growing body of opinion in criminal justice, supported by an impressive amount of scholarly research, that such a purpose is a mistake. Human beings inherently resist coercion and correctional coercion elicits failure more often than success. But the current return in corrections to neoclassical concepts of punishment and "just deserts for evil deeds" will also fail. Despite the intuitive attraction and appealing simplicity of these concepts, it must be recognized that they too are built on faulty premises which deny the complexity of human behavior and ignore the multiplicity of purposes served by criminal justice and corrections. Most importantly, the advocates of greater punitiveness toward offenders and of higher rates of incarceration fail to consider the social and political costs of their recommendations. Rising jail and prison populations have exacerbated conditions under which inmates must live to intolerable levels. Too often, correctional institutions are characterized by inhumane conditions, crippling idleness, anonymous brutality, lawlessness, discrimination, and arbitrary decisions concerning the disposition and lives of offenders. An increasing number of judicial interpretations of offenders' rights reflect the plight of the corrections system and the belief that such practices are unlawful and counterproductive to instilling respect for the law in offenders. Yet, in spite of these developments, state legislatures and the public continue to deny the criminal justice system the tools and facilities it needs to develop a swift and effective criminal justice system that is respectful of due process and equity. Finally, it is essential to remember that in a democracy there is a need to maintain a delicate balance between the will of the majority and the rights and liberty of the individual. Since the defense of the rights of social misfits and criminals is unappreciated by most and odious to many, a society's willingness to grant these rights is probably the most sensitive indicator of the degree to which that society is willing to uphold the rights of all of its citizens. President Madison, in The Federalist, No. 51, stated the issue well:

It is of great importance in a republic, not only
to guard the society against the oppression of
its rulers, but to guard one part of the society
against the injustice of the other part. Justice
is the end of government. It is the end of civil
society. It ever has been, and ever will be,
pursued until it be obtained, or until liberty be
lost in the pursuit.

Even a cursory examination of the public attitude and the prevailing political climate concerning crime control in this country
reveals that individual liberty is in distinct danger. Whenever the
rights of society are deemed more important than the rights of individuals and whenever there are some who are willing to sacrifice
these rights in the name of law and order, or the safety of the
streets, the very fabric of our society is threatened.

The following chapter on the presumption of innocence and the
U.S. jail by William Nagel has special relevance and significance
for the field. Nagel, director of the American Foundation in Philadelphia, is the author of The New Red Barn and is a leading corrections reformer. He is nationally known as a person of deep compassion for the suffering and the oppressed in our society. For
those who might perceive him as too idealistic in his assumptions
and prescriptions for criminal justice reform, it should be noted
that Nagel has had many years of direct experience with prison administration and has had to deal extensively with the breadth and
depth of human needs. The National Council on Crime and Delinquency chose to recognize Nagel's achievements by giving him the
1977 Roscoe Pound Award at the occasion of their annual meeting in
Salt Lake City in June of that year.

15

QUEST OR QUESTION:
THE PRESUMPTION OF
INNOCENCE AND THE U.S. JAIL
William G. Nagel

Certainly there can be few more glaring dichotomies than that dividing pretrial justice in the United States. I refer, on one hand, to the "presumption of innocence" and, on the other, to the U.S. jail. That dichotomy has fundamental significance to those who finance, plan, build, or run our jails.

It is not necessary to tell you that lawyers do not agree as to the significance of presumption of innocence. Ex-Attorney General John Mitchell, for example, arguing _for_ preventive detention, said: "The presumption of innocence is not a presumption in the strict sense of the term. It is simply a rule of evidence . . . there is no basis for thinking that the presumption of innocence has any application to proceedings prior to trial." One of Mitchell's predecessors as attorney general, Ramsey Clark, arguing _against_ preventive detention, wrote:

> The presumption of innocence should not be light-
> ly discarded. It has elemental force. Its spirit
> is embodied in the Eighth Amendment. It estab-
> lishes the relationship between the individual and
> the state, implying that every person is worth
> something, may have dignity and be deserving of
> trust. In questions between citizen and state,
> the presumption is--and must remain--that the
> individual will prevail until society proves him
> a criminal beyond a reasonable doubt.[1]

Address delivered at the Fourth National Symposium on Criminal Justice Planning and Architecture, New Orleans, April 8, 1977.

Legal scholars have lined up on both sides of this issue, one calling it the "bedrock, axiomatic, and elementary principle . . . of our criminal law" (In Re Winship 1970), while another termed it an "indulgence in self-deception . . . pretense and fiction" (Fletcher 1968).

There is no reference to "presumption of innocence" in our federal Constitution. Jeff Thaler of the Yale Law School recently has done some research on the subject and traced the concept back to Deuteronomy and through the Greek and Roman law to the English and then to the American colonies. In 1657 the Massachusetts Codes held that "in the law every man is honest and innocent unless it be proved to the contrary."

The Judiciary Act of 1789, which translated the Judicial Articles of the Constitution into practice, equated the right-to-bail provision of the Eighth Amendment to the presumption of innocence. Since then there has been a long line of court opinions and rules of procedure which uphold the concept and its corollary, the right to bail. For example, in Stack v. Boyle (1951), the Supreme Court held that "the traditional right to freedom before conviction permits the unhampered preparation of a defense, and serves to prevent the infliction of punishment prior to conviction . . . unless this right is preserved, the presumption of innocence, secured only after centuries of struggle, would lose its meaning."

Whatever the doubts in the minds of legal scholars may be, there appear to have been no such doubts until very recently in the minds of the people who planned, built, and operated our jails.

Here is one example: Between 1940 and 1970 Roy Casey was undoubtedly the most influential force in jail construction and operations in the United States. He prided himself in the title "Certified Jail Consultant." For many years he was Chief of the Jail Inspection Services to the Federal Bureau of Prisons and after his retirement in 1957 he crisscrossed this country helping counties to design their jails. He was much sought after by the steel companies who fabricated jail equipment. In 1958 he wrote a book called The Modern Jail--Design, Equipment, Operations. Until the creation of the National Clearinghouse on Criminal Justice, Planning and Architecture in 1971, this little book served as the "bible" of sheriffs and jail wardens, of steel companies, and of architects. For some it still does.

Page 1, Chapter 1 of Casey's (1958) book sets the tone: The "jail is a highly specialized institution and is built for only one purpose--that of detaining criminals. . . ." There is no indulgence in self-deception, no pretense or fiction, in that statement. It is straight to the point and in the 89 pages which followed Casey spelled out how to build and operate jails that would indeed hold "criminals." He designed hard, hard jails with inside cells, multiple iron grilles, small "bull-pen" types of day rooms, closed visiting, and limited movements. Most of these jails were inoffensive--even pretty--on the outside but all boiler plate and cages on the inside.

In my own book (Nagel 1973: 20) I described the result as follows:

> Our first impression of almost all the new jails we inspected was that they were designed in hypocrisy. Often built as part of a criminal justice complex or civic center, they are frequently, on the exterior, inoffensive and even attractive structures. The approaches are attractively landscaped, sometimes even including fountains and reflection pools. One warden proudly noted that no bars are visible to outsiders--a now frequent ploy.
>
> The overwhelming impression, once inside, is that the modern American jail, like its predecessor of the last century, is a cage and has changed only superficially. The concepts of repression and human degradation are remarkably intact.

There is nothing about these jails that would suggest the possibility of innocence, that would permit the untampered preparation of a defense, or would not add up to the infliction of punishment prior to conviction.

I have visited literally hundreds of U.S. jails: one built as early as 1817 and another scheduled to be opened in April 1977. Almost all of them, the architecture and the operations, speak loud and clear to Casey's single purpose, "that of detaining criminals." They are mute on the subject of "presumption of innocence." In fact, they are in general the most restrictive, most repressive, most inhumane, most punitive segment of our entire penal-correctional system.

We who work in correctional and especially in jail operations have not been in the vanguard of those demanding that our jails be basically transformed. There are many reasons for this. From our experience we know that among those who are presumed to be innocent are men and women who are, in fact, notorious, vicious, hardened, and dangerous criminals. They would go to any length to escape. We know, too, that apparently harmless and tractable inmates become violent. Even worse, trusted prisoners who are granted movement rights every so often aid the dangerous person to escape. The "loving kiss" during the contact visit can introduce heroin or other drugs. As I heard a guard say, "Those bastards have twenty-four hours a day to figure out how to beat us and they will if we don't beat them first."

All the grilles, prison locks, restrictions, electronic devices, rectal searches, telephonic visiting stalls, remote controlled doors, and sally ports are the ways we have devised to "beat them first."

In short, we question the applicability of the "presumption" principle to the design and operation of the U.S. jail. Our quest is for security and control. In the last few years, however, courts around the country have been demanding that presumption should indeed become part of the design and operation of the American jail. Borrowing from Blackstone (Commentaries 300) federal judges are increasingly demanding that "in this dubious interval between commitment and trial a person ought to be used with the utmost humanity and neither be loaded with needless fetters nor be subjected to other hardships except such as are absolutely requisite for the purpose of confinement only."

Court decision after court decision has affirmed Blackstone's principle. In Jones v. Sharkey (1972), for example, the judge held that "detainees retain all rights of bailees except for the curtailment of mobility deemed necessary to secure attendance at trial."

Compare the "retain all rights of bailees" with Casey's (1958: 84-88) principles for jail administration. "All visiting must be through visiting panels. Visiting periods should not exceed twenty minutes and be restricted to one per week. All mail written and received by prisoners must be censored and carefully examined." And so on.

And in Hamilton v. Love (1971), another landmark decision, the opinion stated that "it is manifestly obvious that the conditions of incarceration for detainees must, cumulatively, add up to the least restrictive means of achieving the purpose requiring and justifying the deprivation of liberty."

In establishing "least restrictive" as a principle of jail design and operation, courts have insisted upon differentiation in cell design, availability of both inside and outside recreation, elimination of rectal searches, greater freedom of movement, single-occupancy rooms, extensive contact visits, uncensored mail, access to telephones, right to privacy, restriction on search and seizure, and many other requirements that are anathema to jailers.

It has been a disappointment to me, as a corrections man, to hear and feel the arguments of other corrections persons defending buildings and policies that are diametrically opposed to the "least restrictive" principle required by our Constitution as interpreted by the courts. Because they are prison people, they argue so often for controls, against movement, against normalcy in visits, against all

the things that add up to "least restrictive" and in behalf of all those
gadgets and practices that add up to "most restrictive. "

I will present one example. Jails, traditionally, have inside
windowless cells with open grilles. Groups of cells are surrounded
by a wall of bars. Together this design creates the "cage" syndrome. In addition, the open grilles deprive the detainees of privacy while the windowless inside cells prevent the prisoner from
getting so much as a glimpse of the outside world, which has been
denied to him only because of his inability to make bail.

Recently a federal judge (Lasker) closed such a huge, cage-
like jail in New York City--the Tombs--because its conditions added
up to a situation far in excess of any least restrictive" facility that
could be tolerated under the Constitution. New York City, anxious
to reopen it, hired an architect who proposed some cosmetic changes.
The City then went back before Judge Lasker requesting permission
to reopen the place. The petitioners, after careful analysis of the
proposed changes, held that the Tombs, under the suggested altera-
tions, would still violate the "least restrictive" provisions. The
City engaged some of correction's brightest luminaries who argued,
as expert witnesses, that the proposed changes would make the
Tombs, constitutionally, just fine.

In regard to the cage-like inside cells, one correctional leader
testified that cells with an exterior view would merely provide "an
invitation to attempts at escapes. " With complete callousness to the
importance of a person's retaining some connection with his outside
world, with complete insensitivity to what a person might feel as he
toileted behind the open grille required by inside cells, with total
disregard for the importance of the privacy provided by outside
rooms with their solid, rather than barred, doors, he testified:
"From the standpoint of being in the cell itself, I see very little
difference whether it is inside or whether it is outside. "

The petitioners had argued that the untried had a right to exercise in the open air--to be able to experience the sensory stimu-
lation of the cold wind, the bright sun, or even the gentle rain. To
that the correctional expert testified: "I think if a person is confined two, three, four months . . . that an actual outdoor, physically out of doors facility is not necessarily that important" (Rhem
v. Malcolm 1974).

Why do we have to defend the past, or the status quo? Why do
we always have to defend the rectal search? Oppose the contact or
even conjugal visit? Deny freedom of movement from the cell to
the law library? Argue against the introduction of work, or play,
or school into the lives of detainees? Deny the wearing of personal
clothing? Defend the absurd but enforced wearing of red or yellow
monkey suits? Invent and support "modular functional units" that

would ensure the denial of "least restrictive conditions" for genera-
tions to come?

We defend all these because our horizon--at least in regard to
those who are untried, presumed to be innocent--is limited by our
total absorption with control. Preoccupied with that purpose, we
have been oblivious to the basic law of the land.

I paraphrase Orwell's 1984: Left to ourselves, we would continue, century after century, working and dying not only without any
impulse to change but without the power of grasping that the jail
could be other than it is.

We have not, however, been left to ourselves. First, there
have been the courts, already mentioned. Then, in 1971, the
Clearinghouse was created with its unfettered, untraditional staff of
bright young people questioning the old, questing for the new. Then
came the National Advisory Commission and the resulting impetus
toward new state standards and goals for jails, followed by the vol-
umes of the National Sheriff's Association and soon the revised
Standards of the American Correctional Association. Sometimes the
movement has been slow, causing the courts to prick us again. For
example, a member of the National Advisory Commission on Criminal Justice Standards and Goals, testifying in the Tombs case, said
that standards were really goals to be obtained one future day, but
in the meanwhile the very restrictive conditions of the Tombs were
quite acceptable. The court retorted, "With regards to the presumption of innocence and the least restrictive conditions looking to the
future is altogether absurd" (Rhem v. Malcolm 1974).

I agree with Judge Lasker's impatience. What is a constitutional right, he suggests, is today's right. It cannot be delayed until
tomorrow. But we know, as he knows, that the meaning and impact
of the U.S. Constitution evolved as our nation evolved and both are
still evolving. In 1789 the Constitution affected, essentially, only
white male landowners. In the ensuing 188 years it has spread its
protections to the merchant, the craftsman, the laborer, the slave,
the freedman, the woman, the child, and now to the prisoner. It
has become the twentieth century's secular expression of a twenty-
century-old enjoinder, "As you do it unto the least of these, my
brethren, you do it unto me."

Court decisions which impel us, and standards and goals that
guide us, are and should be visions. By their very nature they are
something to be attained. Born of the present, they are the future
which so soon will be the present. Our responsibility is to both generate and actualize those visions. In this, the twenty-first decade of
the American experiment, our task no longer is to question the applicability of the presumption of innocence to the pretrial experience.

We must make the pretrial jail constitutional or we must abolish it.

That may sound like the impossible dream, the unreachable star, but that must be our quest.

NOTE

1. Both quotes are from Jeff Thaler's unpublished paper, "The Presumption of Innocence and Its Application Prior to Trial," Yale Law School, July 1976.

Mr. Thaler participated with me in a workshop on the Judiciary and the Jail at the Yale Law School. The workshop was financed by the Guggenheim Foundation and conducted by Professor Dan Freed. I very much appreciate Mr. Thaler's sharing this important paper with me. I am indebted to him for widening my understanding of the subject.

REFERENCES

Blackstone's Commentaries, 4, 300.

Casey, R.
1958   The Modern Jail. Continental Press.

Fletcher, G. P.
1968   The presumption of innocence and the Soviet Union. UCLA Law Review.

Hamilton v. Love
1971   328 F. Supp. at 1194 (E.D. Ark. W.D.).

Jones v. Sharkey
1972   Civ. No. 4948 (D.R.I. June 7).

Nagel, W. G.
1973   The New Red Barn. New York: Walker.

Rhem v. Malcolm
1974   507 F. 2d 333.

Stack v. Boyle
1951   342 U.S. 1.

In Re Winship
1970   90 S. Ct. 1068, 1072.

PART

VIII

PAROLE

Parole, as a form of correctional treatment, originated in the rehabilitation model of corrections. The underlying assumption of this approach is that offenders can be rehabilitated in prison and then best reintegrated into the communities when subject to some continuing supervision. Parole also provides a politically convenient way to reduce prison populations, without affecting (or interfering with) sentencing practices. Parole boards tend to be composed of a mixture of experts in the fields of psychology, social work, criminology, and law and frequently include some lay citizens. Criteria for release decisions often circumscribe little more than an unintegrated consideration of public safety, the crime for which the offender was sentenced, the person's general and work histories, and behavior in prison.

Since the 1970s, parole--just when it had become the predominant mode of release for prison inmates in the United States--came under increasing attack from every conceivable quarter: liberals, conservatives, prisoners, and from many criminal justice practitioners. In essence, parole is criticized for being too lenient a disposition; for pursuing the treatment model, now deemed defunct by many, if not all, knowledgeable in the field; for exercising entirely too much and unwarranted discretion; for imposing more severe penalties in a criminal justice system that already imposes too much control; and for being intolerable for inmates who cannot take the uncertainty of it. In contrast, defenders of parole view it as a compensatory system, which counteracts unchecked judicial discretion, and as an important form of graduated return of offenders to the community, providing assistance to the releasees and protection to the community.

Recommendations concerning the future of parole range from advocating restrictions on discretion, to delimitation of parole-board functions, to the development of hybrid parole agencies pursuing a combination of functions, to abolition. To date, some states, such as Maine and California, have abolished parole altogether.

There can be no question that the current situation in criminal justice is complex. There is a desperate need to maintain public confidence in the criminal justice system. There is also a critical need to bring about changes in attitudes among criminal justice practitioners, and especially in judges. It appears that criminological thought has traveled full circle, from classical theory, based on the assumption of free will, to notions of determinism and limited

257

retribution, to concepts of social contract, to neoclassicism, in which free will, individual responsibility, and punishment reign supreme. As a result, it appears that criminal justice in the United States is about to embark on yet another experiment based on faulty premises.

But let a cautionary voice be raised here. It is simply unlikely that the abolition of parole and the concomitant reduction of judicial discretion (by means of instituting flat-time, fixed, and/or determinate sentences) will provide the much-needed solution to the problems of crime or to the dilemma of the criminal justice system. While indeterminate sentences can no longer be defended on the basis of available evidence which shows clearly that inmates released on parole in the United States actually serve more time than those released through unconditional discharge, the elimination of all discretion and flexibility on the part of the judiciary is too extreme a remedy. Some flexibility in sentencing--perhaps a two- to five-year leeway depending on the seriousness of the crime--should be preserved for criminal justice decision makers, whether they be parole agencies (and not necessarily parole boards), sentencing review boards broadly representing the community of the returning offender, or other structures. Pursuing such avenues seems warranted for the following reasons. First, if sentencing is left entirely to the discretion of legislatures, it will in all probability be more severe and punitive than it presently is. California, for example, which enacted a definite sentencing structure and abolished the Adult Authority in July 1977, is now constantly in the process of revising its legislation. In the process of dealing with vested interests and political pressures, the tendency is strong to opt for greater and stiffer penalties. There is little reason to assume that other states would act differently, and such developments will no doubt produce catastrophic rises in prison populations at a time when such institutions are already brimful. Second, in spite of the prevailing rhetoric, the discarding of rehabilitation is without a doubt premature. The facts are that we know more about the effectiveness of rehabilitation than we know about the effectiveness of punishment. Too many criminal justice practitioners have accepted uncritically the present negative view concerning correctional effectiveness. Just because there are findings of "no difference" in outcome between two or more correctional alternatives does not demonstrate that correctional programs have no effect. It may well be that offender differences cancel out positive and negative effects of particular programs. In addition, there is now a growing body of information that some programs do indeed have a positive effect (in terms of reducing recidivism, among other variables) on certain kinds of offenders. Third, there is little evidence that the way in which the criminal justice system operates exerts any measurable deterrent effect, regardless of whether parole exists or is abolished, or whether sentencing is flat, mandatory, or indeterminate. As long as the majority of criminals escape apprehension, it is unlikely that criminal justice operations will affect the crime rate one way or another.

The following two chapters by Joseph Scott, John Stahura, and Richard Vandiver, and by Albert Simkus, Edwin Hall, and Taylor Griffiths are most timely in view of their thorough empirical examination of parole decision making. Simkus et al. show parole-board decisions to be more rational than most critics would admit. They found, for example, that parole decisions seem to be influenced the most by such factors as seriousness of the offense and the length and consistency of an inmate's criminal history. Considerations such as these are certainly consonant with public expectations of protection from offenders having committed serious crimes. Another interesting finding is that personal-biographical characteristics of inmates on parole decisions--long-suspected major determinants of parole release decisions--are negligible, if they exist at all. The chapter by Scott et al. also suggests that parole boards tend to base their decisions basically on legal criteria, especially the legal seriousness of the committed crime. While such considerations are once again consistent with public safety, they point to the fact that parole decisions do not seem to consider questions of offender adjustment to institutional life or, more importantly, rehabilitation. And since the authors view these activities as primary tasks, for which parole had been created to begin with, they now doubt the value of parole and call for a reexamination of the concept at this point in time.

In sum, sufficiently serious questions are being raised today concerning the effectiveness and equity of parole decisions to warrant a serious reanalysis of the issues. However, wholesale abandonment of the concept and practice is surely premature. In view of the proven efficacy of community corrections, the field needs more community dispositions for offenders rather than fewer. Further, consider the fact that virtually all inmates, including those sentenced under fixed terms, become eligible for release before the expiration of their sentences. As a result, the question of "who" should be paroled might better be shifted to "when" a particular inmate is optimally paroled or released. Given valid and reliable data, prediction devices currently in existence could help assess optimal release dates. At this time, some departments of corrections--Michigan, for example--are beginning to combine predictive devices with typological models which should greatly enhance a system's capacity to identify low- as well as high-risk groups in terms of future recidivism or violent crime. Offenders belonging to low-risk groups could then be released with little or no supervision,

while high-risk group members could be released but more closely
supervised to provide community protection. Would it not be ironic
that just when criminal justice appears to stand of the threshold of
a predictive breakthrough the avenues for acting on these developments become closed? Finally, a wide variety of alternatives to
(or modifications of) current practices should first be explored,
tried, and tested before we relegate parole to the annals of correctional history.

16

PAROLE BOARD DECISION MAKING: AN EXAMINATION OF THE CRITERIA UTILIZED

Joseph E. Scott
John Stahura
Richard Vandiver

Decision making by social-control agencies has received considerable attention by behavioral scientists. Many studies have been conducted concerning the discretionary practices of police, prosecutors, judges, and juries. Such studies have provided considerable insight into both legal and nonlegal factors which affect people who came into contact with representatives of such agencies. Nevertheless, there is one area or agency of the criminal justice system which has received little attention by behavioral scientists, namely, parole boards.[1] Few studies have investigated the processes which determine when, how, and why legal-norm violators, who have been found guilty and incarcerated, should be released from our penal institutions. This situation prevails despite the fact that the decision making at this stage is not generally governed by "due process," subject to appeal, or open to public scrutiny.

In most states today, the determination of the nature and the extent of an offender's sentence has become a divided task. A portion of the task is still assumed by the legislature when it sets lower and upper limits to the sentence which a court may impose for each offense.[2] The courts in their separate decisions on each case do another part. The parole board can exercise discretion after the legislature and the courts are through. The extent of the parole boards' discretion varies greatly from one jurisdiction to another.[3] However, the discretionary power of parole boards has apparently increased concomitantly with the apparent shift in the ideology of the criminal justice system from an almost exclusive "retributive" basis to a more "retributive-reformative" approach. This change in ideology has resulted in more frequent use by several states of the indefinite or indeterminate type of sentence. This increased usage has transferred the primary responsibility of determining the proper length of incarceration for each defendant from the judiciary to the parole board. Simply by imposing the statutory sentence passed by the legislature for the specific offense for which the defendant was found guilty, the judiciary, in many states, has left any reconciliation of the seriousness of the crime with the severity of the sentence entirely at the discretion of the parole board. Not only does the parole board have the responsibility of determining the proper length of incarceration for each offender given an indefinite sentence, but, in addition, many parole boards also function as the state clemency commission. In this capacity they have the prerogative to overrule legislatively enacted minimum sentences or judicially imposed minimum or definite sentences and release inmates when they, the clemency commission, feel they should be released.

Being one of the later stages in the criminal justice system, the decision-making process to release inmates from prison has received little attention from criminologists, perhaps because of the correctional ideology that release from prison before the maximum portion of the sentence has been served "is a privilege rather than a right."[4] This theory and justification appears to have been closely linked with the courts' "hands off" doctrine in dealing with correctional issues. Both doctrines have recently come under severe attack and appear no longer to be governing policy. With the increasing concern for due process and the curtailment and control of arbitrary use of power in administering justice, the correctional process and, in particular, the paroling process become likely candidates for scrutiny at this time.[5]

Despite the numerous constitutional procedural safeguards applicable at the preadjudicative decision-making states, the need for still greater control over the discretion utilized by these social-control agents is seldom denied. Lacking even such procedural safeguards in the postadjudicative process, the innumerable parole-board decisions made on the basis of administrative policy have not only lacked judicial safeguards but have, in addition, not been subject to public scrutiny.

The specific focus of this study is on the criteria utilized by parole boards in determining the proper amount of punishment a convicted adult felony offender should receive. Specific attention is focused on three principal factors: legal, institutional, and personal-biographical.[6] These three factors were selected because of their relationship to correctional ideology and criminological theory. The legal factor was the primary consideration in determining the punishment according to the retributive school of thought. The severity of punishment was to be determined by the seriousness of the crime. The institutional approach (factor) is closely associated with the reformative approach to corrections, which advocates the incarceration of individuals only until they are rehabilitated. Perhaps the most commonly used indicator of an individual's rehabilitation while incarcerated is his institutional behavior. Finally, the personal-biographical factor is closely associated with the conflict of power theory of criminology. This theory maintains that those individuals with more power in society will receive more consideration and more favorable treatment by representatives of our legal institutions.

METHOD

The data for this research was gathered from the prison records from one Midwestern state's adult penal institution for felony offenders. The principal source of data consists of information recorded in prison records compiled and submitted to the parole board before each inmate's parole hearing.

The research sample consists of the records of all female and male inmates released from the two Midwestern prisons between 1965 and 1971 (one male, one female penal institution). Partial data were also obtained for the years 1961-65 from the Midwestern prisons. The sample was partitioned by individual years and year groupings for purposes of analyses with the primary analysis focusing on the period 1966-71 (N = 890). Table 16.1 contains a description of the partitioned samples and the mean level of punishment for inmates by year.

Correlation and multiple regression techniques are used to analyze the data. Pearson correlation coefficients provide an indication of each independent variable's relationship to the dependent variable. By using multiple regression analysis, the effects of variation within each independent variable upon the dependent variable are provided (unstandardized B) as is the importance of various independent variables' ability to explain variation in the dependent variable (beta, standardized coefficient). In addition, using this type of analysis allows one to examine variables categorized as legal, institutional, or sociobiological as sets and thereby determine the relationship of each set to the dependent variable. The Bs (unstandardized) and betas (standardized) reported (see Tables 16.3, 16.5, 16.7) are calculated for each of the sets of variables and represent their relative effect within each set of variables on the dependent variable. Statistical significance for the correlation coefficients was determined by employing a simple student's t-test. The Bs and betas were subjected to both a t-test and f-test in testing for significance. The .05 level of probability was predetermined to indicate a significant result.

TABLE 16.1

Severity of Punishment for Prison Inmates, in Months, 1961-71

Year	N	Mean	Standard Deviation
1961-65	77	29.4545	26.6560
1966	110	14.5000	13.0108
1967	132	15.6894	24.6691
1968	157	19.8981	27.4056
1969	185	16.7243	19.8339
1970	191	18.4031	26.6037
1971	115	19.7478	38.8042
1966-69	584	16.9247	22.3018
1970-71	306	18.9085	31.6881
1966-71	890	17.6067	25.9145
1960-71[a]	953	16.3914	18.8141
1967-71[b]	1,195	26.5498	174.9267

[a]Figures are for sample where the severity of punishment was less than 500 months.

[b]Includes 242 cases not identifiable by year of release. The results of the analysis of this sample are not reported because the data for the unidentifiable cases are unverified.

Source: Compiled by the authors.

The variables examined for their possible effect upon variations in the severity of punishment comprise three factors:

Legal factor: This is the seriousness of crime (the legal minimum sentence, in months, imposed by the courts),[7] and the prior criminal involvement of each inmate (prior criminal involvement was quantified by weighting prior prison incarcerations, felony and misdemeanor arrests, and convictions).[8] Table 16.4 contains the zero-order correlations for the legal-factor variables and their multiple effects on the severity of punishment by year. Table 16.5 contains the standardized and unstandardized regression coefficients for the legal-factor variables. (Standardized coefficients are also interpretable as path coefficients.)

Institutional factor: Institutional adjustment is the sole variable used in gauging the institutional factor. The only available information on an inmate's institutional adjustment for the parole board to consider was whether the inmate had attended school or not.

TABLE 16.2

Coefficients of Correlation for Severity of Punishment
with Institutional Adjustment, by Year, 1961-71

Year	Pearson's r	r^2	N
1961-65	-.248[a]	.061	77
1966	.024	.001	110
1967	-.138	.019	132
1968	-.119	.014	157
1969	-.147[a]	.021	185
1970	-.079	.006	191
1971	-.223[a]	.050	115
1966-69	-.115[a]	.013	584
1970-71	-.149[a]	.022	306
1966-71	-.125	.015	890
1960-71[b]	-.090[a]	.008	953

[a]Significant at the .05 level.
[b]Figures are for sample where the severity of punishment was less than 500 months.
Source: Compiled by the authors.

TABLE 16.3

Regression and Beta Coefficients for the Institutional
Variable, by Year, 1961-71

Year	B	Beta	N
1961-65	-13.573	-.272	77
1966	+1.175	.042	110
1967	-6.388	-.119	132
1968	-7.165	-.125	157
1969	-5.943	-.147	185
1970	-5.083	-.084	191
1971	-22.498	-.269	115
1966-69	-5.211	-.111	584
1970-71	-11.491	-.163	306
1966-71	-7.074	-.127	890
1960-71*	-3.662	-.012	953

*Figures are for sample where the severity of punishment was less than 500 months.
Source: Compiled by the authors.

Institutional adjustment for the two Midwestern prisons consists solely of having enrolled in school at some time during an inmate's incarceration or not having so participated. Table 16.2 contains the zero-order correlations by year for the institutional factor. The betas and Bs are reported in Table 16.3 for the institutional factor.

Sociobiographical: This consists of age (at the time of release), education (number of years of school completed), marital status (single, separated, widowed, or divorced; or married at the time of inmate's appearance before the parole board), race (white or nonwhite), residence (resident of state in which incarcerated or not), and occupation (full-time employed, part-time, or unemployed at the time of arrest). In Table 16.6 are found the zero-order correlations of the sociobiographical variables with the severity of punishment. The Bs and betas are shown in Table 16.7.

The severity of punishment (number of months an inmate was incarcerated) was used as the dependent variable.[9] Table 16.8 summarizes the results of the multiple analysis using all three factors as predictors of the severity of punishment by year.

FINDINGS

Legal Factor

Seriousness of Crime

The seriousness of crime (SC) for which inmates were convicted was the best predictor of the severity of punishment for all of the year samples. The correlation coefficients (Table 16.4) indicate a strong relationship between the seriousness of crime and the severity of punishment. The strong zero-order relationship implies that parole boards operate on the assumption that an inmate is not ready for parole until he has suffered commensurately for the crime he committed. The magnitude of the zero-order relationship did change across time to a significant degree. The zero-order relationship for the 1966-69 aggregate was significantly different from the 1970-71 aggregate sample. In 1970 the significance of the seriousness of crime as an indicator of the severity of punishment diminished. The partial effects of SC are reported in Table 16.5. In every year subsample, SC was found to be statistically significant. SC remained the best predictor across time but diminished in importance in 1970-71. The change that occurred for 1970 and 1971 releases in the decision-making process evidence by the SC findings will be discussed in some detail in the conclusion section.

TABLE 16.4

Coefficients of Correlation for Severity of Punishment with the Legal Factor
(Seriousness of Crime and Prior Criminal Involvement), by Year, 1961-71

Year	Seriousness of Crime	Prior Criminal Involvement	R	R^2	N
1961-65	.870[a]	.221[a]	.878	.770	77
1966	.842[a]	.313[a]	.861	.740	110
1967	.966[a]	.228[a]	.969	.939	132
1968	.869[a]	.150[a]	.883	.780	157
1969	.869[a]	.116	.869	.756	185
1970	.647[a]	.020	.648	.420	191
1971	.689[a]	-.030	.690	.476	115
1966-69	.892[a]	.170[a]	.897	.804	584
1970-71	.668[a]	-.004	.668	.446	306
1966-71	.772[a]	-.096[a]	.775	.601	890
1960-71[b]	.680[a]	.226[a]	.693	.481	953

[a]Significant at the .05 level.
[b]Figures are for sample where the severity of punishment was less than
500 months.
Source: Compiled by the authors.

TABLE 16.5

Regression and Beta Coefficients for the Legal-Factor
Variables, by Year, 1961-71

Year	Seriousness of Crime		Prior Criminal Involvement[a]		N
	B	Beta	B	Beta	
1961-65	.188[b]	.855[b]	.016	.120	77
1966	.254[b]	.812[b]	.015	.182	110
1967	.268[b]	.954[b]	.013	.079	132
1968	.281[b]	.870[b]	.024	.155	157
1969	.225[b]	.866[b]	.004	.032	185
1970	.161[b]	.647[b]	.003	.020	191
1971	.201[b]	.692[b]	.008	.034	115
1966-69	.258[b]	.884[b]	.013	.097	584
1970-71	.180[b]	.669[b]	.005	.023	306
1966-71	.215[b]	.770[b]	.012	.074	890
1960-71[c]	.190[b]	.661[b]	.016	.138	953

[a]After eliminating cases from the analysis where the severity of punishment was greater than 500 months, several of the coefficients for year
subsamples become significant. PCI was significant for 1968, 1970, and
1970-71 subsamples.
[b]Significant at the .05 level.
[c]Figures are for sample where the severity of punishment was less
than 500 months.

Prior Criminal Involvement

The importance of prior criminal involvement (PCI) in the parole-board decision-making process varies across time. In Table 16.4 several of the zero-order relationships between PCI and the severity of punishment were statistically significant, but after controlling for the effect of SC (Table 16.5), PCI becomes an insignificant predictor. Note a in Table 16.5 is worth mention in that, after eliminating the most serious crimes from the sample, PCI did become a significant predictor for several of the subsamples, that is, 1966-69 and 1960-71. No discernible trend, however, or distinct change in PCI as a predictor is readily evident from the data.

Institutional Factor (Institutional Adjustment)

The law stipulates that an inmate's institutional behavior is one of the major factors to be considered by the parole board in determining whether to grant parole or not. The data (Tables 16.2 and 16.3) suggest, however, that institutional adjustment (IA) is not significantly related to the severity of punishment. The zero-order relationships (Table 16.2) for each of the year subsamples indicate that IA appears to be inversely related to SP as expected. The partial effects (Table 16.3) show that, after controlling for the seriousness of crime, IA becomes an insignificant factor in the parole decision-making process. No distinct patterns or changes are in evidence across time. The significance of the partial effects are the most interpretable of all the measures reported since each of the subsamples represents a unique sample of inmates. The interpretation of the partial effects, however, should be a cautious one, noting the N of each of the samples.

Sociobiographical Factor

Tables 16.6 and 16.7 summarize the effects of the sociobiographical variables, that is, race, marital status (MS), sex, education (ED), age, occupation (OCC), and residence (RES). Several of the zero-order effects were significant for some of the variables as reported in Table 16.6, but none of the partial effects were significant after controlling for the seriousness of crime. Evidently, the sociobiographical factor plays an insignificant role in the parole-board decision-making process.

TABLE 16.6

Coefficients of Correlation for Severity of Punishment with the Sociobiographical Variables, by Year, 1961-71

Year	Race[a]	MS[a]	Sex[a]	ED	Age	OCC[a]	RES[a]	R	R²	N
1961–65	-.146	-.005	-.135	-.105	.061	-.231[b]	.042	.352	.124	77
1966	.004	.009	-.082	.066	.031	.132	-.004	.197	.039	110
1967	-.024	-.051	-.091	-.070	-.024	.163[b]	-.020	.221	.049	132
1968	-.022	.092	-.079	-.087	.169[b]	-.040	-.014	.202	.041	157
1969	-.024	.069	.103	-.063	.010	.021	-.035	.135	.018	185
1970	-.113	-.056	-.080	-.230[b]	.163[b]	-.055	-.060	.324	.105	191
1971	-.090	.024	-.061	-.055	.073	-.081	-.140	.204	.042	115
1966–69	-.025	.033	.014	-.054	.052	.047	-.019	.102	.010	584
1970–71	-.100[b]	-.018	-.055	-.149[b]	.119[b]	-.063	-.093	.243	.059	306
1966–71	-.053	.011	-.024	-.092[b]	.080[b]	-.000	-.051	.143	.021	890
1960–71[c]	-.032	.010	-.026	-.097[b]	.110[b]	.001	-.021	.153	.023	953

[a]Dichotomously coded.
[b]Significant at the .05 level.
[c]Figures are for sample where the severity of punishment was less than 500 months.
Source: Compiled by the authors.

TABLE 16.7

Regression and Beta Coefficients for Severity of Punishment with the Sociobiographical Variables, by Year, 1961-71

Year	Race[a]		Marital Status[a]		Sex[a]		Education		Age		Occupation[a]		Residence[a]		N
	B	Beta	B	Beta	B	Beta	B	Beta	B	Beta	B	Beta	B	Beta	
1961-65	-4.506	-.195	.076	.004	-10.134	-.061	-2.241	-.225	-.314	-.117	-6.796	-.308	-.524	-.008	77
1966	-.029	-.002	.351	.034	-7.071	-.102	.338	.064	.093	.076	1.636	.175	-2.049	-.066	110
1967	-.739	-.031	.171	.009	-12.334	-.120	-.859	-.084	-.018	-.008	3.298	.191	-1.545	-.025	132
1968	-.662	-.018	.697	.030	-13.086	-.084	-.891	-.073	.385	.148	.425	.020	-1.014	-.016	157
1969	-.727	-.026	.664	.041	3.098	.094	-.582	-.068	-.049	-.026	.186	.012	-1.028	-.024	185
1970	-5.596	-.157	-2.056	-.098	-2.846	-.020	-2.823	-.248	.356	.141	-.350	-.019	.727	.012	191
1971	-6.156	-.104	-1.223	-.041	-1.948	-.053	-.999	-.052	.273	.073	-.886	-.036	-13.391	-.134	115
1966-69	-.878	-.033	.278	.015	.057	.001	-.476	-.050	.110	.053	1.099	.067	-1.072	-.021	584
1970-71	-5.734	-.129	-1.656	-.067	-1.793	-.038	-2.185	-.153	.326	.108	-.560	-.027	-4.285	-.059	306
1966-71	-2.192	-.067	-.369	-.018	-1.197	-.023	-1.018	-.091	.184	.076	.494	.027	-2.678	-.044	890
1960-71[b]	-1.042	-.046	-.443	-.030	-1.004	-.026	-.718	-.090	.201	.113	.407	.030	-.780	-.018	953

[a]Dichotomously coded.
[b]Figures are for sample where the severity of punishment was less than 500 months.
Source: Compiled by the authors.

The direction of the relationships between the sociobiographical variables and SC were as expected. Older offenders are punished more severely than younger offenders.[10] The rationale underlying the decision is that young offenders are perceived as being immature and simply having made a mistake. Women were incarcerated for shorter periods of time than were men. Whites received more severe punishment than nonwhites (most of the nonwhites in the Midwestern state's prisons were Indians, with few blacks). Residents were punished more severely than nonresidents. (These relationships may have been stronger if comparisons had been made exclusively for residents and nonresidents not being paroled to detainers. Inmates who have detainers filed against them are generally paroled and discharged to the detainers, which absolves the paroling state from any parole supervision responsibility. Inmates who have detainers filed against them are most often nonresidents.) Inmates with higher educational attainment served less time. Marital status and occupation showed no distinct pattern in terms of the nature of the zero-order relationship. Again, when the seriousness of crime and other independent variables are controlled, variation in the sociobiographical variables has an insignificant effect on the severity of punishment. An interpretation of nonsignificant partial effects is meaningless. Hence, no specific attempt is made to specify the relationships of the sociobiographical variables to the severity of punisnment.

Analyzing Data in Aggregates

When the variables categorized as legal, sociobiographical, and institutional are treated as sets and examined with regard to their relationship to the severity of punishment, the legal set (SC, PCI) is the most significant.[11] Comparing the explained variation (R^2) for the legal factor by year subsamples (Table 16.4) with the R^2 for combined effect of all three factors by year subsamples (Table 16.8; values not enclosed in parentheses), very little is added by the inclusion of the institutional and sociobiographical factors in terms of explained variation. This was expected since no variable other than SC was a significant predictor of the severity of punishment. Between 1960 and 1969, 76 to 94 percent of the variation in severity of punishment is accounted for by the seriousness of crime. In 1970 and 1971 the amount of explained variance by the legal factor drops considerably in importance (42 percent and 48 percent explained), but the other factors still do not account for a significant percentage of the explained variance.

TABLE 16.8

Multiple Rs and R^2 for Severity of Punishment with the Legal, Institutional, and Sociobiographical Factors, by Year, 1961-71

Year	R	R^2	N
1961-65	.883 (.822)[a]	.779 (.676)[a]	77 (74)[a]
1966	.869 (.869)	.755 (.755)	110 (110)
1967	.970 (.905)	.941 (.819)	132 (131)
1968	.887 (.797)	.786 (.635)	157 (154)
1969	.873 (.747)	.762 (.557)	185 (182)
1970	.684 (.564)	.467 (.318)	191 (187)
1971	.713 (.642)	.508 (.412)	115 (111)
1966-69	.898 (.804)	.806 (.647)	584 (577)
1970-71	.683 (.539)	.466 (.291)	306 (298)
1960-71[b]	.800 (.696)	.640 (.485)	974 (953)
1966-71	.778 (.653)	.605 (.427)	890 (875)
1960-71[c]	.923	.853	1,195

[a]The values in parentheses are for the same year samples but exclude the cases where the severity of punishment was greater than 500 months.

[b]Figures are for sample where the severity of punishment was less than 500 months.

[c]Figures are for entire sample including cases unidentifiable by year.

Source: Compiled by the authors.

The figures in parentheses in Table 16.8 represent the multiple effects of the three factors on the severity of punishment for samples where cases with reported severity of punishment exceeding 500 months were eliminated. In effect, inmates convicted of the most serious crimes (capital offenses) were eliminated from the analysis. The amount of variation explained by all factors in the truncated sample decreases for all of the year subsamples. The rationale for the reduced sample analysis is that for inmates convicted of less-serious crimes, where the inmate is thought to be rehabilitatable, the parole-board process would vary and more closely approximate the stated policy of the board. Seriousness of crime did decrease in relative importance as a predictor, but only prior criminal involvement emerged as a significant predictor of the severity of punishment for some of the year subsamples (see note b on Table 16.4). Again, none of the institutional and socio-biographical variables emerged as a significant predictor. A drop in explained variation across time for the reduced samples would lead one to assume that factors other than those available to the parole board on inmate's records are entering into the decision-making process.

DISCUSSION AND CONCLUSION

As was referenced earlier in the discussion of the legal factor, seriousness of crime diminished as a predictor of the severity of punishment in the late 1960s and early 1970s (specifically for releases occurring in 1970 and 1971). During this period the parole policy of the state did change dramatically. The governor of the state and the Department of Corrections felt there were too many people in the state prisons. As a consequence, policy shifted in such a way to expedite the parole and discharge of inmates and consequent reduction in inmate population. The case of every inmate was reviewed more often by the board of pardons. As a result, there were increased commutations, pardons, paroles, and discharges from supervision by the board of pardons. As a result of the change in policy, the normal decision-making process was somewhat altered. However, the data show that the board of pardons still did not use the available objective information in the decision-making process after the policy change. The reduction in explained variance due to objective information diminished after 1969.

Until 1970 the decision to parole an inmate was based almost exclusively on the seriousness of crime. On the basis of the objective data available to the board, the decision-making process was a reaffirmation of the preadjudicatory and/or the adjudicatory stages, apparently using little if any information that had not previously been available to the trial judge.

The positivists' ideology that an inmate should be sentenced to prison until he is rehabilitated or "ready" to return to society would appear still far removed from realization. Perhaps what should be seriously questioned at this point is the present usefulness of either indefinite sentences and/or of parole boards.

As indicated earlier, the extent of the parole boards' discretion has apparently increased concomitantly with the apparent shift in the ideology of the criminal justice system from a "retributive" basis to a more "retributive-reformative" approach, resulting in more frequent use of the indefinite or indeterminate sentence, and transferring the primary responsibility of determining the proper length of incarceration for each defendant from the judiciary to the parole board. This broad power was conferred on the parole board in order to implement the "reformative" approach to corrections. The idea was for an agency or board to review each inmate's case periodically and release him at the optimum time for him to adjust and function adequately in society. The thinking was that the judge, schooled in law and not human behavior, would not be as well qualified to determine how much treatment (punishment) specific inmates needed. Similarly, it would be difficult to predict in advance how offenders would respond to the various treatment programs provided. A solution to both of these problems was to create parole boards, composed of citizens trained in understanding human behavior, which would determine on the basis of the offender's response to institutional treatment his degree of readiness to return to society.

The data analyzed from one Midwestern state's prisons certainly do not demonstrate that parole boards function in the manner expected. The data suggest that parole boards base their decisions basically on one legal criterion (the legal seriousness of the crime). The variables which parole boards might use in determining the offender's adjustment and improvement while incarcerated either are not provided for their use or, if provided, appear to be utilized very little in determining when an inmate should be released.

The parole board does not appear to be fulfilling any function that the courts could not perhaps handle better with the possible exception of keeping the inmates locked up for shorter periods than otherwise might be the case. Whether they are even serving this function is open to discussion.[12] The innumerable parole-board decisions have lacked judicial safeguards and, in addition, have not been subject to public scrutiny. Inasmuch as one of the reasons often given for prison riots is poor and unjust parole policies,[13] the entire parole concept should be reexamined at this time.[14] If parole boards are not acting or functioning on any basis other than that available for the judiciary, it seems rather redundant, expensive, and ridiculous simply to append one more agency making decisions with real consequences for individual lives.

As was recently pointed out in a policy statement by the National Council on Crime and Delinquency (1973, 137):

> . . . the prisoner, comparing his case to that of others who were granted parole, may see the denial as a capricious decision. He is often at a loss to understand what he has done wrong or how he can improve his performance. Parole board silence compounds his cynicism and his hostility to authority.

> At the very least, unexplained parole denials obstruct rehabilitation yet they are quite common in many state and local jurisdictions.

Given the manner in which parole boards operate, other alternatives should certainly be considered for deciding when offenders should be released. Several have been suggested, including strict administrative guidelines for parole decision making.[15] This would require parole boards to follow strict rules and regulations in making decisions and possibly grant certain rights to inmates previously unavailable (for example, the right to examine records for the accuracy upon which decisions are based, or the right to appeal or have the decision reviewed).[16] Others have suggested the utilization of an independent ombudsman to intervene when injustices are observed (Fitzharris 1973; Badillo 1972). Still another alternative (although not necessarily desirable) would be simply to return the punishing power strictly to the courts.[17] The courts could then determine the punishment a particular offender should receive either by returning to the utilization of more definite-type sentences or by utilizing indefinite-type sentences with specific rules and regulations concerning eligibility for release from prison. This approach would at least provide due process to the releasing procedure and would eliminate much of the uncertainty prevalent in prisons today.

If an inmate's institutional adjustment and development are not being used to determine the amount of punishment he needs, there would be little justification for the continued use of parole boards and for that matter the continued utilization of indefinite or indeterminate-type sentences. As Morris (1966) recently demanded of various segments of the criminal justice system, "practices must cease to rest on surmise and good intentions; they must be based on facts." This is certainly applicable for parole boards. If they are not operating as expected and not fulfilling some other unsurmised purpose, then their usefulness must be reconsidered. There is little justification for a social control agency simply to increase the apprehension and uncertainty of offenders unless they are providing some legitimate social function.

Research has already indicated that there is little if any relationship between institutional adjustment and recidivism (Glaser 1964; Miller 1971). Therefore, the continued use of parole boards and indefinite-type sentences on the assumption that parole boards can better determine than a judge when an inmate is ready for release appears to be based on a false assumption at the outset.

Certainly additional research is needed on parole-board decision making. If parole boards in other states are basing their decisions almost exclusively on the legal seriousness of the crime, as the parole boards are in the Midwestern state studied, this will certainly be added justification for seeking other alternatives to utilize in determining offenders' "proper" length of incarceration.[18]

SUMMARY

This research investigates the criteria utilized by parole boards in determining when an inmate is ready for release. Variables are grouped under three factors: legal, institutional, and sociobiographical. The major finding is that one variable, the legal seriousness of the crime, accounts for almost all the variation in punishment. The seriousness of the crime's importance, however, has diminished somewhat in the last three years. An inmate's prior criminal involvement and institutional adjustment were found for the most part insignificantly related with the severity of punishment. Finally, the usefulness of parole boards in general is examined and several alternatives suggested for determining when and how an inmate should be released from prison.

NOTES

1. There have been a few studies conducted on the operation of parole boards, but these have been primarily ethnographic in nature. See, for example, Paul A. Thomas, "An Analysis of Parole Selection," 9 Crime and Delinquency 173-79 (April 1963); Scovel Richardson, "Parole and the Law," 2 Crime and Delinquency 27-32 (January 1956); Robert O. Dawson, Sentencing: The Decision as to Type, Length and Conditions of Sentence 222-424 (1969); Robert O. Dawson, "The Decision to Grant or Deny Parole; A Study of Parole Criteria in Law and Practice," Washington University Law Quarterly 243-303 (June 1966); Michael Gottesman and Lewis J. Hecker, "Parole: A Critique of Its Legal Foundations and Conditions," 38 New York Law Review 702-39 (1963); "The Parole System in Canada," 15:2 Canadian Journal of Criminology and Corrections 144-69; John D. Quinn, "The Parole Board's Duty of Self-Regulation," 6:1 University of Michigan Journal of Law Reform 131-53 (1972); Ramsey Clark, "The Report of the New York Task Force on Parole," presented at the 1973 Annual Meeting of the American Society of Criminology, New York. Other studies have outlined parole rules used by various states: Don M. Gottfredson, Kelly B. Ballard, Jr., and Vincent O'Leary, "Uniform Parole Reports: A Feasibility Study," 3 Journal of Research in Crime and Delinquency 104-10 (July 1966); Nat R. Arluke, "A Summary of Parole Rules--Thirteen Years Later,"

15 Crime and Delinquency 267-74 (April 1969). Still other studies have attempted to compare differences between parole boards with regard to parole decisions and have been much more quantitative: Don M. Gottfredson, "Differences in Parole Decisions Associated with Decision Makers," 3 Journal of Research in Crime and Delinquency 114-19 (July 1966); Donald Gottfredson and Leslie T. Wilkins, "Parole Decision Making--A Progress Report," published by the National Criminal Justice Reference Service, 1973; and Peter B. Hoffman, "Paroling Policy Feedback," 9:2 Journal of Research in Crime and Delinquency 117-31 (1972).

2. For an excellent analysis of the use of differing sentencing procedures, see Robert H. Vasoli, "Growth and Consequences of Judicial Discretion in Sentencing," 40 Notre Dame Lawyer 404-16; Editorial Note, "Statutory Structures for Sentencing Felons to Prison," 60:6 Columbia Law Review 1134-72.

3. For a summary of the statutes and practices of the parole agencies in the 50 states and federal parole, see W. Parker's "Parole (Origins, Development, Current Practices and Statutes)," (Springfield, Va.: National Technical Information Service, 1972).

4. For a review of the theoretical foundation of parole, see David Dressler, Practice and Theory of Probation and Parole, 2nd ed. (1967), especially Chapters 1, 4, and 5; Editorial Comment, "The Parole System," 120 University of Pennsylvania Law Review 282-377.

5. The Fifth Circuit Court of Appeals' decision in Scarpa v. United States Board of Parole, 468 F. 2d 31 (5th Cir. 1973) held that the actual bestowal or denial of parole need not be accompanied by a hearing and any change in procedures must be made by the legislative branch and not the judicial. One justification the court gave in reaching this decision was a dearth of information available to them on parole-board decision making.

6. These three factors are similar to those examined by Edward Green in his "Sentencing Practices of Criminal Court Judges," 22 American Journal of Corrections 32-35 (July-August 1966).

7. For those inmates originally given a death sentence subsequently reduced to life and those given life sentences, a score of 500 was assigned. This was arrived at in a somewhat arbitrary manner.

8. Each inmate's prior criminal record was ascertained from the FBI report. From these reports five separate indicators of prior criminal involvement were recorded: total number of previous misdemeanor arrests, total number of previous felony arrests, total number of previous misdemeanor convictions, total number of previous felony convictions, and total number of previous prison incarcerations. These five indicators were combined to form a prior

criminal involvement scale in the following manner: First, the total
number of misdemeanor arrests and the total number of felony arrests in the United States for 1968 were ascertained, as were the
number of misdemeanor and felony convictions. These numbers
were then divided by the U.S. population as of July 1, 1968, to get
the percentage of the population arrested and/or convicted of misdemeanors and/or felonies during this period. The same procedure
was followed for individuals sentenced to prison during 1968--the
total number was divided by the U.S. population. The respective
percentages were: 0.04 percent of the population received by prisons
in 1968, 0.49 percent of the population convicted of a felony in 1968,
1.41 percent of the population arrested for a felony in 1968, 1.49
percent of the population convicted of a misdemeanor in 1968, 2.58
percent of the population arrested for a misdemeanor in 1968.

The percentage of the population received by prisons in 1968
was approximately 50 times smaller than the percentage of the population arrested for misdemeanors, 30 times smaller than the percentage convicted of a misdemeanor or arrested for a felony, and
10 times smaller than the percentage convicted of a felony. Therefore, the respective weights of 50, 30, 30, 10, and 1 (corresponding
to the five items above) were used to calculate each inmate's prior
criminal involvement score. This score was computed for each individual by weighting each time he or she had been arrested, convicted, or incarcerated in prison by the above weights and summing
the total for each individual.

Although the weights utilized in constructing this prior criminal involvement scale were derived in a somewhat crude, albeit
nonarbitrary, manner, the prior criminal involvement scale was
calculated in a number of other ways in an attempt to ascertain the
effect of weighting indicators differently. A second scale was constructed by squaring each of the weights used in the first scale.
The weights 2,500, 900, 900, 100, and 1 were then utilized to multiply each individual's raw score on each of the indicators. A third
scale was constructed by simply assigning Likert scores of 5, 4, 3,
2, and 1 to each of the indicators. Those weights were then used to
multiply the raw score of each individual and then summed for the
five indicators. Finally a fourth scale was calculated by assigning
a weight of 1 to all of the five indicators and multiplying each individual raw score and summing. The correlation between the original scale and the second scale was .98; between the original scale
and the third, .98; and between the original scale and the fourth,
.89. This appears to indicate that the weights assigned the various
indicators have little overall influence on the scale score. Others
have already argued this same point quite convincingly. See, for
example, Julian C. Stanley and Marilyn D. Wand, "Weighting Test

Items and Test Item Options: An Overview of the Analytical and Empirical Literature," 30 Educational and Psychological Measurement 21-35 (1970).

For an even more detailed explanation of how prior criminal involvement was quantified, see Joseph Elmo Scott, "An Examination of the Factors Utilized by Parole Boards in Determining the Severity of Punishment," Ph.D. dissertation, Department of Sociology, Indiana University, 1972, pp. 57-59.

9. This number includes possible jail time served by an inmate for the same offense either before trial or sentencing if so recorded in the summary report. The Midwestern state in which these parole boards were studied had the policy of counting time served in jail on the same offense in determining when the inmate was eligible for a parole hearing.

10. This finding was completely unexpected not only in light of conflict theory predictions but perhaps even more so because of the consistent finding that younger offenders are more likely to recidivate than older offenders. Ralph W. England, "A Study of Postprobation Recidivism among Five Hundred Federal Offenders," 19:3 Federal Probation 11-16 (1965); Daniel Glaser and Vincent O'Leary, Personal Characteristics and Parole Outcome (Washington, D.C.: U.S. Government Printing Office, 1966). Glaser and O'Leary argue that perhaps the most established piece of statistical knowledge about criminals is that the older a man is when released from prison the less likely he is to be rearrested. Assuming that the likelihood of rearrest is a crucial consideration in parole decisions, the relationship found in this research is rather surprising.

11. In analyzing data categorized as sets, one simply takes the entire variation of the dependent variable (punishment) and allows one set to explain all it can separately; then using the entire variation again, one allows the next set to explain all it can, and so on. Thus, the percent due to the fact that some of the same variation in the dependent variable is being accounted for by each data set, indicating perhaps some multicollinearity.

For an example and justification for using similar type data in analyzing sets, see Jacob Cohen, "Prognostic Factors in Functional Psychosis: A Study in Multivariate Methodology," 30:6 Transactions of the New York Academy of Sciences 833-40 (1968), and Jacob Cohen, "Multiple Regression as a General Data-Analytic System," 70:6 Psychological Bulletin 426-43 (1968).

Although many of the independent variables are nominal, by using dummy variables they are treated as interval for regression analysis. See Daniel B. Suits, "Use of Dummy Variables in Regression Equations," 52:280 Journal of the American Statistical Association 548-51 (1957).

12. See Daniel Glaser's discussion of whether having indeterminate-type sentencing laws and utilizing parole boards increases the average length of confinement in prison, in "Correction of Adult Offenders in the Community," Prisoners in America, ed. Lloyd Ohlin, 90-93 (1973).

13. Richard W. Wilsnack and Lloyd E. Ohlin, in a paper presented at the American Sociological Association annual meeting in New York, August 1973, on "Preconditions for Major Prison Disturbances," reported that instability in correctional administration and the uncertainty it created was often a precondition for a major prison disturbance. The uncertainty of parole creates numerous problems and much anxiety for inmates. See Joseph E. Scott and Jack L. Franklin, "Inmates' Evaluation of the Indeterminate Sentence," Journal of Correctional Education (Spring 1970). G. David Garson also discusses conditions favorable to prison unrest and disturbances in "The Disruption of Prison Administration: An Investigation of Alternative Theories of the Relationship among Administrators, Reformers, and Involuntary Social Service Clients," 6:4 Law and Society Review 531-61 (May 1972); Jessica Mitford, "Kind and Unusual Punishment in California," Atlantic Monthly, March 1971.

14. The courts are already doing this in several areas since repudiating the "hands off doctrine" and apparently adopting a "balancing of interest test" or the "least restrictive means test." Behavioral scientists, it would seem, have an equal responsibility to contribute in this examination as well. In fact, the Second Circuit in Sostre v. McGinnis, 442 F. 2d 197 (2d Cir. 1971), indicated an unwillingness to interfere any more in prison administration because of the dearth of reliable, empirical studies on the subject of prison procedures.

15. John W. Palmer, "A Preliminary Inquiry into the Exercise of Correctional Discretion," paper presented at the 1973 Annual Meeting of the American Society of Criminology, New York, November 4.

16. Several district courts have recently intervened and imposed procedural safeguards on prison disciplinary hearings: Clutchette v. Procunier, 328 F. Supp. 767 (N.D. Cal. 1971); Bundy v. Cannon, 328 F. Supp. 165 (D. Md. 1971); and Morris v. Travisono, 310 F. Supp. 857 (D. R.I. 1970). For an excellent review of judicial intervention in prison discipline and in particular the impact of the Morris case in Rhode Island, see Harvard Center for Criminal Justice, "Judicial Intervention in Prison Discipline," 63:2 Journal of Criminal Law, Criminology, and Police Science 200-28 (1972).

17. Gerhard O. W. Mueller, in an address to the Citizens' Task Force on Corrections for Ohio on July 27, 1971, advocated the use of institutionally based judges. See Mueller's "Correctional Law: Inmates' Rights, Legal Criteria, Reforms, and Futures" (Columbus, Ohio: Program for the Study of Crime and Delinquency, 1971; available in photocopied typescript). For a review of other countries' use of institutionally based judges, see Gerhard O. W. Mueller, "Punishment, Corrections and the Law," 45 Nebraska Law Review 58-95 (1966). Mueller argues that it is certainly not illogical for the judiciary to take the initiative in determining when an offender should be released. After all, everyone in an institution is there by judicial order. However, it is not to be expected that the judge who sentenced an offender to prison is to check on him daily. A viable alternative would be an institutional judge--one whose court room and facilities would be located at each penal institution. This judge would receive complaints by inmates with respect to anything that should come to judicial attention. He would be in charge of reviewing writs of habeas corpus and requests for writs of mandamus which "flow" from our institutions today. An institutionally based judge would also handle inmates' civil problems which require adjudication such as divorces or child custody cases and he could also perform marriages. In addition, he would have the authority to review inmates' sentences and he could, if necessary by judicial order, have all relevant information provided concerning each inmate and his institutional adjustment. Such procedures would at the very least provide inmates additional legal rights.

The idea of having institutionally based judges is not new. Several European countries have already initiated such procedures. Such a plan is a viable alternative to the present system which is apparently not working as expected or as desired. The use of institutional judges may provide the dignity and the concern our prisons have repeatedly demanded.

18. Scott has found similar results for a Midwestern parole board's decision making; see note 12.

REFERENCES

Arluke, N. R.
1969 A summary of parole rules--thirteen years later. Crime and Delinquency 15 (April).

Badillo, H.
1972 The need for an ombudsman. Social Action 38:8.

Cohen, J.
    1968   Prognostic factors in functional psychosis: a study in
            multivariate methodology. Transactions of the New York
            Academy of Sciences 30:6.

    1968   Multiple regression as a general data-analytic system.
            Psychological Bulletin 70:6.

Dawson, R. O.
    1966   The decision to grant or deny parole: a study of parole
            criteria in law and practice. Washington University Law
            Quarterly (June).

Dressler, D.
    1967   Practice and Theory of Probation and Parole. 2d ed.

England, R. W.
    1965   A study of postprobation recidivism among five hundred
            federal offenders. Federal Probation 19:3.

Fitzharris, T. L.
    1973   The desirability of a correctional ombudsman. Institute
            of Government Studies, University of California, Berkeley.

Garson, D. G.
    1972   The disruption of prison administration: an investigation
            of alternative theories of the relationship among adminis-
            trators, reformers, and involuntary social service clients.
            Law and Society Review (May).

Glaser, D.
    1964   The Effectiveness of a Prison and Parole System.
            Indianapolis: Bobbs-Merrill.

Glaser, D., and V. O'Leary
    1966   Personal Characteristics and Parole Outcome. Washing-
            ton, D.C.: U.S. Government Printing Office.

Gottesman, M., and L. J. Hecker
    1963   Parole: a critique of its legal foundations and conditions.
            New York Law Review 38.

Gottfredson, D. M.
    1966   Differences in parole decisions associated with decision
            makers. Journal of Research in Crime and Delinquency 3
            (July).

Gottfredson, D. M., K. B. Ballard, Jr., and V. O'Leary
   1966   Uniform parole reports: a feasibility study. Journal of
          Crime and Delinquency 3 (July).

Green, E.
   1966   Sentencing practices of criminal court judges. American
          Journal of Corrections (July-August).

Hoffman, P. B.
   1972   Paroling policy feedback. Journal of Research in Crime
          and Delinquency 9:2.

Journal of Criminal Law, Criminology, and Police Science
   1972   Judicial intervention in prison discipline. Harvard Center
          for Criminal Justice.

Miller, S. J.
   1971   Post-institutional adjustment of 433 consecutive TICO
          releasees. Ph.D. dissertation, Department of Sociology,
          Ohio State University.

Mitford, J.
   1971   Kind and unusual punishment in California. Atlantic
          Monthly (March).

Morris, N.
   1966   Impediments to penal reform. University of Chicago Law
          Review 33.

Mueller, G. O. W.
   1966   Punishment, corrections and the law. Nebraska Law
          Review 45.

National Council on Crime and Delinquency
   1973   Parole decisions. A policy statement. Crime and De-
          linquency 19, no. 2 (April): 137.

Ohlin, L.
   1973   Prisoners in America. New York: Columbia University
          Press for The American Assembly.

Palmer, J. W.
   1973   A preliminary inquiry into the exercise of correctional
          discretion. Paper presented at the 1973 Annual Meeting
          of the American Society of Criminology, New York.

Quinn, J. D.
    1972   The parole board's duty of self-regulation. University
            of Michigan Journal of Law Reform 6:1.

Richardson, S.
    1956   Parole and the law. Crime and Delinquency 2 (January).

Scott, J. E.
    1972   An examination of the factors utilized by parole boards in
            determining the severity of punishment. Ph. D. disserta-
            tion, Department of Sociology, Indiana University.

Scott, J. E., and J. L. Franklin
    1970   Inmates' evaluation of the indeterminate sentence.
            Journal of Correctional Education (Spring).

Stanley, J. C., and M. D. Wand
    1970   Weighting test items and test item options: an overview
            of the analytical and empirical literature. Educational
            and Psychological Measurement 30.

Suits, D. B.
    1957   Use of dummy variables in regression equations. Journal
            of the American Statistics Association 52:280.

Thomas, P. A.
    1963   An analysis of parole selection. Crime and Delinquency 9
            (April).

17

PAROLE BOARD DECISIONS AND THE SEVERITY OF PUNISHMENT: A CRITICAL REEXAMINATION OF THE EVIDENCE

Albert A. Simkus
Edwin L. Hall
C. Taylor Griffiths

The use of parole has increased in recent years to the point where a majority of prisoners released in the United States are released on parole.[1] Depending on the particular state involved, the length of time a prisoner remains incarcerated beyond the legal minimum set by the court depends to varying degrees on the discretion of the parole board. Thus, the severity of punishment, in terms of the length of imprisonment, imposed upon a criminal offender should be related to if or when the parole board decides to grant parole. Despite the important role now played by the parole boards as arbiters of the final length of incarceration of the inmate, knowledge about the criteria used by these boards in the rendering of their decisions is relatively incomplete.

The parole boards of many states publish the official criteria upon which their decisions are based, and a number of studies have involved interviews or surveys of board members asking those members to describe, list, and rank the considerations that they discuss and take into account in making their judgments (Board of Pardons, State of Montana 1971; National Parole Institutes 1966; Dawson 1969). It is doubtful, however, that the board members themselves can estimate very precisely the relative degree to which particular characteristics of inmates have influenced their decisions over the long

This chapter was originally a paper presented to the American Society of Criminology meetings, 1974. The authors wish to express their gratitude to Dr. Gordon Browder for access to data analyzed in this report. We also wish to thank Drs. Rob Balch, William McBroom, and Browder for their comments on an earlier draft.

run. Without examining the outcomes of a large number of hearings, it is difficult to translate a board member's statement that he sees younger or first-time offenders as "better risks" into a statement specifying that being ten years older or having committed a previous felony resulted in a specific increase in the probability that an inmate's hearing would result in a denial of parole. Since older offenders are also more likely to have committed prior offenses, it is difficult to separate the possible "effects" of age from the "effects" of previous offenses on the board's decision. In order to isolate the effect of one particular factor, one must be able to simultaneously control the influence of the other important factors.

Recent papers have examined the cases of a large number of inmates in an attempt to estimate the amount of effect particular personal-biographical characteristics of the inmate (such as age, education, and sex) appeared to have on the decisions of a parole board (Scott and Vandiver 1973; Griffiths 1974). In these studies the evident effects of personal-biographical characteristics of the inmate were compared to the influences of certain aspects of the inmate's legal background, such as the number of previous felonies and aspects of the inmate's record of behavior while imprisoned. Of these previous studies, only that done by Scott and Vandiver examined the influence of each of these factors while simultaneously controlling the other factors.

Using multiple regression techniques, Scott and Vandiver evaluated the ability of individual inmate characteristics and sets of these characteristics to predict the eventual severity of punishment of the inmate, in terms of the length of incarceration. They then interpreted differences in the length of incarceration as being due to the decisions of the parole board. They concluded that the personal-biographical characteristics of the inmate "are substantially better predictors than the institutional factors" involving reports on the inmate's behavior in prison. Since the board's decision appeared least influenced by information related to whether or not an offender had been "reformed" while imprisoned, they maintained that the boards, since evidently not functioning in a manner consistent with the "reformative" interpretation of the function of imprisonment, should perhaps be eliminated.

The Scott and Vandiver paper has been well received; however, it may easily escape the attention of the reader that the research reported by Scott and Vandiver contained no direct indicators of the decisions actually made by the parole board. Scott and Vandiver examined the correlations between inmate characteristics and length of incarceration and then interpreted these correlations as being entirely due to the decisions of the parole board. Nowhere in their paper do they acknowledge the possibility that these inmate characteristics may have resulted in the offender's spending longer in prison because of the effect of these characteristics on the sentence imposed by the court, rather than because of the effect of these characteristics on the decisions made by the parole board. The length of incarceration is not only a function of the parole board's decision but also of other factors, such as the sentence imposed by the court and the accumulation of "good time" reductions of sentence. If the exercise of discretion by parole boards does not account for the greater portion of the variation in length of incarceration, length of incarceration is an inaccurate indicator of the actions taken by the boards. The analysis by Scott and Vandiver reveals that the minimum length of sentence imposed by the judge alone accounts for 70 to 76 percent of the variation in length of incarceration.[2] This suggests that attributing differences in length of incarceration primarily to the parole board may be a mistake. If this is the case, these particular studies cannot be interpreted as accurate descriptions of the influence of various factors on parole-board decision making. They should instead be interpreted as descriptions of the impact of these variables on the overall effect of all aspects of the criminal justice system.

In the research reported here, the same data from a Western state parole board used in the studies done by Scott and Vandiver (1973) and Griffiths (1974) have been reexamined. Additional cases and two direct measures of the actual decisions made by the parole board regarding each case were added to the data used in the Scott and Vandiver study.[3] The influences of those background characteristics which have been previously reported as significantly influencing parole-board decisions have been reexamined in an attempt to identify whether their primary effect is through the parole board or through the sentencing process. An attempt has been made to gather evidence which might begin to answer two questions. First, in which particular phase of the criminal justice system--that is, court, parole board, or correctional institution--do various characteristics of the inmate have an effect on the eventual length of incarceration? Second, how much of the variation in the length of time spent in prison can be attributed to the decisions made by the parole board?

DATA AND METHODOLOGY

The data were drawn from the records of prisoner characteristics used by the parole board of a Western state during the five-year period from June 1966 to July 1971 (N = 710).[4] Part of the analysis involved comparing those 710 inmates who were paroled with an additional 182 inmates who either voluntarily or involuntarily were never released on parole (N = 892).

Using multiple regression techniques[5] to simultaneously control all other available relevant variables, we studied the influence of individual legal and personal-biographical background characteristics of the inmate upon the length of sentence imposed by the court, the number of times an inmate's case appeared before the board resulting in the denial of parole, whether the inmate was ever granted parole, and the resultant length of incarceration of the inmate.[6] Four separate equations were calculated from the multiple regression of each of the above dependent variables on all those inmate attributes which could be assumed to precede each of those dependent variables in time (see Table 17.1). By examining the relative sizes of the standardized regression coefficients (β) and unstandardized regression coefficients (b) displayed in Table 17.1, we may estimate the relative influence exerted by each of the inmate's characteristics on the dependent variables representing the outcome of each of the processes: sentencing, granting of parole, and incarceration.[7] The personal-biographical characteristics included as independent variables were the sex, marital status, ethnicity, educational attainment, employment history, and age of each inmate.[8] The number of prior felony convictions, whether a detainer had been filed against the inmate, and whether or not he had been in a juvenile institution were included as attributes of the legal background of the inmate.

FINDINGS

The Effects of Inmate Attributes on the Sentencing Process

All of the inmate characteristics in combination accounted for only a small amount of the variation in length of sentence ($R^2 = .055$). More of the variance could have been accounted for if other independent variables, such as a measure of the seriousness of the crime, had been introduced. The sole purpose of this analysis, however, was to discover whether the effects of these particular attributes on the length of incarceration were a result of their direct influence on the parole board's decisions, or if those end effects were the result of the influences of those attributes on sentencing.

The number of prior felony convictions had the greatest influence on the length of sentence ($\beta = .13$, b = 5.7). Of the personal-biographical variables, marital status appeared to make the most difference with married persons receiving, on the average, sentences 15.2 months shorter than those received by inmates who were

TABLE 17.1
Elements of the Regression Equations

Population	Dependent Variable	Independent Variables	Zero-order Correlation (r)	Multiple Correlation Coefficient (R)	Partial Regression Coefficient (b)	Standard Partial Regression Coefficient ( )	Standard Error of (b)
Parolees[a] (N = 710)	Sentence	Prior felonies	.163		5.714	.132	1.837
		Married	-.098	R = .235	-15.212	-.130	4.958
		Sex	-.101	R² = .005	-20.830	-.079	9.837
		Age	.124		2.873	.082	1.676
		Ethnicity	-.064		-7.028	-.057	4.712
		Divorced	.064		-4.510	-.044	3.758
		Unemployed	-.034		-2.751	-.028	4.606
		Prior incarceration juvenile institution	-.047		-2.860	-.026	4.462
		Detainers	-.010		-1.850	-.012	5.752
		Education	-.001		.931	.010	3.401
Parolees[a] (N = 710)	Parole deferments	Prior felonies	.257	R = .514	.155	.195	.030
		Detainers	-.072	R² = .264	-.253	-.090	.093
		Married	-.089		-.082	-.038	.081
		Prior incarceration juvenile institution	.062		.158	.078	.072
		Employed	-.018		-.050	-.028	.061
		Sex	-.073		-.013	-.003	.160
		Education	-.048		-.045	-.027	.055
		Ethnicity	-.055		.003	.001	.055
		Age	.110		-.011	-.017	.076
		Sentence	.462		.008	.429	.027
		Divorced	.077		.035	.019	.075
Inmates[b] (N = 892)	Paroled or not paroled	Prior felonies	-.157	R = .299	-.051	-.149	.013
		Education	.104	R² = .089	.048	.065	.024
		Detainers	.067		.093	.071	.043
		Ethnicity	-.064		-.045	-.045	.033
		Employed	-.068		-.036	-.045	.027
		Age	-.106		-.018	-.061	.011
		Married	.039		.051	.053	.035
		Sex	.033		.083	.037	.075
		Divorced	-.035		.010	.011	.032
		Sentence	.187		.002	.210	.003
Parolees[a] (N = 710)	Length of Incarceration	Sentence	.766	R = .846	.204	.578	.008
		Appears	.673	R² = .716	7.816	.406	.436

[a]Offenders who were eventually paroled.
[b]Includes 182 offenders who were not or who would not accept parole and served to discharge from the institution.
Source: Compiled by the authors.

single (β = -.13, b = -15.2). The age of the offender was next in importance,[9] indicating that even when other factors were controlled, older offenders were more likely to have long sentences (β = .08). Sex was also a significant factor, women having received sentences which averaged 20.8 months shorter than those received by men (β = -.08, b = -20.8). The influence of ethnicity was marginal; the sentences of native Americans averaged seven months shorter than those of whites (β = -.06, b = -7.0).[10] Employment history, being divorced, having been incarcerated in a juvenile institution, and education had insignificant (β < .050) effects on the length of sentence.

The Effects of Inmate Characteristics on Parole Board Decisions

The length of sentence imposed by the court had the most substantial effect on the number of times an inmate's case appeared before the board before parole was granted (β = .43). This effect may indicate that the parole boards tended to treat the inmates in a manner consistent with the severity of the punishment imposed by the court. Assuming the length of sentence to be an indicator of the seriousness of the crime, it could also reflect a tendency of the parole board to hold back offenders who have committed more serious crimes, perhaps feeling that those convicted of more serious crimes were a greater threat to society.[11] The number of prior felony convictions also had a positive effect on the number of deferments of parole (β = .20). Inmates who had been incarcerated in juvenile institutions, though evidently not treated differently in regard to the length of sentence, appeared before the boards a slightly greater number of times than those who had not been incarcerated in juvenile institutions (β = .08).

A previous study has reported that the largest percentage of parole-board members ranked the statement "My estimate of the chances that the prisoner would or would not commit a serious crime if paroled," as one of the five most important considerations influencing their decisions (National Advisory Commission 1973). It is reasonable to believe that the length, consistency, and seriousness of an inmate's criminal record tended to influence the board's estimation of the likelihood of that inmate committing a serious crime while on parole. Scott and Vandiver reported an interview in which a parole-board member indicated that the board liked to "pass on" inmates against whom detainers had been filed. Consistent with this view, it was found that inmates with detainers were more likely to be released early (β = -.09).

None of personal-biographical characteristics showed a significant ($\beta <$ .050) direct influence on the number of times parole was denied.

Approximately 20 percent of the inmates from the Western prison were never released on parole. Those prisoners with longer sentences were more likely to be paroled ($\beta =$ .21), while those inmates who had been convicted of a larger number of prior felonies were less likely to be paroled ($\beta =$ -.15). The tendency of some offenders, particularly those with prior records and/or shorter sentences, to elect to serve to discharge rather than face the "hassle" of parole supervision may explain these findings. Prior incarceration in a juvenile institution had a negative effect on the chance of receiving parole. Of the personal-biographical set of variables, education ($\beta =$ .07) and marriage ($\beta =$ .05) had a marginally positive effect. Age seemed to have an equally small negative effect ($\beta =$ -.06). The effects of ethnicity, employment, history, sex, and divorce appeared to be unimportant ($\beta <$ .050).

The Influence of Sentence and Parole Deferments on the Length of Incarceration

The regression problem utilizing both the length of sentence and number of parole deferments as independent variables in predicting the length of incarceration indicated that of the two, the length of sentence had the greater influence ($\beta =$ .58 and .41, respectively).[12] For each year of sentence the average inmate spent .20 years in prison (b = .20). An inmate spent on the average an additional 7.8 months in prison (b = 7.8) for each time his parole was deferred by the board. The impact of the board's decisions relative to the impact of sentencing was small primarily because the board released most inmates upon their first hearing. Of the variation (R = .85) in length of incarceration, 72 percent was accounted for by these two factors together; much of the remaining 28 percent probably being due to differences in the accumulation of "good time."

The Process as a Whole

The important relationships which apparently took place within the sentencing, parole hearing, and incarceration process are summarized by a path model[13] (see Figure 17.1) including only those paths which resulted in path coefficients greater than .050. The path model summarizes the more important relationships between the various variables considered.

FIGURE 17.1

Path Model Showing Relationships between Sentencing, Parole Hearings, and Incarceration Processes

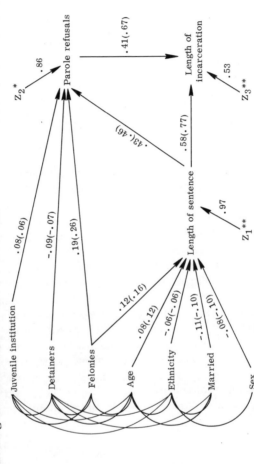

Note: A correlation matrix of the intercorrelations among the exogenous variables representing the inmate background characteristics is included in the Appendix to this chapter.

*These are "random shock" terms and refer to the residual variation in the dependent variables which is unaccounted for by the independent variables included in the model ($Z_i = 1 - R_i^2$). In path analysis these terms are assumed to be uncorrelated with either each other or the independent variables explicitly included in the model.

Source: Compiled by the authors.

TABLE 17.2

Correlation Matrix of Pearson Correlations (r) between
the Variables Included in the Path Model

	Juvenile Institutions	Detainers	Felonies	Age	Marriage	Sex	Ethnicity	Sentence	Prior Deferments	Length of Incarceration
Prior incarceration in juvenile institutions										
Detainers	.075									
Felonies	.058	.096								
Age	-.297	-.051	.424							
Marriage	.003	.059	.017	.104						
Sex	-.051	-.024	-.119	.023	.017					
Ethnicity	.158	-.082	-.003	-.102	-.073	.072				
Sentence	-.047	-.006	.163	.124	-.098	-.101	-.065			
Prior deferments	.062	-.072	.257	.110	-.089	-.073	-.005	.462		
Length of incarceration	.001	-.050	.234	.150	-.109	-.082	-.043	.766	.673	

Source: Compiled by the authors.

The arrows in the figure represent what is assumed to be the unidirectional influence of each variable considered as a "cause" on the variable considered as an "effect." Such arrows are not drawn if a relationship was logically impossible because of the time order involved or if the previous regression analysis had shown it to be relatively unimportant ($\beta < .050$). The directions of the relationships between the variables representing inmate characteristics are presumed to be unclear, and the intercorrelations among them are simply represented by symmetrical curved lines. The values placed in parentheses on each arrow represent the zero-order correlation (r) between the two variables connected by the arrows. The "path coefficient," the value outside the parenthesis to the left of the correlation coefficient, corresponds to the standard partial regression coefficient (β), which expresses the amount of change in the dependent variable (measured in standard scores) associated with the same amount of change in the independent variable (also in standard form) when the value of all other variables shown as having an effect upon the dependent variable are held constant. In a sense, the "path coefficient" represents the direct "effects" of the variable at the tail of the arrow on the variable at the head of the arrow. The difference between the zero-order correlation coefficient and the "path coefficient" represents the total of the indirect effects of the independent variable on the dependent variable which are derived from the intercorrelations of the two with other variables.[14] We caution against interpreting this model in any strict "causal" sense. The model is presented as a means of parsimoniously providing a decomposition of the relationships among the variables considered.

Several conclusions may be inferred from the path diagram. First, the influence of the personal-biographical background characteristics on the length of incarceration is small and is exerted primarily through their direct effects on sentencing. Second, the number of prior felonies has significant direct effects on the decisions of both the courts and the parole board. Third, of the variables examined, only the legal characteristics of the inmate had significant effects on the number of parole refusals. Finally, the length of incarceration is not solely or even primarily a result of the deferment of parole by the parole board.

Although, not surprisingly, parole refusals and the length of sentence together account for 72 percent of the variation in length of incarceration, only 26 percent of the variation in parole deferments ($R = .51$, $R^2 = .26$), and 9 percent of the variation in whether or not a prisoner was ever paroled ($R = .30$, $R^2 = .09$), are explained by the combination of all of the independent variables studied. This suggests either that the parole board's decisions are largely arbitrary, that the relationships of interest are either nonlinear or nonadditive, or that the major factors influencing the parole board have been excluded or inadequately measured.

CONCLUSIONS

Scott and Vandiver's conclusion that "the fact that an inmate's personal social-biographical characteristics are substantially better predictors of the punishment he will receive than his entire institutional adjustment, cooperation and participation, and the prison's evaluation of his rehabilitation," and their portrayal of this outcome as a result of the decisions by the parole board cannot be supported convincingly by their data. In their study the influence of "institutional factors" on parole discretion is underestimated due to both the inadequacy of their measures of "institutional factors"[15] and their lack of a measure of the direct effects of such factors on parole-board decision making. At the same time, they overestimate the influence of the personal-biographical factors both by virtually ignoring the role of sentencing and by including age at time of release as an independent variable. The correlation between age at release and length of sentence is inflated by the linear but very uninteresting effect of staying in prison on becoming older.

The reexamination of the data reported here did not involve an evaluation of the importance of the "institutional factors" because no adequate indicator of those factors was included in the data gathered from the Western state. Such information was available for a Midwestern state (Scott and Vandiver 1973), but the data from the Midwestern state included no information on the actual decisions of the parole board.

This reexamination did indicate that the influence of the personal-biographical characteristics of an inmate is very small and is exerted mainly on the sentencing process. It has also shown that the factors studied, the seriousness, length, and consistency of an inmate's criminal history, seemed to have the greatest influence on the parole board's decisions. Primarily because of the lack of adequate data, neither this nor such previous studies have yet convincingly measured the "really important" influences on the decision to parole. What we hope has been demonstrated is that the influence of personal-biographical characteristics of the inmate on the decisions of the parole board studied may have been overestimated in the previous studies.

NOTES

1. According to National Prisoner Statistics: Prisoners in State and Federal Institutions for Adult Felons, 1970, 72 percent of the felons leaving prison in 1970 were released as parolees.

2. The "seriousness of the crime" was operationally defined by Scott and Vandiver as the legal minimum sentence imposed on the offender by the court. Thus, the strong relationship they found between the "seriousness of the crime" and the severity of the punishment was no more than the relationship between the sentence imposed by the court and the length of imprisonment.

3. The samples studied by Scott and Vandiver consisted of the records of all female inmates released from two prisons in the Midwest in 1968 (N = 39), and a 25 percent sample of the records of all male inmates released from two prisons in the Midwest in 1968 (N = 325), plus the records of all inmates released on parole from the Western prison in 1968 (N = 152).

4. Those receiving life sentences, involving commutations, as well as those cases which were of neither white nor native American ethnic background, were excluded. Such excluded cases comprised a very small percentage of the offenders incarcerated in this state.

5. One of the clearest explanations of the use of multiple regression in social research may be found in Kerlinger and Pedhazur (1973).

6. These dependent variables were defined in the following ways: length of sentence = the length of sentence imposed by the courts, subtracting that portion of the sentence suspended (measured in months); parole deferments = the number of times an inmate's case appeared before the board, resulting in denial of parole; paroled–not paroled = a dummy variable coded as "1" if the inmate was ever granted parole, and "0" if the inmate served until release without parole.

7. denotes the standardized partial regression coefficient which reveals the ability of the independent variable to account for the variation in the dependent variable while all other variables are being controlled. b, the unstandardized regression coefficient, may be interpreted as the average amount of change in the dependent variable associated with one unit of change in the independent variable. In those cases where we have collapsed together values of the independent variable (such as was done with age), the interpretation of b is difficult and often misleading. The values of b are therefore not listed in the text in the discussion of the effects of those variables whose interval level of measurement was negated in the process of collapsing.

8. The independent variables were assigned values in the following ways: felonies--the number of previous felony convictions, collapsed in the following manner: (0 = 0) (1 = 1) (2 = 2) (3 or more = 3); juvenile institutions--a dummy variable coded as a "0" if the inmate had never been incarcerated in a juvenile institution and coded as a "1" if the inmate had been previously incarcerated in such an institution; detainers--coded as "0" if the inmate's record showed no detainers filed against the inmate during his incarceration; age, in years, at time of incarceration, recoded in the following manner: (18 through 20 = 1) (21 through 24 = 2) (25 through 29 = 3) (30 through 39 = 4) (40 and above = 5); sex--women were coded "1" and males were coded as "0"; education--the number of years of formal education completed by the inmate prior to his incarceration, recoded in the following manner: (0 through 8 = 1) (9 through 12 = 2) (13 or more = 3); ethnicity--the self-reported ethnic background listed on the inmates' parole records. Native Americans were coded as "1," while whites were coded as "0"; divorced--inmates who were presently divorced were coded "1," all others as "0"; employment--inmates whose records indicated frequent or permanent unemployment were coded as "0," those who were usually employed prior to incarceration were assigned "1."

9. The correlation between age at time of release, as measured in the Scott and Vandiver paper and the length of incarceration partially reflected the linear relationship between aging and spending time in prison.

10. Other research conducted by the authors has shown that native Americans in this state were significantly more likely to be incarcerated and significantly less likely to receive deferred sentences than were similar whites. The shorter sentences given native Americans may be a reflection of the fact that whites who had committed less serious crimes were less likely to be incarcerated and were thus missing from the prison data.

11. See note 2.

12. Limitations in the data prevented us from including those prisoners who were always denied parole by the board. The contribution of the board's decisions would have been greater if those cases could have been included. It is highly doubtful, however, that the importance of sentencing would have been reduced to an insignificant level.

13. For a more extended discussion of path analysis, see Kerlinger and Pedhazur (1973), Land (1969), or Duncan (1966).

14. For a fuller explanation see Kerlinger and Pedhazur (1973).

15. The only measure of "institutional adjustment" available to Scott and Vandiver from the Western prison data was information regarding whether or not an inmate had ever enrolled in the prison school program.

REFERENCES

Board of Pardons, State of Montana
  1971   Annual Report of the State Board of Pardons for Fiscal
          Year Ended June 30, 1971. Deer Lodge, Mont.: Board
          of Pardons.

Dawson, R. O.
  1969   Sentencing: The Decision as to Type, Length, and Condi-
          tions of Sentence. Boston: Little, Brown.

Duncan, O. D.
  1966   Path analysis: sociological examples. In Causal Models
          in the Social Sciences, ed. H. M. Blalock, Jr. Chicago:
          Aldine.

Griffiths, C. T.
  1974   Factors associated with parole board decision making.
          M.A. thesis, University of Montana.

Kerlinger, F. N., and E. J. Pedhazur
  1973   Multiple Regression in Behavioral Research. New York:
          Holt, Rinehart and Winston.

Land, K. C.
  1969   Principles of path analysis. In Sociological Methodology,
          ed. E. F. Borgatta. San Francisco: Jossey-Bass.

National Advisory Commission on Criminal Justice Standards and
Goals
  1973   Corrections. Washington, D.C.: U.S. Department of
          Justice.

National Parole Institutes
  1966   Selection for Parole. New York: National Council on
          Crime and Delinquency.

Scott, J. E., and R. D. Vandiver
  1973   The use of discretion in punishing convicted adult offender
          parole boards and their decisions. Paper presented at
          American Criminological Society Meetings.

APPLIED CRIMINOLOGY:
IMPROVING THE SYSTEM

Today, we are facing ever-accelerating change in society as a whole. Most futurists agree that the years from 1990 to 2000 will bring overwhelmingly more change to mankind than will the coming 13 years. And since social change touches every society and every social institution, we would do well to ask what significance this change will have for our concepts of equity and justice, our institutions for social control, and our human service agencies, whose task it is to provide for those who cannot provide for themselves. One thing seems certain: Unless major adjustments are made in the immediate future, the criminal justice system will be unprepared to face the oncoming change. Criminologists know only too well that criminal justice has always tended to be reactive when faced with change. It has certainly never been proactive. Critical situations and problems tend to arise. Only then are procedures worked out to cope with the change that has befallen the system. The history of criminal justice is replete with examples of unpreparedness. When in the early 1970s Attica and other prisons exploded, no one was prepared to deal with the problems and underlying issues that had been smoldering and continue to do so. Even though ample research had documented many avenues for reducing and preventing prison violence, no action had been taken. More recently, when riots and civil disobedience brought unprecedented numbers of detainees, as happened in New Hampshire and New York City, the system was unprepared to handle them. There are very few efforts under way that seek to measure the impact of the mania for mandatory sentencing legislation that is currently sweeping the nation. In fact, few systems have the necessary information systems and sophisticated data bases that would permit the assessment of such legislation. The examples could go on and on. Perusing the state of the art, one thing seems clear. Not only is criminal justice in the United States unprepared for the coming change, but the chances are more than even that our entire machinery for social control will soon break down.

What can be done to ward off such a development? Obviously, planning for criminal justice is one important answer. While never a panacea, planning will be necessary if the system is to anticipate, adjust, and deal with change. Clearly, planning is useful because the guideposts to the future can usually be found in the present. However, we need to note that most of the current planning effort in criminal justice, which is not regressive, is in terms of dabbling with system improvements and solutions seeking "more of the same."

All this has the regrettable but obvious characteristic of rearranging the deck chairs on the Titanic. Again we need to ask, what kind of planning is needed to prevent the predicted collapse of the system? Clearly, we must quickly become aware of the contingencies of our present courses of action, of the repercussions of our inactions, and begin to divert the present trends by strategic planning and developing appropriate alternative plans for action. Most of all, we need strategic criminal justice planning which is synonymous with innovating planning and which seeks to produce structural change in the system.

At this time there are few students of criminal justice who would disagree on the critical need for immediate action based on a conscientious effort of strategic planning and contingency-plan development. All the more surprising, then, are the recommendations listed in a recent report to the Attorney General of the United States, developed by a special study group whose task it was to review the mission and activities of the Law Enforcement Assistance Administration and to recommend changes (Report to the Attorney General, Department of Justice Study Group, June 23, 1977). As is well known, LEAA's congressional mandate requires that the organization work in a partnership with state and local units of government to reduce crime and delinquency. To achieve that goal, LEAA adopted two subgoals: to develop, test, and evaluate effective programs, projects, and techniques to reduce crime and delinquency; and to build the capacity for comprehensive crime-reduction planning, program development, and evaluation. Organizationally, this meant an LEAA headquarters in Washington, D.C., the development of 50 state planning agencies and 10 regional offices to execute the mission of the agency as a whole. It is not the purpose here to prepare a treatise on the problems and ills of LEAA. There is a growing body of literature on that subject. We wish only to comment on the recommended changes of the report cited above in view of the vast implication these changes would have for criminal justice as a whole and for planning in particular, if they were to be implemented.

In essence, the report recommends that the present block grant portions of the LEAA program be replaced by a simpler program of direct assistance to state and local governments under which federal funds would be distributed among these governments on a basis whereby they would be entitled to a specific level of funding with no requirement for detailed plan submission. This direct assistance program would include those portions of the LEAA block program which are currently utilized in planning, action programs, and corrections construction. In addition, the study group recommends that these funds be integrated into the legislative and budgetary processes of the eligible jurisdictions and simply be treated as general revenue. A minority report of that study group recommends the outright abolition of the state planning agencies. The majority report, fudging on this issue, simply says that receipt of funding be made contingent upon a state government's (or local government's) ability to prove that it had an existing organization or agency which could conduct a "coordinating function" among the various criminal justice components.

Now it is true, as the report says, that systemwide criminal justice planning is not taking place in the United States, except on a highly limited scale and on an exception basis. It is also true that many planning agencies had little impact on the allocation of total state and local criminal justice funds. Most states seem to plan for only the 3-5 percent of their criminal justice expenditures which they receive from LEAA. And planning for block grant funds amounts to little more than the paperwork exercise required to qualify for the money. We must agree with the report up to this point and to the extent that the state planning agencies--with a few notable exceptions-- have failed to affect the system in any significant way. But Massachusetts did impact the juvenile justice system to an unprecedented degree during the Sargent administration by deinstitutionalizing its juvenile justice system. This feat has yet to be implemented anywhere else and could never have been done without LEAA funds. Hawaii did develop a long-range master plan which, if implemented in its entirety, has the potential to revolutionize the criminal justice system as we know it. A small number of agencies did try to live up to the congressional charge; but little can be said for the majority of the state planning agencies. In most instances, the agencies are wholly politically oriented, serve the will of their governors, and function as pork-barrel operations, distributing money as a result of political considerations. Directorships and key posts are part and parcel of the patronage system. Little attention, if any, is paid to enlisting professionals knowledgeable in the field. Too often, funding goes to those persons with the strongest political pull or to those who clamored the loudest, rather than on the basis of rational planning or merit. A pervasive and remarkably enduring view held by many legislators and echoed by most of the LEAA leadership, that the agency and its satellites should principally be "check-writing agencies," did not help the record. But this is as far as one should go with the criticism of LEAA. Serious exception should be taken to the study group's observation that "the requirement for state comprehensive criminal justice planning proved unworkable in most instances because of the different responsibilities and authorities of State and local governments, and because of the great difficulties experienced in specifying planning roles, responsibilities, and relationships among State, regional and local governments in ways that all levels of government agree meet their needs." This is nothing short of a capitulation, saying that because criminal justice still operates in the manner of feudal fiefdoms, and because there are inordinate difficulties, one should throw in the towel and just dole out the people's hard-earned tax money on some predetermined apportioned basis, regardless of whether there is merit and innovation or not. Even if receipt of the money were dependent on a jurisdiction's proof of coordination, what assurance can be given that state and local governments would not go to any length to convince the federal government as to their compliance, even if they had to erect an entire Potemkin village to do so?

It is ironic indeed that in 1977 we have to defend criminal justice planning. The need for systematic, continuous, formal, and organized planning is recognized the world over. Nations would not long survive if they did not plan for food, for their defense, and for the various needs of their people. In the face of fleeting depletion of resources, such as fuel, precious metals, and so on, paired with population explosions, almost every country has begun to plan for meeting their population's needs. And criminal justice, whose machinery is at the breaking point, is not supposed to plan because it is too difficult? Surely, a nation as innovative and energetic as ours cannot and must not give up that easily. There is no reason why one cannot benefit from the lessons and errors of the past and modify LEAA (or some comparable agency) to the point that the system can enable all of us to face the future with some modicum of confidence. For example, there should be support for the study group's recommendation that LEAA refocus its national research and development role into a coherent strategy of basic and applied research and that a systematic national program be developed that is designed to test, demonstrate, and evaluate innovating programs. But in addition, a leadership role needs to be developed similar to the national school integration and affirmative action programs, which stand in the forefront and assist tangibly the activities of the federal courts in the implementation of equity and justice in criminal justice. And there will have to be more planning, not less, and improved total system planning, if we wish only to avoid the cataclysm that is almost upon us.

The last chapter of the book (by Edith Elisabeth Flynn) recounts the development of the National Clearinghouse on Criminal Justice Planning and Architecture at the University of Illinois and the evolution of a planning document which was first geared at corrections planning but then grew to encompass a total systems approach, promulgated extensively by the work of the National Advisory Commission on Criminal Justice Standards and Goals (1973). It should be remembered that in the early 1970s, criminal justice planning, that is, planning that looks at the police, courts, corrections, and relevant human service agencies as an entity and in terms of their impact on each other, was not known. As a result, the research team at the University of Illinois had to grapple with formidable difficulties. Just getting decision makers in the various subsystems of criminal justice to talk to one another and to begin considering one another's problems and needs was a major challenge. The difficulties were compounded by the absence of national leadership required by such coordination. Whatever LEAA's faults, the agency deserves full credit for creating the setting and structure for key representatives of the various components of criminal justice to begin talking to one another. Taking advantage of what little leverage LEAA could provide under its legislative mandate (that is, the "carrot" of Part E and Part C funding), the study team developed a corrections planning document (<u>Guidelines for the Planning and Design of Regional and Community Correctional Centers for Adults</u>) that calls for the consideration and analysis of law enforcement and judicial and corrections practices. It also calls for every planning effort to assess developing trends in criminal justice and to inventory community resources in order to modify the workings of particular parts of the criminal justice machinery. For example, following the planning process, a jurisdiction could plan for the diversion of socioeconomic problem cases from criminal justice altogether. It could also explore alternatives to incarceration on the pretrial and postconviction level, based on an analysis of their own data. Planning can occur on a local, regional, or statewide basis, depending on the willingness of the involved jurisdictions to cooperate with one another. (Remember, at this time there is no leverage to force jurisdictions to cooperate with one another.) Taking into cognizance the fact that the implementation of change in criminal justice is always contingent upon the political realities of the jurisdiction(s) concerned, the planning document provides the flexibility for decision makers to proceed incrementally, in accordance with the community's or state's readiness to accept change.

Much has happened since the development of the planning document. Hundreds of jurisdictions at various governmental levels have applied it. While few followed it to the degree that major modifications of system components occurred, none who used it confined their planning just to corrections alone.

One final note of historical interest. The National Clearinghouse has been in existence since 1971. Since that time, the agency has been involved in thousands of corrections planning efforts, especially in projects involving construction. While not the extensive hindrance to corrections construction as some would have it, today the Clearinghouse is the only agency advising the federal government that has thwarted the construction of many jail and prison construction projects that would most assuredly have replicated the worst in corrections construction, brick by brick. It is important to note that this agency did it solely on the basis of its powers of persuasion and whatever incentive a 2-3 percent federal subsidy represents on a particular construction bill. There are precious few obstacles in the road to prison and jail construction, once a jurisdiction decides that it wants a new facility. At the time of this writing, the fate of the Clearinghouse at the University of Illinois is an open question. There are major changes impacting LEAA, as was seen above. The LEAA regional offices have already been abolished. The Clearinghouse, which is serving on a sole-source contracting basis, has been notified that in March 1978 its contract will go out on bid, as if it were so easy to replicate and accumulate the knowledge of eight years in this difficult field. It is to be hoped that its contributions in the area of comprehensive, total system planning and innovative architectural practices will not be lost to a criminal justice system that badly needs to pursue these directions.

18

SYSTEMS PLANNING IN CRIMINAL JUSTICE: AN EXAMPLE OF AN INTERDISCIPLINARY ENDEAVOR
Edith Elisabeth Flynn

Late in 1969 the Law Enforcement Assistance Administration was faced with a multimillion-dollar problem. Congress was about to pass the Part E Amendment to the Omnibus Crime Control and Safe Streets Act, which would authorize LEAA to make grants to states for "the construction, acquisition and renovation of correctional institutions and facilities, and for the improvement of correctional programs and practices."

It soon became apparent that little current information was available as to the special ways in which architectural design affects the process of corrections. Furthermore, there was consensus among those working in the field that the acute failures of corrections were at least in part attributable to the grossly inadequate, frequently dehumanizing and deadly effect of the physical structures in which most prisoners are housed. A repetition of the disastrous errors of the early nineteenth century was to be avoided; and if scarce resources were to be applied constructively and not wasted in the replication of obsolete molds, a number of vital questions had to be quickly answered. What kinds of jails and prisons should be built? Can physical design improve the effectiveness of the correctional institution? Have architects through earlier prison design contributed to the abysmal failure of our so-called correctional institutions? How should correctional institutions be financed? Should the focus be on bricks and mortar, or should LEAA concentrate on the diversion of offenders from the correctional system and on alternatives to incarceration?

The pressure on LEAA to fund buildings--jails and prisons-- would be enormous. A large percentage of prisons and jails are over 50 years old. Some institutions were built as early as the War of 1812 and are still in use. And, too frequently, the physical conditions defy explanation in a supposedly civilized country.

To prepare itself for the anticipated boom in correctional construction, LEAA underwrote three studies and had a private foundation carry out a fourth study. The University of California at Davis was asked to pinpoint areas in correctional architecture which were in urgent need of investigation and research. The University of Pennsylvania addressed itself to issues of correctional environment planning for juvenile offenders (Management and Behavioral Sciences Center 1972); the Institute of Corrections of the American Foundation in Philadelphia conducted an evaluation of the state of the art in correctional architecture (Nagel 1973); and the University of Illinois developed some guidelines for correctional administrators and architects in the planning and development of treatment programs within the community context, and in the planning and design of regional and community correctional centers for adults (University of Illinois 1972). This chapter reports on the development findings of this last study.

CONCEPTUALIZATION OF THE PLANNING MODEL

The U.S. correctional system in general and the prison system in particular are currently experiencing intense and growing criticism by both national and state study commissions for the apparent failure to reduce recidivism.[1]

Although inferences about crime and delinquency are at best hazardous, because of the general unreliability of criminal statistics and the lack of uniformity in recording techniques, it is generally estimated that juvenile and adult offenders are recommitted to correctional institutions and agencies at unacceptably high rates. It may be argued that recidivism should not be the sole index of the effectiveness of correctional programs, and that success may well be measured in terms of reduction of the seriousness of offenses or in the lengthening of the time period in which offenders refrain from committing further criminal acts.

We cannot agree with this logic. Offenses, regardless of their severity, still add to the total burden of crime and point to the failure of correctional programs to achieve their often-stated goals of resocialization and reintegration. In addition to its high failure rates, the U.S. prison system has failed to keep pace with the rapidly progressing social, political, and economic changes of today's society. It is tenaciously clinging to nineteenth-century policies and practices which have long since lost their viability in the urban, heterogeneous, and postindustrialized society of the twentieth century. As a result, public confidence in present correctional efforts is eroded, and there is great public anxiety about the system's ability to control and reduce crime, which is now at its peak.

Responding to the furor and attempting to meet the challenge facing the prison system, such influential organizations as the National Advisory Commission on Criminal Justice Standards and Goals, the American Bar Association's Commission on Correctional Facilities and Services, the National Council of Crime and Delinquency, and the Law Enforcement Assistance Administration of the U.S. Department of Justice launched their attacks.

Under the auspices of these organizations, a virtual plethora of research efforts, studies, and experiments have been conducted. All were designed to contribute to the existing fund of knowledge in the field of penology and corrections and to bring about reform in the correctional field. The research efforts of the University of Illinois, under the sponsorship of the Law Enforcement Assistance Administration, resulted in the establishment in 1971 of the National Clearinghouse for Criminal Justice Planning and Architecture on the Urbana campus. The specific goal of the project was to prepare some guidelines that would aid states and local governments in more innovative correctional program and facility planning. The guidelines were to reflect the high priority of the federal government to reform the nation's correctional systems and to improve or initiate community-based correctional programs, such as diagnostic services, probation and parole, halfway houses, work release, and a host of other supervisory programs for juvenile and adult offenders. In addition, the guidelines were to serve as a bench mark for the evaluation of correctional construction projects seeking federal funding under the Part E Amendment to the Safe Streets Act and to assure that such funding would not be used to perpetuate the kinds of prisons, jails, and programs that contributed to the failures of the past.

To accomplish the task, an interdisciplinary research team of one sociologist and three architects was assembled. Additional support came from the areas of law, survey research, and a broad array of correctional administrators, practitioners, and members of the academic and professional communities of corrections and of architecture. Guidelines for the Planning and Design of Regional and Community Correctional Centers for Adults was published in 1971 (Moyer et al. 1971).

The basic guiding philosophy for the manual had been given in broad strokes by LEAA. Nonetheless, Guidelines could easily have taken the shape of a series of blueprints and prototypes for a host of facilities ranging from prisons, to jails, to halfway houses, and to similar correctional institutions. Also, the interdisciplinary research could have applied the microperspective of predominant man-environment relations and sociophysical technology--topics which currently are treated in many promising multidisciplinary research projects.[2] Instead, the team producing Guidelines came to grips with some of the most crucial and fundamental issues facing corrections and the prison system today.

The theoretical and empirical articulation between the discipline of sociology (particularly, the substantive areas of criminology and penology), and the field of architecture resulted in the development of a planning instrument that bridges the gap between theory and practice in criminal justice and represents the first comprehensive social planning model designed to improve criminal justice planning.

The planning model is permeated by the following five principles and key considerations. First, there is the recognition that defective theory and lack of information as to correctional methods have long impeded our efforts to deal rationally with the problems of delinquency and crime. As a result, a theoretical perspective and guiding conceptual tether were developed.

Second, there is the concern--a concern shared by innovators and leaders in the field--that the prevention and treatment of crime cannot possibly be solved by corrections alone; that progress in this field is firmly tied to advancement in the entire criminal justice system. As a result, the model considers the entire spectrum of the criminal justice system as an integral whole on the macrospective and provides for the assessment of practices of the current autonomous systems of courts, law enforcement, and corrections in the planning process, all under the concept of total system planning.

Third, there is the realization that the etiology of crime is deeply embedded in the social structure of our society and that the task of crime control can no longer remain the exclusive domain of the criminal justice system. The problem of crime will not be solved merely by increasing the number of judges, prosecutors, police, or correctional staff. Nor will it be solved by focusing narrowly on rebuilding or refurbishing our correctional facilities. We must concentrate on the reduction of those social conditions that are clearly identified as breeding grounds for crime: poverty, disease, unemployment, illiteracy, and, above all, lack of equal opportunity because of racial discrimination. Success in the reduction of a significant proportion of crime will be contingent only upon our success in the reduction of these grave social ills. Although such a comprehensive approach exceeds what may be theoretically and technically possible, as far as corrections is concerned, the planning model does provide for a coordinated, multipronged effort that involves the community in the correctional process in order to make progress in this direction.

Fourth, the model is committed to the concept of community-based corrections. It provides a blueprint for the deprisonization of corrections. In contrast to the documented failure of most prison programs, there are reasonable indications that community-based corrections programs can have a positive effect on crime and delinquency control.[3] Underlying this approach is the assumption that, in most cases, treatment of offenders in the community is preferable to institutional treatment as long as the treatment can be implemented without detriment to the community. Individualization of treatment and differential handling of offenders are also more easily facilitated on the community level.

Finally, the deleterious isolating effects caused by prisonization can also be substantially reduced. Even though community corrections seems to provide the most promising approach to the problem of crime, a caveat must be voiced for those seeking instant solutions. The many faces of crime, the complexity of human life and of our society preclude, from the start, a single course of action. Community-based corrections is not a panacea for our prison and recidivism problems. In fact, even with good indications that such corrections may reduce crime, there is still a lack of verified data to measure the success of community treatment as well as the success or efficacy of any particular treatment technique. Nonetheless, there are compelling reasons for committing ourselves to the implementation of community corrections.

A considerable amount of crime and delinquency is a symptom of failure both on the part of the community and the individual who commits a crime. Community corrections, with its emphasis on changing the viewpoints of both community and individual, seems to be an appropriate response. Since the majority of offenders return to the community after their release from prison, corrective efforts must emphasize the process of reintegration into the community as the best way to protect the community. There is growing evidence that the current use of prisons intensifies and compounds the very problems professedly being treated. Prisons seldom accomplish reform. In fact, a large percentage of released offenders commit additional and often more serious crimes (Uniform Crime Reports 1975).

The notion of gaining community protection by confinement of convicted offenders to prison is largely a myth because most of these offenders are eventually released. The concept of protection rests on the unproven assumption that incarceration is synonymous with rehabilitation, but the evidence seems to point in the other direction. Time spent in prison is inversely related to success upon release. In addition, temporary quarantine of prisoners in jails and penitentiaries under dehumanizing conditions frequently has the effect of a lethal time bomb: once released, prisoners vent their frustrations on the citizenry at large. Community-based programs, in contrast to traditional confinement in prison, are much more effective in reducing recidivism.

Finally, community-based corrections is less expensive than institutionalization. It avails itself of community resources and the whole breadth of already established and functioning human service agencies. Obviously, the correctional dollar will never be large enough to refurbish and renovate this country's prisons. As a result, the economic advantage of community corrections may well make the pursuit of such programs worthwhile.

DISCUSSION OF THE THEORETICAL PERSPECTIVE OF THE PLANNING MODEL

Historically, correctional philosophy has been dominated by theories of punishment, which served as the guiding rationale for dealing with the adjudicated delinquent and the adult criminal. These theories are epitomized by the key words retribution, restraint, deterrence, and rehabilitation. Rehabilitation, the more recent approach, puts emphasis on changing the attitude of the offender. It is based on the "medical" or psychogenic model that reflects the belief that delinquency and crime are largely the result of emotional maladjustment, which, after proper identification and diagnosis, requires individual treatment. The theoretical base of this model is traceable to the growing influence of psychology and psychoanalysis earlier in the twentieth century. Compelling evidence of the model's ineffectiveness, in the majority of cases, and undiminished crime rates have brought growing dissatisfaction with the approach to individualized treatment (American Friends Service Committee 1971). The difficulty in identifying and defining individual pathology, the failure to account for social and environmental factors that are frequently correlated with crime, and exiguous information on the causation and treatment of crime have led to the search for more ecumenical approaches to the problem of crime. We know today that no one theoretical perspective on delinquent and criminal behavior is useful for all purposes and that no one model can sufficiently account for the great variety of behavior patterns found in the total population of those who commit criminal acts. There is also growing evidence that favorable change in behavior seldom, if ever, occurs in the compulsory, coercive setting of correctional institutions. Further, whatever changes do occur are seldom translated to the community where the offender's adjustment is ultimately tested. This recognition, coupled with theoretical and conceptual advances that link crime chiefly to social factors, has led to the development of the chronologically most recent theoretical perspective in dealing with crime. The perspective is characterized by the words (re)socialization and reintegration; the theory behind it rests on at least three interrelated propositions and assumptions.

First, since crime and delinquency are at least in part attributable to society's failure to provide for some of its citizens even the basic environment for law-abiding conduct--adequate educational and vocational training and employment opportunities (President's Commission 1968)--we recognize today that we must place more emphasis on the offender's social and cultural milieu if any substantial relief from crime is to result. This is not to say that individual differences and responsibility no longer remain important factors in our response to criminal behavior but that these simply need to be considered within the setting of the offender's social group, the community, and the subcultural matrix. For example, if the vexing pressures of an offender's social milieu contribute to his criminal behavior, the social milieu itself must be changed.

Second, since the ways in which society responds to deviant behavior can influence the effectiveness of social control, societal responses are an integral part of the crime and delinquency problem. In this respect, a useful distinction can be made between primary and secondary deviation. With primary deviation assumed to result from a wide variety of social, cultural, and psychological contexts, secondary deviation is deviant behavior which becomes a means of defense, attack, or adaptation to the overt and covert problems created by societal reaction to the primary deviation (Lemert 1951). The analysis, therefore, of the mechanisms of social response to deviance becomes vital in dealing with the problem.

Third, the theory is based on the philosophical consideration that the act of punishing offenders can never wipe out the harm done to both the individual and to society. As a result, concentrated efforts at influencing future behavior are deemed more desirable than the imposition of suffering and discomfort.

Fourth, criminal law is not equally effective in dealing with all forms of deviant behavior. It characteristically overreaches itself in a host of moralistic "victimless" crimes. Hence, "decriminalization" or legal reform is proposed for such manifestations of individual or social deviance as narcotics and drug use, gambling, alcoholism, abortion, certain types of consensual adult sexual practices, and a wide range of noncriminal aspects of juvenile delinquent behavior.

Finally, the relative ineffectiveness of the current arsenal of social responses to deviance, particularly the failure of traditional penal institutions, calls for the development of alternative, more effective approaches to the problem. Among these are institutional methods for dealing with the reduction of criminal stigmatization by diverting social deviants by means of noncriminal procedures into more appropriate human service agencies, and by minimizing as much as possible the penetration of persons into the criminal justice system.

In conclusion, the concepts of (re)socialization and the social reintegration of offenders into free society are based on theoretical concepts vastly different from those that guided earlier correctional philosophies. Although this latest theoretical perspective is not entirely new, it is important to note that it has yet to be pursued in a systematic way in the formulation of a more coherent social response to delinquency and crime and in the development of policy guidelines, which focus all major decisional responses on these phenomena.
One final caveat seems in order. In spite of the fact that the theory of reintegration represents by far the most plausible and rational social response to deviance, its effect has yet to be verified by empirical research.

Having discussed the theoretical and intellectual frame of reference of the planning model, we are now ready to examine implications for directions of action and the new modes of intervention proposed by the model.

TOTAL SYSTEMS PLANNING

It is difficult to conceive of any social problem area that is more in need of coordinated and uniform planning than that of adult crime and juvenile delinquency. This country's juvenile and criminal justice system is so complex, and the interrelations among its components are so varied, that even loyal supporters view the system as an incomprehensible, administrative maze. Correctional services have developed more by default than by design; they may be centralized at the state level, decentralized in cities and counties, or shared by the federal, state, county, and city governments in an almost infinite number of permutations. On every level of service the question of integrated planning arises.[4] The need for full-scale coordination is acute.

To overcome the fragmentation of the correctional system and to avoid the dissipation of energies and meager resources, effective relationships must be established among the various components of the criminal justice system--a system which thus far continues to function in resplendent social and political isolation. Beyond these essential requirements, however, lies the need for well-defined objectives, definitions, and standards, appropriate techniques for crime prevention and correction, careful allocation of resources, and meticulous research and program designs. Such requirements perforce suggest that planning activities be coordinated to the highest possible degree.

Uniform state planning is probably the sine qua non for optimal planning results. It has, in fact, been adopted with notable success by several states. Such planning, however, may remain a long-range goal for many of the remaining states, in view of the competing value orientations that characterize U.S. society (Lerman 1970). On the one hand, there is a preference for a rational approach to social problems, which stresses the application of science and technology in an integrated and coordinated way. On the other hand is the desire to disperse centers of authority and to defer decision making to the level of the local community. Given the reality of this value conflict, social planning in criminal justice either will need to compromise and accommodate these concerns or require an impetus from a vis major to pursue the more rational state-planning approach. The impetus could come in a variety of ways: recommendations of special study or advisory commissions, special incentives of federally financed planning or requirements of planning as a condition of eligibility for large-scale federal or state aid, or, more preferably, by means of executive orders. In the absence of centrally directed planning efforts, it is safe to assume that planning on the local level will no doubt continue to take place, at least until more coordinated services can be established.

To allow for the diversity of planning considerations, the planning model is explicitly designed to accommodate planning efforts at the state, regional, and local levels. With an open-ended approach, it unites with community resources all the efforts of the law-enforcement, judiciary, and corrections branches. To facilitate adding new information as it becomes obsolete, the model features a loose-leaf format and an open-index system. To assure empirical grounding of the instrument, the research methodology includes an assessment and synthesis of all pertinent theoretical and empirical socioenvironmental data in the field. In accordance with its conceptual scheme of socialization and reintegration, the methodology represents a comprehensive and systematic approach to planning in which institutionalization is seen as the last, not the first, dispositional alternative. Field testing has occurred at the state level in Hawaii, where a long-range correctional master plan has been developed that combines juvenile and adult planning (University of Illinois 1972). Field testing has also been used at over 100 regional and local levels elsewhere in the nation.

It should be noted that the concepts of total systems and even statewide correctional planning are not in philosophical or practical conflict with the concept of community-based corrections. The concepts are not synonymous with remote control of corrections from capital cities. Nor are they a continuation of the erroneous policy of isolating offenders in distant state institutions. What they do imply is systems planning as opposed to subsystems planning--anticipation of crime control needs as opposed to eclectic responses to periodically emerging crises and problems in the correctional system.

In summary, total systems planning provides the conceptual framework necessary for the identification of changing state and planning area needs to guarantee the optimal development of comprehensive crime prevention and crime reduction programs and maximum utilization of available resources. Such an approach obviates the fallacy of singling out in the planning process any one item, such as a minimum- or maximum-security prison, without fully assessing the total service needs of the convicted offender population that is not served in the planning area. For example, planning might reveal that optimum service delivery would require an expansion of existing probation and parole programs in preference to the construction of a new prison facility.

Among the particular considerations included in the total systems approach, employed by the planning model, are a thorough assessment of present practices, an evaluation of resources, an analysis of trends based on sufficient statistical information, and an exploration of community-based alternatives to current dispositions. Furthermore, the concept of total environment planning always implies coordination with and input from the courts, probation departments, law-enforcement agencies, state corrections agencies, and public and private agencies already involved in treating and preventing crime and juvenile delinquency. Planning efforts also include the participation of social welfare agencies, academic and vocational departments in education, physical and mental health services, employment agencies, public recreation departments, and representatives from youth groups.

The model assists administrators in the identification of the correctional problems for specified target areas by means of problem definition, survey and analysis, program linkage, and systems concept. On this basis, current and future correctional needs can be determined. Because of the many variations and fluctuations in the quality and quantity of information available to planners, the survey process is designed primarily to collect basic information generally available to all. Key components of the survey include an assessment of existing correctional practices: programs, personnel, and facilities; an analysis of law-enforcement and judicial practices and trends; and an assessment of community resources.

In terms of overall planning concepts, the model recognizes two general service delivery systems: a regional system in which correctional programs and facilities are centralized for a multicounty or city-county area; and a network system in which programs and facilities are dispersed to accommodate metropolitan areas. The model develops a clear rationale for the regionalization of correctional services in sparsely settled rural areas and for program specialization in high-density urban locations.

Remaining within the general boundaries of the legalistic framework and continuing to protect the safety of the public, the model identifies, for any given target area, the theoretical minimum of offenders for whom detention and postsentence in correction must be provided in order to protect the safety of the community. It further identifies the theoretical maximum of offenders for whom alternatives to incarceration could be utilized. A series of program linkages are then provided, stressing the divestment of social, medical, and psychiatric problem cases from corrections, which is particularly important if the current overloads of the system are to be overcome. In addition, the criminal justice system is singularly ineffective in dealing with the mentally ill, the alcoholic, and the drug addict. We know today that applying criminal sanctions to such persons only exacerbates their problems and contributes heavily to the revolving-door syndrome that characterizes our jails and penal institutions. The model makes similar recommendations for the divestment of juveniles in need of care and supervision who have not committed criminal offenses. Their removal from the aegis of juvenile justice to more appropriate youth-service agencies--family services or the newly emerging youth service bureaus (Norman 1971)-- represents a much more viable approach to the prevention of juvenile delinquency and the avoidance of the criminogenic influence of stigmatization and isolation.

In keeping with its conceptual tether, the model identifies a host of community-based correctional programs, in accordance with previously identified offender needs, and approaches systematically the deprisonization of our large correctional facilities. This development is based on the recognition that the traditional institutional approach, with its coercive settings and inadequate programs, has failed to an inordinate degree. There is ample evidence that penitentiaries create more crime than they prevent. The banishment of offenders into isolated institutions, warehousing in crippling idleness, under conditions of stark deprivation and anonymous brutality, all insure failure. For these reasons the days of the megaprison, as we know it, must be numbered.

In an effort to provide alternative approaches to the existing system, the planning model recommends a substantial redefinition of the role of the traditional penitentiary as well as the jail. Although the model recognizes the continued need for the incarceration of the convicted, unusually refractory, offender, because of the many inadequacies of our knowledge and because of our techniques in treatment, it recommends such drastic measures for only a few and uses greater selectivity and sophistication in the application of crime control and correctional methods. To achieve greater selectivity and sophistication, new theoretical concepts for correctional programs

and facilities were needed. The field testing of <u>Guidelines</u> in the development of the Correctional Master Plan for the state of Hawaii
and other states, such as Oklahoma and Rhode Island, presented the
necessary empirical setting for the development of such concepts.

DEVELOPING THE MASTER PLAN: A REVIEW OF CRITICAL COMPONENTS

Correctional practice today provides the convicted felon with
a considerable amount of diagnostic service. But professional resources are often spent at a time when the criminal's career has
long since been established, when rehabilitation is much more difficult, so that the returns on society's investments are predictably
low.

Intake Service Center

In view of these considerations, the need is obvious to focus
on juvenile and adult offenders at the earliest possible time--at the
first point of contact with the juvenile and criminal justice system.
Thus the concept of the Intake Service Center emerges. In typical
Hegelian fashion, it turns our system's current approach to corrections upside down. The center is a public agency, established to
receive and screen all youth and adults referred to it by the police
and public and private agencies for court referral. Ideally, the
center is operated by the state government under the auspices of
some blanket state agency: Department of Health and Rehabilitative
Services, State Department of Social Welfare, or Department of
Social Services. The selection of particular departments is less
important than the fact that the Intake Service Center should be free
from the stigma usually attached to a Department of Corrections or
a Division of Youth Services, as well as being free from the influence of the judiciary and probation system. Persons referred to the
agency have not been adjudicated and are therefore not screened for
diversion into programs outside the juvenile and criminal justice
system. The center thus provides a second screening process and
diverts as many persons as possible from the criminal justice system, at the same time referring to the appropriate court those for
whom court action is deemed necessary. The center replaces traditional jail and intake units of juvenile probation offices. Only
after full exploration of a range of alternatives to detention does the
center provide for the safe and secure detention of persons in a
social and physical environment that is conducive to their mental,
physical, and social well-being.

The Intake Service Center functions in close cooperation with other private and public agencies: youth service bureaus, family and mental health services, employment counseling, and so on, all toward the goals of prevention of delinquency and reduction of crime.

Three prototypes of Intake Service Centers can be distinguished: the nonresidential, community-based center, the community-based residential center, and a combination of the first and second. The latter features nonresidential as well as residential services. In addition, the centers should be available on a local or regional basis, dependent on population distribution and service needs.

The functions of the Intake Service Center include the diversion of socially deprived, dependent, and nondelinquent children and adults with sociomedical problems into appropriate alternative programs; predetention screening of eligible youth and adults to programs involving alternatives to pretrial incarceration; the provision of assessment and evaluative services for each person, on the basis of which, recommendations for appropriate programs and services can be made to receiving agencies and the court systems (such activities include diagnostic services relating to voluntary pretrial programs, presentence investigations, and correctional programs for sentenced offenders); ongoing evaluation of offender performance in given programs; systematic coordination of the entire juvenile and criminal justice system to include reintegrative and after-care services; and evaluation of all correctional programs and activities serving the system.

The key characteristic of the Intake Service Center is to bring to bear on the particular problems of offenders a multifaceted, interdisciplinary approach. The cause of the difficulties is examined and a treatment modality and program approach is developed to divert the offender, at the earliest possible state, from progressing in criminal careers.

Community Correctional Centers

Much has been said and written about Community Correctional Centers (CCC). The term "community," however, is frequently a euphemism for "jail," and it is sometimes used to designate a closed population of inmates living in a prison setting with only fragmented and very limited contacts with the outside community. The concept, as developed at the National Clearinghouse, refers to a facility in which a comprehensive program of both noninstitutionalized and institutionalized methods of treatment and care are coordinated. In terms of complexity, it may range from a community-based "nerve center" to a plan that coordinates a network of separate residential and nonresidential care, counseling, educational and vocational

training programs, work release, prerelease programs, halfway
house programs, and other services for offenders with special
problems.

Although the CCC's primary mission is to provide a carefully
devised combination of control that offers a range of treatment programs for differentiated types of offenders, it also performs an important function in the area of crime prevention by educating the public and actively involving it in the offender's rehabilitation and resocialization processes. In terms of other functions, the CCC provides for long-term, pretrial detention, detention of sentenced mis-
demeanants, and selected felony offenders requiring low- and
medium-security considerations. Many of the program activities
for convicted offenders can be administered and coordinated from
the CCC. Usually, office, clerical, and interview areas are the
only spaces needed; in some cases, group meeting and counseling
spaces are required. Such spaces should be accessible to the area
where the programs are administered. In addition, administrative
links to the Intake Service Center must be highly developed so that
the management of incarceration alternatives can be facilitated.

Because of the highly interactive program (that is, the high
degree of staff and client movement in and out of the facility) and
the usual apprehensiveness of the community about detention facilities, the overall size of in-house activities needs to be minimized.
In addition to the fluctuations in size, the three basic components of
the CCC (client housing, program support, and administrative facilities) may vary drastically, depending upon the availability of existing resources.

High-Security Correctional Facility

The concept of a high-security correctional facility has been
developed for certain types of offenders whose record of violent behavior is grave enough to require such disposition for the safety of
the community. In essence, it replaces the prison as we know it.
The purpose of the facility is to provide a carefully controlled physical environment and program based on the Institutional Community
Model first described by Street et al. (1966). The institution has as
its goal to control and treat the serious predatory offender and
habitual, serious recidivist. Since this category of offender is
characteristically difficult to deal with, a small institution is vital
to assure individualized treatment. Furthermore, the facility should
be designed with small living units for not more than 10 to 12 men
each, in an environment conducive to the development of a constructive, socializing interaction among residents and staff. Basic

program components are guided group interaction offered in con-
junction with intrainstitutional programs: academic and vocational
education, recreation, extrainstitutional programs of the community-
college variety, and work-release programs for selected residents.
In view of the type of client involved, emphasis is given to providing
various levels of security, with a relatively high degree of security
for clients in the beginning phases of the program.

A principal feature of the high-security program is to offer a
safe, therapeutic milieu in which individuals are given the opportunity to express their inner drives and innate abilities, rather than
to provide them with the traditional training and instruction programs
so characteristic of the present practice in our prison system. Design considerations complement and enhance such program activities
as intensive staff/client interaction, reality confrontations and reality testing, free discussions, optimal living and constructive learning situations involving varied degrees of resident autonomy, and a
host of community and group activities and programs.

Conclusion

In conclusion, the model provides a validated approach to comprehensive planning in crime control by which current agencies and
institutions can be transformed into a more responsive criminal
justice system. It permits a systematic response to previously
identified needs of an offender population and offers a diversity of
programs and individual responses for each major category of offense. It utilizes to the maximum extent possible existing human
service resources and thus goes beyond the traditional boundaries
of corrections into the law-enforcement and judicial subsystems of
the criminal justice system. It deemphasizes imprisonization as
the most expensive and least effective response to deviance and
stresses utilization of alternatives to incarceration to the extent
that such dispositions are consistent with the protection of the community.

Two final considerations are important. The first concerns
the need for continued evaluation of the crime-control effectiveness
of the planning model. The second concerns the machinery necessary for conducting the planning process and for the implementation
of its recommendations. Since ultimate validation of the model is
contingent upon the success or failure of the wide range of programs
generated by the plan, the validation will be slow in coming. The
process will be particularly cumbersome in view of the fact that
good evaluations of programs require essentially two to three years
of ongoing research. In the face of the model's increased emphasis

on community-based programs, research and evaluation assume
particular importance. In the last analysis, only research can
prove whether or not innovative programs can continue to protect
the safety of the public. Evaluation techniques will require explicit
statements of objectives to permit adequate measurement and testing of their achievement. They should focus on the attainment of
both the system's capability goals and its performance goals for a
new evaluation of effectiveness (Suchman 1967). Regardless of the
effort involved, there is a clear need for performance evaluation of
the model to assure its effectiveness in crime control and to maintain its viability as a planning instrument.

Overall, effective usage of the model, and implementation of
its recommendations, will be highly dependent upon the quality and
degree of authority of the planning organization. In view of the
model's total system approach, adequate representation of all interests from the various subsystems of criminal justice is especially
critical. Also, without adequate and completely capable staff that
encompasses all human-service and criminal-justice specialities,
the integration of planning components into a comprehensive long-
range goal may be seriously jeopardized. In addition, the ultimate
responsibility for the implementation of the plan will need to be
placed in a single unit--preferably on the state level--and will require the full-fledged support of that state's legislative and executive authorities, in terms of sanction as well as in liberal funding.
With the existing criminal justice system being characterized not
only by severe fragmentation of services but also by many vested
interests, power conflicts, and an acute scarcity of resources, a
wider application of the planning model may well be contingent upon
the influence of a national policy statement and on the promise of
large-scale funding.

NOTES

1. Among the many influential study efforts in the field of
corrections are those of the President's Commission on Law Enforcement and the Administration of Justice of 1967; the National
Advisory Commission on Criminal Justice Standards and Goals,
1973; the National Commission on Violence in 1969; the American
Friends Service Committee's Struggle for Justice, 1971; the American Bar Association's Commission on Correctional Facilities and
Services, which has produced many studies; and the American
Foundation, Inc., Institute of Corrections in Philadelphia, which
has undertaken many research and planning efforts in the United
States.

   2. "Man-Environment Systems," Association for the Study of
Man-Environment Relations, Inc. (Orangeburg, N.Y., March 1972).
See also Thomas E. Lasswell and C. M. Deasy, "The Measurement
of Values, Goals, and Strains in Architectural Programming," a
paper presented at the 65th Annual Meeting of the American Sociological Association, Washington, D.C., August 1970.
   3. See Robert L. Smith, "A Quiet Revolution: Probation
Subsidy" (Washington, D.C.: U.S. Department of Health, Education
and Welfare, 1971), for a good description of the California probation subsidy program. Also, "Programs in Criminal Justice Reform" (New York: Vera Institute of Justice, Ten-Year Report
1961–1971, May 1972).
   4. The need for comprehensive planning as a prerequisite to
improvement of the criminal justice system was recognized by the
President's Commission on Law Enforcement and Administration of
Justice, <u>The Challenge of Crime in a Free Society</u> (1968), which
called for the early establishment of a formal machinery for planning by state and local government.

REFERENCES

American Friends Service Committee
   1971   Struggle for Justice. New York: Hill and Wang.

Association for the Study of Man-Environment Relations
   1972   Man-environment systems. Orangeburg, N.Y. (March).

Lasswell, T. E., and C. M. Deasy
   1970   The measurement of values, goals, and strains in archi-
          tectural programming. Paper presented at the 65th
          Annual Meeting of the American Sociological Association,
          Washington, D.C. (August).

Lemert, E. M.
   1951   Social Pathology. New York: McGraw-Hill.

Lerman, P.
   1970   Delinquency and Social Policy. New York: Praeger.

Management and Behavioral Sciences Center
   1972   Planning and designing for juvenile justice. Law Enforce-
          ment Assistance Administration, U.S. Department of
          Justice (August).

Moyer, F. D., E. E. Flynn, F. A. Powers, and M. J. Plautz
  1971   Guidelines for the Planning and Design of Regional and
         Community Correctional Centers for Adults. University
         of Illinois at Urbana.

Nagel, W. G.
  1973   The New Red Barn. New York: Walker.

Norman, S.
  1971   The Youth Service Bureau. Paramus, N.J.: National
         Council on Crime and Delinquency.

President's Commission on Law Enforcement and Administration of
Justice
  1968   The Challenge of Crime in a Free Society. New York:
         Hearst Corporation.

Street, D. et al.
  1966   Organization for Treatment. New York: The Free Press.

Suchman, E.
  1967   Evaluative Research. New York: Russell Sage Foundation.

Uniform Crime Reports
  1975   Washington, D.C.: U.S. Government Printing Office.

University of Illinois
  1972   Correctional Master Plan for Hawaii. Urbana: National
         Clearinghouse for Criminal Justice Planning and Archi-
         tecture.

ABOUT THE EDITORS AND CONTRIBUTORS

JOHN P. CONRAD, Senior Fellow, Academy for Contemporary Problems, Columbus, Ohio; Adjunct Professor of Sociology, Ohio State University. Formerly lecturer in sociology, University of California at Davis, University of Pennsylvania; Chief of Research, U.S. Bureau of Prisons; Chief, Center for Crime Prevention and Rehabilitation, National Institute on Law Enforcement and Criminal Justice. Senior Fullbright Fellow, London School of Economics, 1958-59.

EDITH ELISABETH FLYNN, Professor of Criminal Justice, Northeastern University; Academic Director, Northeastern University Criminal Justice Training Center, Boston; Executive Councillor, American Society of Criminology; member, Corrections Council, National Council on Crime and Delinquency. Formerly member, Task Force on Corrections, National Advisory Commission on Criminal Justice Standards and Goals; U.S. Delegate, 5th Congress of the United Nations on the Prevention of Crime and the Treatment of Offenders; Commissioner, Illinois Law Enforcement Commission; founder and Associate Director, National Clearinghouse for Criminal Justice Planning and Architecture.

DONALD J. ARTICOLO, Computer Systems Analyst, Judicial Information System, Hartford, Connecticut.

ANN WOLBERT BURGESS, Professor of Nursing, Boston College, Chestnut Hill, Massachusetts.

WILLIAM G. DOERNER, Assistant Professor, School of Criminology, Florida State University, Tallahassee.

CARL A. EKLUND, Assistant Director, American Academy of Judicial Education, Washington, D.C.

DON C. GIBBONS, Professor, Portland State University, Portland, Oregon.

C. TAYLOR GRIFFITHS, Department of Criminology, Simon Frazier University, Burnaby, B.C., Canada.

EDWIN L. HALL, Research Specialist, Department of Institutions, State of Montana.

R. KELLY HANCOCK, Graduate Student, Portland State University, Portland, Oregon.

LYNDA LYTLE HOLMSTROM, Associate Professor and Chairperson, Department of Sociology, Boston College, Chestnut Hill, Massachusetts.

JEAN C. JESTER, Graduate Student, School of Criminal Justice, The State University of New York at Albany.

MARY S. KNUDTEN, Assistant Professor, Department of Sociology and Anthropology, Marquette University, Milwaukee, Wisconsin.

RICHARD D. KNUDTEN, Professor, Department of Sociology and Anthropology, Marquette University, Milwaukee, Wisconsin.

SARA LEE, New York State Department of Mental Hygiene, Albany, New York.

ANTHONY C. MEADE, Senior Research Scientist, Institute for Juvenile Research, State of Illinois, Department of Mental Health, Chicago.

WILLIAM G. NAGEL, Executive Vice President, American Foundation Inc., Institute of Corrections, Philadelphia.

GRAEME R. NEWMAN, Professor of Criminal Justice, School of Criminal Justice, The State University of New York at Albany.

ALAN R. ROWE, Associate Professor, Department of Sociology and Social Psychology, Florida Atlantic University, Boca Raton.

JOSEPH A. SCIMECCA, Chairman of the Department of Sociology, George Mason University, Fairfax, Virginia.

JOSEPH E. SCOTT, Associate Professor of Sociology, Ohio State University, Columbus.

ALBERT A. SIMKUS, Department of Sociology, University of Wisconsin, Madison.

GLENN SNODGRASS, Department of Sociology, Temple University, Philadelphia.

JOHN STAHURA, Associate at The Center for Vocational and Technical Education, Ohio State University, Columbus.

CHARLES R. TITTLE, Professor, Department of Sociology and Social Psychology, Florida Atlantic University, Boca Raton.

RICHARD VANDIVER, Assistant Professor of Sociology, University of Montana, Missoula.

KURT WEIS, Assistant Professor, Department of Sociology, University of the Saarland, Saarbruecken, West Germany.

MARGARET A. ZAHN, Associate Professor of Sociology, Temple University, Philadelphia.

CRIME AND DELINQUENCY: Dimensions of
Deviance
>
> edited by
> Marc Riedel
> Terence P. Thornberry

CRIMINAL JUSTICE PLANNING
>
> edited by
> Joseph E. Scott
> Simon Dinitz

DRUGS, CRIME, AND PUBLIC POLICY
>
> edited by
> Arnold S. Trebach

ISSUES IN CRIMINAL JUSTICE: Planning and
Evaluation
>
> edited by
> Marc Riedel
> Duncan Chappell

TREATING THE OFFENDER: Problems and Issues
>
> edited by
> Marc Riedel
> Pedro A. Vales

YOUTH CRIME AND JUVENILE JUSTICE:
International Perspectives
>
> edited by
> Paul C. Friday
> V. Lorne Stewart

AMERICAN INSTITUTE OF BIOLOGICAL SCIENCES